THE
Weekend
Woodworker
ANNUAL
1991
40 Easy-to-Build Projects

Selected by the Editors of Rodale Books

Edited by Rob Yoder

Rodale Press, Emmaus, Pennsylvania

The authors and editors who compiled this book have tried to make all of the contents as accurate and as correct as possible. Plans, illustrations, photographs, and text have all been carefully checked and cross-checked. However, due to the variability of local conditions, construction materials, personal skill, and so on, neither the author nor Rodale Press assumes any responsibility for any injuries suffered or for damages and other losses incurred that result from the material presented herein. All instructions and plans should be carefully studied and clearly understood before beginning construction.

This book is being simultaneously published by Rodale Press as a book entitled *The Weekend Woodworker 40 Easy-to-Build Projects.*

Editor in Chief: William Gottlieb

Senior Managing Editor: Margaret Lydic Balitas

Senior Editor: Jeff Day

Assistant Editor: Rob Yoder

Writers: Roger Holmes, William Hylton, Josh Markel, David Page, David Schiff, Edward J. Schoen, Jim Tolpin, Roger Yepsen, and Rob Yoder

Copy Editor: Candace Levy

Editorial Assistance: Stacy Brobst and Deborah Maher

Cover Designer: Darlene Schneck

Cover Photographer: Mitch Mandel

Book Designer: Ayers/Johanek, PUBLICATION DESIGN

Illustrator: Sally Onopa

Printed in the United States of America on acid-free ⊗, recycled paper ♻

If you have any questions or comments concerning this book, please write:

Rodale Press
Book Reader Service
33 East Minor Street
Emmaus, PA 18098

ISBN 0–87857–926–5 hardcover

2 4 6 8 10 9 7 5 3 1 hardcover

Contributors, Sources, and Craftsmen:

Möbelslöjd by Hans Keijser and Lars Sjöberg, ICA bokförlag, Västerås, Sweden, 1981. (Plate Rack, Armoire, Country Chair, Farm Table, Tilt Top Table)

Snickra till barnen by Hans Mårtensson, ICA bokförlag, Västerås, Sweden, 1983. (Wall Clock, Bookshelf, Cradle, Child's Bench, Child's Chair, Noise Machine, Race Cars, Front-End Loader, Dump Truck, Pleasure Boat, Biplane, Steam Train, Sled, Child's Wagon)

Stora boken om Hobbysnickeri by Hans Mårtensson, ICA bokförlag, Västerås, Sweden, 1986. (Tea Cabinet, Display Cabinet, Hall Mirror, Dovetail Mirror, Peg Shelf, Jewelry Cabinet, Dressing Mirror, Sewing Box, Blanket Chest, Liar's Bench, Jumping Jack, Pickin' Chicken)

Ronald Day (Quilt Rack)

Fred Matlack (Bathroom Cabinet, Cassette Box, Footstool)

Fred Matlack and Phil Gehret of the Rodale Design Center (Lamp Stand, Gateleg Table)

Sarah Terry (Magazine Rack)

Rob Yoder (Little Boxes)

CONTENTS

PART THREE: Tables and Seating

PART FOUR: Toys

INTRODUCTION

Let's face it. Shop time is precious: You manage to squeeze in whatever's left of the weekend after you mow the lawn and perhaps an evening here or there. But no matter how good you are, there's never enough time to build half the things you'd like to build.

This book is the first in a series that helps you build quality projects in the time you have. The 40 projects you'll find here are sleek, simple, and manageable enough to build in a weekend or two.

To help save you time, we've had professional cabinetmakers help write this book. The directions they wrote tell you, step-by-step, every shortcut and every trick used by the guys who do this for a living. Shop tips, scattered throughout the book, will save you time and frustration. The exploded and measured drawings show you how each piece goes together. A special comments column in the Cutting List helps you get each piece just right.

This book is as important as any tool you own. It won't make your life any less hectic. It won't give you more shop time. But it will ensure that every moment spent in the shop is well spent, enjoyable, and productive.

PART ONE

WALL-HUNG PROJECTS

TEA CABINET

This pear wood cabinet is perfect for small knicknacks, like tea tins, coffee mugs, or even those small kitchen implements that keep getting lost in the drawer.

The doweled construction is simple and adequate for a small cabinet like this. Pear wood may be hard to find. Cedar, fir, or pine would work equally well.

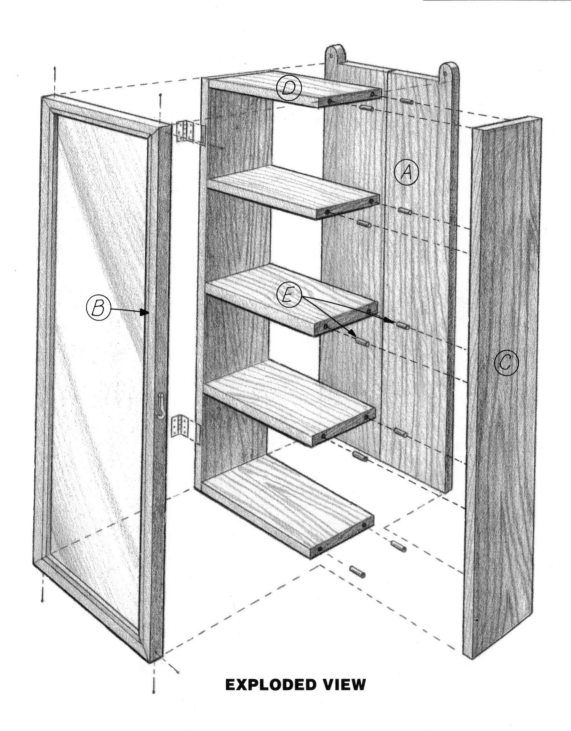

EXPLODED VIEW

1 Select the stock and cut the parts. Choose straight, flat stock. Joint, plane, rip, and cut the parts to the sizes given in the Cutting List.

2 Cut the hangers in the back boards. The back is longer than the cabinet sides and is cut away to create the hangers shown in the *Front View.* Lay out and cut the hangers to the profile shown. When you have cut the hangers, drill a ¼-inch-diameter hole through them, as shown.

SHOP TIP: To get two identical hangers, cut both at once. First stack the pieces together and secure by putting double-sided tape between them. Then cut both hangers in one operation.

3 Rabbet the backs, door stock, and sides. Put a rabbeting bit in your router. Secure the router in a router table. Put a fence on the table and adjust the setup to rout a ¼ × ¼-inch rabbet. Cut a rabbet in one edge of each back board positioned so that the rabbets will overlap as shown in the *Top View.*

With the router still set up for the ¼ × ¼-inch rabbet, rabbet one edge of the door stock to hold the door glass.

After you cut rabbets in the back boards and door stock, set the router table to rabbet each side to accept the back. Rout the ⅜ × ¼-inch rabbet as shown in the *Top View.*

4 Drill the dowel-pin holes. Lay out the sides for the dowel-pin holes following the dimensions shown in the *Side View.* Drill the ¼-inch-diameter by ¼-inch-deep dowel-pin holes on your drill press.

CUTTING LIST

Part	Quantity	Dimension	Comment
A. Back boards	2	⅜″ × 4¼″ × 23¼″	
B. Door stock	1	¾″ × ¾″ × 64″	Miter to fit.
C. Side	2	½″ × 4½″ × 22″	
D. Shelves	5	½″ × 4⅛″ × 7¾″	
E. Dowel pin stock	1	¼″ dia. × 15″	Makes 20 ⁷⁄₁₆″ pegs

Hardware

2 1-in. butt hinges
1 latch hook. Available from Meisel Hardware Specialties, P.O. Box 70, Mound, MN 55364. Part #309.
1 ⅛-in. × 7 ¹¹⁄₁₆-in. × 20 ¹⁵⁄₁₆-in. piece of glass
As needed, 1″ brads
As needed, pushpins (to hold glass in place)

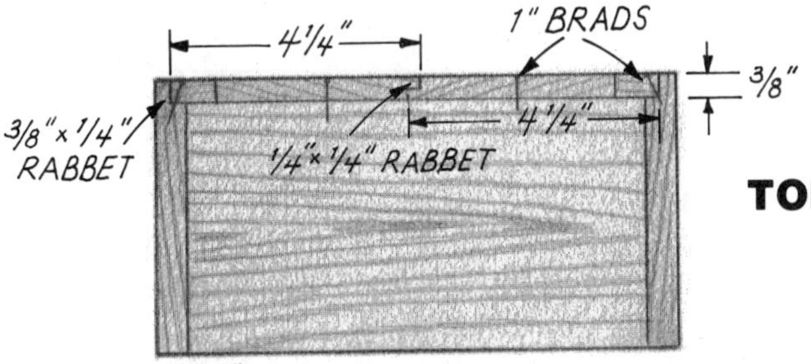
4 1/4"
1" BRADS
3/8"
3/8" × 1/4" RABBET
1/4" × 1/4" RABBET
4 1/4"

TOP VIEW

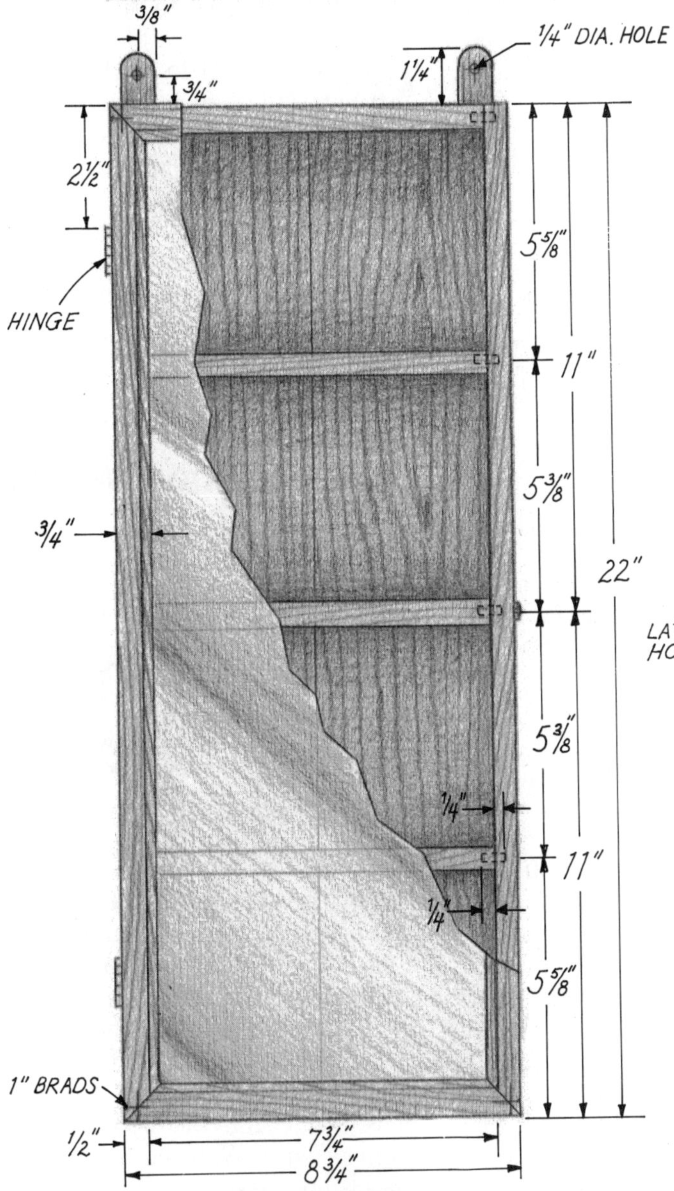
3/8"
1/4" DIA. HOLE
1 1/4"
3/4"
2 1/2"
HINGE
5 5/8"
11"
5 3/8"
22"
3/4"
5 3/8"
1/4"
11"
1/4"
5 5/8"
1" BRADS
1/2"
7 3/4"
8 3/4"

FRONT VIEW

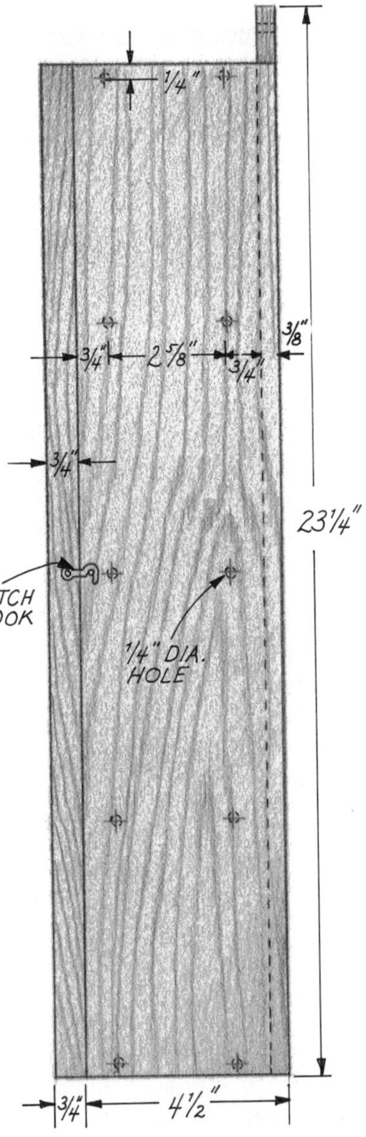
1/4"
3/8"
3/4"
2 5/8"
3/4"
3/4"
23 1/4"
LATCH HOOK
1/4" DIA. HOLE
3/4"
4 1/2"

SIDE VIEW

Locate the exact dowel-pin hole positions on the ends of the shelves with dowel centers. Put the shelves upright in a vise and carefully drill the dowel-pin holes.

SHOP TIP: Drill the dowel holes with the help of a template. Make the template from some scrap wood cut to the exact dimension of the sides. Lay out and drill the dowel-pin holes, shown in the *Side View,* on the template. Clamp the template to the cabinet side. Drill through the holes in the template to locate the holes in the sides.

To make an identical set of holes on the second side, mark the front and top edges of the template and make sure these marks line up with the top and front of the second side. Clamp the template in place on the second side and drill the matching dowel-pin holes.

Drill the holes in the shelves using the top set of holes in the template. Put the shelf in the vise, align the top of the template with the top of the shelf, and drill through the template holes.

5 **Assemble the cabinet.** Cut ¼-inch-diameter dowel stock into ⁷⁄₁₆-inch-long dowel pins with a dovetail saw. Glue the dowel pins into the holes in the shelf ends. While the glue is still wet, glue the shelves and dowels into the sides. Clamp the sides to the shelves, make sure the cabinet is square, and allow the glue to dry.

When the glue has dried, remove the clamps and test fit the back boards. The back boards should have approximately ¹⁄₁₆ inch of play from side to side. Trim if necessary.

When the back boards fit properly, apply glue to the rabbets cut for the backs.

Put the back boards in place and nail them to the cabinet with 1-inch brads. Nail, but do not glue, the back boards to the shelves.

Allow the glue to dry.

6 **Cut the profile in the door stock.** Put a 1⁵⁄₁₆-inch-diameter cove and bead bit in the router. Secure the router in a router table. Before you cut the door stock, cut a test profile in some scrap wood. Cut the scrap to the thickness and width of the door stock. Adjust the height of the bit to approximate the profile shown in the *Door Stock Detail*. When you are satisfied with the scrap profile, rout the profile in the door stock.

DOOR STOCK DETAIL

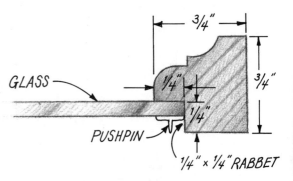

7 **Miter the door stock and assemble the door.** When you miter the door stock to make the door, cut the miters one at a time and compare them to the front edge of the cabinet for accuracy.

When you've cut all four sides of the door frame, apply glue on the mitered ends and clamp the door together in a corner clamp. With the door frame still in the clamp, tack the miters together with 1-inch brads.

Allow the glue to dry.

To get accurate miters, check your setup on some pieces of scrap. Set your table saw blade to the 45-degree position. Set a miter gauge to 90 degrees and use it to cut miters in two pieces of scrap wood. Put the miters together and make sure that the resulting angle equals 90 degrees. Adjust the blade as necessary.

8 Cut the hinge mortises and hang the door. With the hinge as your guide, mark and cut the hinge mortises in the front edge of the cabinet and the back of the door as shown in the *Front View*. Rout the mortises or cut by hand.

Mark and predrill holes for the hinge screws, then hang the door.

9 Apply finish. Set the brads and fill any brad holes with wood putty. Finish sand all the surfaces.

The tea cabinet shown has an oil finish. Finish your cabinet as you choose. After the finish has dried, screw the latch hook in place and install the glass in the door with small push pins.

HINGE MORTISES

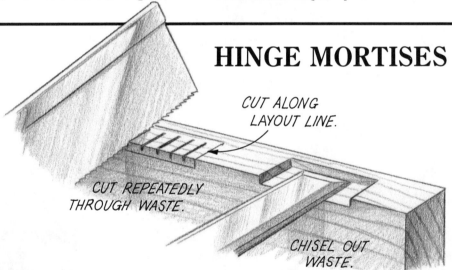

CUT ALONG LAYOUT LINE.

CUT REPEATEDLY THROUGH WASTE.

CHISEL OUT WASTE.

1 Lay out the mortise on the carcase. To cut accurate mortises, lay them out directly from the hinge. Put the hinges in place on the cabinet and trace around one of the leaves with a knife.

The mortise depth should equal half the thickness of the hinge barrel. Scribe a line with a marking gauge to mark the depth of the mortise.

2 Remove the waste. With a backsaw or dovetail saw, cut along the first line you scribed, as shown in the drawing, until you reach the scribe line indicating the mortise depth. Make a series of cuts in the mortise, as shown, and chisel out the waste.

3 Lay out the mortise on the door. Put the hinge in the mortise and position the door on the cabinet. Mark where the hinge barrel meets the door. Remove the door from the cabinet; align the hinge with the barrel marks on the door. Trace around the hinge and remove the waste as before.

DISPLAY CABINET

Have you seen your antique bottle collection lately? How about your mineral collection, or your pocket watch collection? If you're like most people it's probably in a cardboard box in the back of the closet.

If you've been meaning to resurrect your collection, consider this display cabinet as its new home.

The cabinet is made entirely from solid wood, except for the back and drawer bottoms, which are plywood.

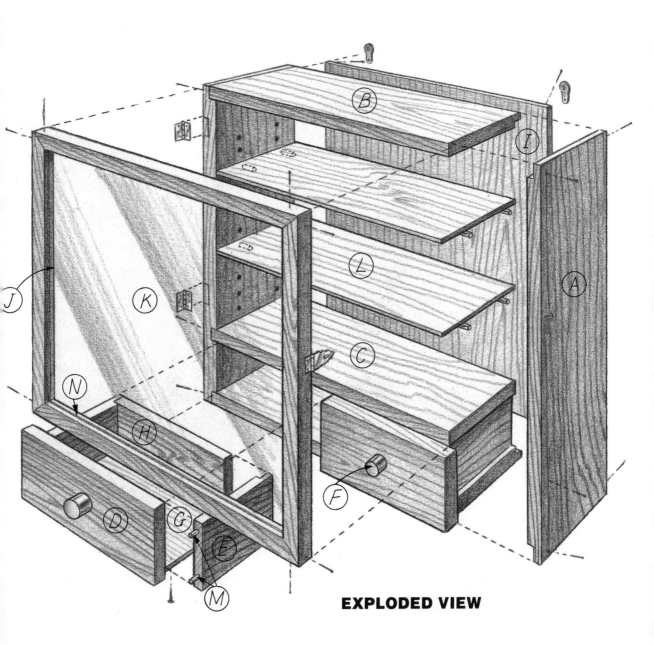

EXPLODED VIEW

1 **Select the stock and cut the parts.** Choose straight, flat stock. Select a cabinet-grade plywood for the back that will match the cabinet's solid wood. Cut the plywood back so that its grain runs parallel with the cabinet sides.

Joint, plane, rip, and cut the parts to the sizes given in the Cutting List.

2 **Cut the dadoes and rabbets in the sides.** Put a ¾-inch straight bit in your router and rout the dadoes and rabbets shown in the *Front View* and *Side View.*

SHOP TIP: To rout a dado or rabbet, clamp a straightedge to the stock and guide the router against it. This will produce a perfectly straight groove and will also give you more control over the router.

3 **Rout a rabbet for the back.** Set up a router table and fence to cut a ⅜ × ¼-inch rabbet. Cut a rabbet in the back edge of the sides, top, and bottom.

CUTTING LIST

Part	Quantity	Dimension	Comment
A. Sides	2	¾" × 4¾" × 19¾"	
B. Top and bottom	2	¾" × 4¾" × 15¼"	
C. Drawer shelf	1	¾" × 4½" × 15¼"	
D. Drawer fronts	2	¾" × 3¹¹⁄₁₆" × 7¹⁵⁄₁₆"	
E. Drawer sides	4	½" × 2¹¹⁄₁₆" × 4½"	
F. Drawer pulls	2	¾" dia. dowel × 1¼"	
G. Drawer bottoms	2	¼" × 4½" × 7³⁄₁₆"	Plywood
H. Drawer backs	2	½" × 2¹¹⁄₁₆" × 6¹¹⁄₁₆"	
I. Cabinet back	1	¼" × 15¼" × 19"	Plywood
J. Door stock	1	¾" × 1" × 70"	Miter to fit.
K. Door glass	1	⅛" × 14⅝" × 14⅝"	Cut to fit.
L. Glass shelves	2	¼" × 4½" × 17⁷⁄₁₆"	Cut to fit.
M. Dowel pin stock	1	¼" dia. × 4"	Cut to size.
N. Glass bead	1	¼" quarter round × 65"	Miter to fit.

Hardware

2 1½ × 1¼-in., open dia. hinges
As needed, 4d finishing nails
8 #4 × ⅝-in. flathead wood screws
As needed, 1-in. brads
1 1¾-in. brass hinge hasp. Available from The Woodworkers' Store, 21801 Industrial Boulevard, Rogers, MN 55374. Part #D3042.
8 ¼-in.-dia. brass shelf pins. Available from the Woodworkers' Store. Part #D5736.
As needed, ½-in. brads
2 2-in. brass hangers. Available from The Woodworkers' Store. Part #D3008.

TOP VIEW

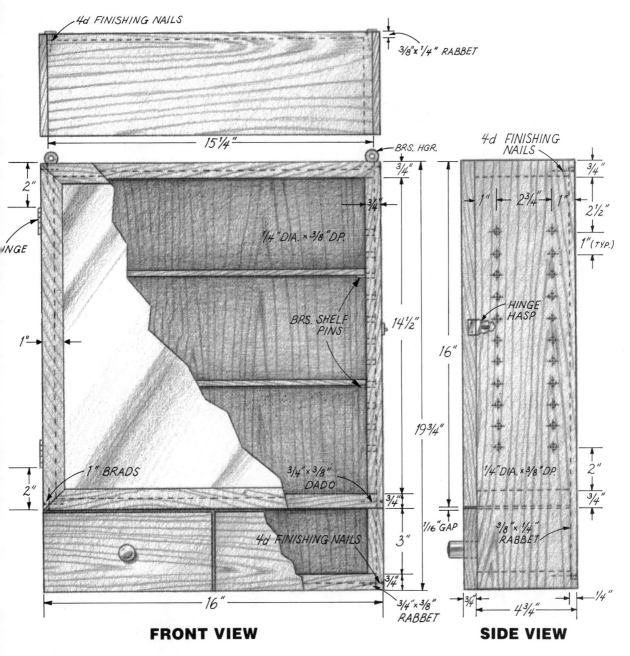

4d FINISHING NAILS

3/8" x 1/4" RABBET

15 1/4"

BRS. HGR.

4d FINISHING NAILS

3/4"

3/4"

1"   2 3/4"   1"

2 1/2"

1" (TYP.)

2"

HINGE

1/4" DIA. x 3/8" DP.

BRS. SHELF PINS

HINGE HASP

14 1/2"

16"

1"

19 3/4"

1/4" DIA. x 3/8" DP.

2"

1" BRADS

3/4" x 3/8" DADO

3/4"

1/16" GAP

2"

3/4"

4d FINISHING NAILS

3"

3/8" x 1/4" RABBET

16"

3/4"

3/4" x 3/8" RABBET

3/4"   4 3/4"   1/4"

FRONT VIEW

SIDE VIEW

4 Drill the shelf-pin holes. Set up and drill the shelf-pin holes in the sides as shown in the *Side View*. Note that the holes do not go all the way through the sides.

SHOP TIP: Drill the holes for the adjustable shelf pins with the help of a template. Make the template from some scrap wood cut to the exact dimension of the sides. Lay out and drill the shelf-pin holes, shown in the *Side View, on the template.* Clamp the template to the cabinet side. Drill through the holes in the template to locate the holes in the side.

To make an identical set of holes on the second side, mark the front and top edges of the template and make sure the marks line up with the top and front of the second side.

5 Assemble the case. Glue and nail the drawer shelf into the side dadoes and glue and nail the top and bottom into the appropriate rabbets. Make sure that the front edge of the drawer shelf is flush with the front edge of the sides.

Before the glue dries, make sure the cabinet is square. Drop the back in place and secure with 4d finishing nails.

6 Make the drawers. The two drawers are not identical. They are mirror images: The left drawer front overhangs the left side of the drawer cabinet, and the right drawer overhangs the right side.

The drawers are simply built. The sides are attached to the drawer front with dowel pins and rabbeted to accept the back. The drawer bottom is screwed in place below the sides and back.

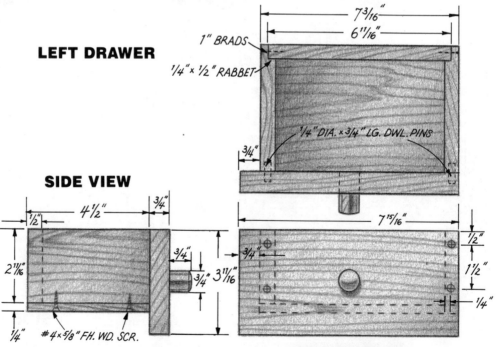

TOP VIEW

LEFT DRAWER

SIDE VIEW

FRONT VIEW

DOOR STOCK DETAIL

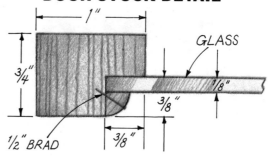

To make the drawer, first drill dowel-pin holes in the front edge of the drawer sides as shown in the *Left Drawer, Front View.*

On the table saw, rabbet the sides to accept the back, using a dado blade. When rabbeting, guide the drawer over the blade by using the miter gauge, set at 90 degrees.

Drill the hole for the drawer pull in the center of each drawer front. Insert the drawer pull made from a ¾-inch dowel in the hole and glue in place.

Assemble the drawer. First, attach the sides to the front with dowel pins and glue. Next, glue and nail the back into the rabbets in the sides. Finally, position the bottom, as shown, and screw it to the sides and back.

7 **Rabbet and miter the door stock to make the door.** The door glass sits in a rabbet in the back of the door frame. To cut the rabbet in the door stock, put a ⅜-inch rabbeting bit in the router. Secure the router in a router table and set it to cut a rabbet as shown in the *Door Stock Detail.*

Miter the door stock to make the door. Cut the miters in the stock one piece at a time and check their size against the front edge of the cabinet. Cut all four sides of the door frame.

Apply glue on the mitered ends and then clamp the door together with corner clamps. With the door frame still in the clamps, tack the miters together with 1-inch brads and allow the glue to dry.

The door glass is held in place by a ¼-inch quarter-round molding. Quarter-round molding can be bought from most lumber and hardware stores, or you can make it yourself with a ¼-inch roundover bit and router. Rout the edge of a wide

board, then rip the molding from it. To avoid kickback, set up the cut so the molding is on the side of the blade farthest from the fence. Miter the molding to fit the rabbeted back of the door.

8 **Hang the door.** With the hinge as your guide, mark and cut the hinge mortises in the front edge of the cabinet and the back of the door as shown in the *Front View.* You can cut the mortises with a chisel or a router and straight bit. Each mortise should take up an equal amount of the closed thickness of the hinge. Make sure that with the hinge in place the door sits flush against the cabinet.

Mark and predrill holes for the hinge screws, then hang the door.

For more information on mortising, see "Hinge Mortises" on page 7.

9 **Apply the finish and install the glass.** Finish sand the cabinet and soften the sharp edges. Round the door pulls with sandpaper.

The cabinet shown has a clear finish, but you can finish yours in any way that best fits your decor. You may want to choose a finish that will accent the objects you'll be displaying.

When the finish has dried, have the glass cut to fit the door. Install the glass with the quarter-round molding and ½-inch brads. Position the brass hangers as shown and screw in place.

BATHROOM CABINET

Walk into almost any bathroom, and you'll find a mirrored medicine cabinet over the sink and a towel rack beside the sink. Here's a variation on the theme: Hang a mirror over the sink and put a cabinet and towel shelf to the side.

The door design for this cabinet makes it particularly easy to build. It has a traditional frame-and-panel look, but the panels are plywood.

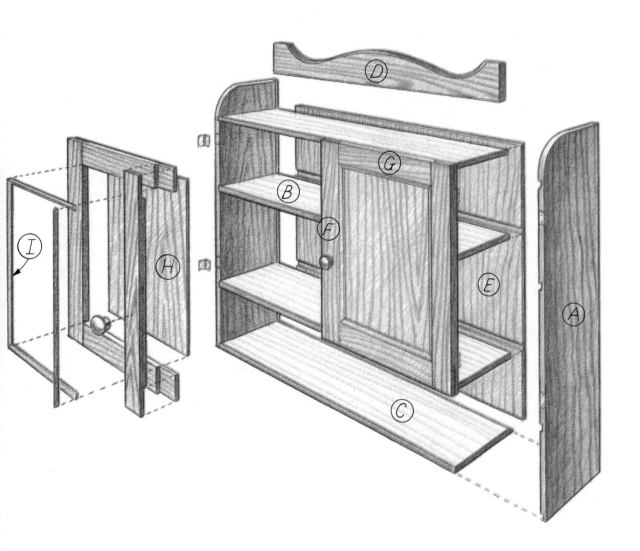

EXPLODED VIEW

1 **Select the stock and cut the carcase parts.** Joint, plane, rip, and cut the sides, shelves, and bottom to the sizes given in the Cutting List. Cut a 3-inch radius on the top front of each side on the band saw as shown in the *Side View*. Sand the sawed surfaces smooth. Lay out the sides as shown in the *Side View*.

2 **Dado the sides.** Cut the dadoes with the dado cutter on your table saw or radial arm saw. On the radial arm saw, align the bottoms of the two sides and dado both in one pass. On the table saw, dado one side at a time. Guide the cuts with the miter gauge, using the fence as a stop. Cut a dado on each side before readjusting the fence. On either saw, rabbet for the bottom using the same dado blade setup. Clamp a wooden auxiliary fence to the table saw fence to protect it from the cutter.

SHOP TIP: Cut sample dadoes in a piece of scrap. Adjust the width of the dado cutter by slipping washers made of paper over the saw arbor between the saw blades.

3 **Rabbet for the back and hanging rail.** The sides are rabbeted in back for the hanging rail and the back. Because the rail is thicker than the back, the rabbet changes from ¾ inch at top to ¼ inch below.

Cut a ¼-inch rabbet along the entire length of the back first. Then rout a ¾-inch rabbet to house the hanging rail. Make both cuts with the same setup on the router table: Put a ¾-inch straight bit in the router and set it to cut a groove ¼ inch deep. Adjust the fence to adjust the width of cut.

CUTTING LIST

Part	Quantity	Dimension	Comment
A. Sides	2	½″ × 5½″ × 26″	
B. Shelves	3	½″ × 5¼″ × 25½″	
C. Bottom	1	½″ × 5½″ × 25½″	
D. Hanging rail	1	¾″ × 3″ × 25½″	
E. Back	1	¼″ × 23″ × 26″	
F. Door stiles	4	¾″ × 2″ × 17¼″	Cut to fit.
G. Door rails	4	¾″ × 2″ × 13¼″	Cut to fit.
H. Door panels	2	¼″ × 10″ × 14″	Cut to fit.
I. Door trim	1	¼″ × ¼″ × 90″	Miter to fit.

Hardware

4 1 × 1-in. butt hinges
2 1¼-in. porcelain knobs
6 2d finishing nails
12 1-in. brads.
2 small magnetic door catches

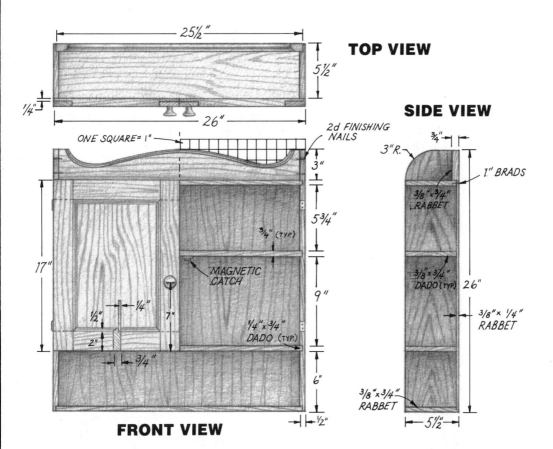

TOP VIEW

25½"

5½"

26"

¼"

SIDE VIEW

ONE SQUARE = 1"

2d FINISHING NAILS

3"

5¾"

¾" (TYP.)

MAGNETIC CATCH

9"

¼" x ¾" DADO (TYP.)

17"

½"

¼"

7"

2"

¾"

6"

½"

FRONT VIEW

¾"

3" R.

1" BRADS

3/8" x ¾" RABBET

3/8" x ¾" DADO (TYP.)

26"

3/8" x ¼" RABBET

3/8" x ¾" RABBET

5½"

4 **Shape the hanging rail.** Draw a 1-inch grid on a piece of paper and draw the hanging rail pattern onto it. Transfer the pattern to one end of the rail, flip it over, and transfer it to the other. Cut the curves. Sand out any saw marks. Rout the molding to the profile shown in the *Molding Detail* with a cove and bead bit with a ball bearing pilot.

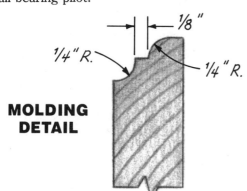

⅛"

¼" R.

¼" R.

MOLDING DETAIL

5 **Assemble the cabinet.** Test fit the cabinet parts and check for square and snug-fitting joints. Make any necessary adjustments.

Put glue in the dadoes and bottom rabbets. Make sure the top of the hanging rail is flush with the sides and clamp the cabinet together. Check to make sure the cabinet is square. When the glue is dry, nail the hanging rail to the sides with 2d finishing nails.

6 **Install the back.** Measure the opening for the back and cut the back to fit. Apply glue to the back rabbet. Put the back in position and nail it in place with 1-inch brads on each side.

7 **Make the door stiles and rails.** Cut the rails and stiles to fit the cabinet. Each rail is half as long as the cabinet

17

is wide. The stiles must be long enough to cover the bottom and top shelves as shown in the *Front View*. Set the dado blade on the table saw or radial arm saw to cut a half-lap joint on each piece as shown in the *Door Detail*. Test the depth and width of the cut on a piece of scrap and adjust as necessary. Cut the joints on the door parts.

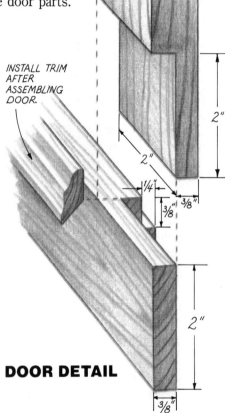

INSTALL TRIM
AFTER
ASSEMBLING
DOOR.

2"

2"

1/4"

3/8"

3/8"

2"

2"

3/8"

DOOR DETAIL

8 **Rabbet the door frames.** Cut ¼ × ⅜-inch rabbets for the plywood panels as shown in the *Door Detail*. To cut the rabbets, put a straight bit in the router. Secure the router in a router table and adjust the fence to get the appropriate size cut.

9 **Assemble the door frames.** Glue and clamp the doors together. Make

sure the doors are square before the glue sets. Cut the panels to fit snugly in the frames. Glue and clamp them into place.

10 **Install the door trim.** Rout a piece of scrap to the profile shown in the *Door Trim Detail*. Rip the molded edge from the scrap on the table saw to produce the door trim. When you rip the scrap, adjust the fence so that the trim is to the left of the saw blade rather than between the fence and the blade. Miter the trim to fit inside the door frame and glue it to the front of the door.

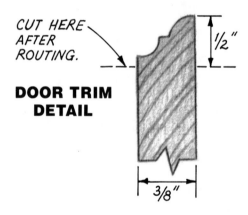

CUT HERE
AFTER
ROUTING.

1/2"

**DOOR TRIM
DETAIL**

3/8"

11 **Hang the doors and install the knobs.** Mortise each door for the butt hinges and hang the door, as explained in "Hinge Mortises" on page 7. Drill holes for the knobs and screw them in place.

12 **Apply finish.** Finish sand the entire piece. Apply stain, if you wish. For a finish that will resist moisture, apply spar varnish. When the finish is dry, attach the magnetic door catches below the middle shelf.

HALL MIRROR

This piece is a good example of how thoughtfully added features improve a design. A mirror can fit into any room of the home. Adding the shelf hooks to this mirror makes this piece special—and more functional.

The construction of this mirror is as simple as the design. First make the mirror frame. Glue the shelf to the frame and then glue the hanging board to the shelf.

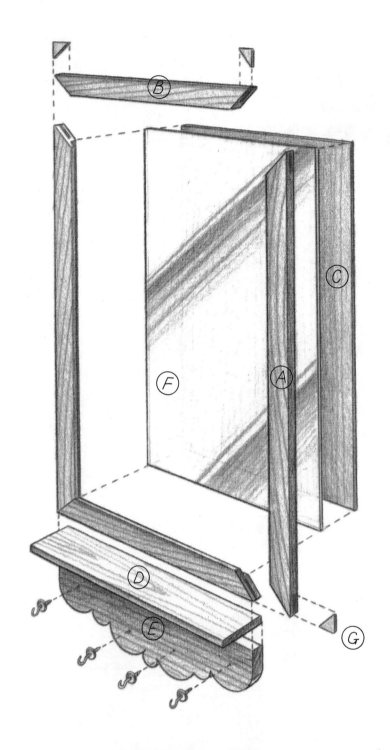

EXPLODED VIEW

1 Select the stock and cut the parts. The mirror shown is made from pine. You can build your hall mirror from any wood you may have on hand. Choose straight, flat stock. Joint, plane, rip, and cut the parts to the sizes given in the Cutting List.

2 Cut a rabbet in the frame stock. The mirror glass sets in a ⅜ × ⅜-inch rabbet in the back of the frame. Put a ⅜-inch straight bit or a ⅜-inch rabbeting bit in your router. Secue the router in a router table and cut the rabbet.

3 Miter the frame. Cut the frame miters on your table saw. Guide the frame stock as you miter with your miter gauge set at 45 degrees. Cut the sides, top, and bottom to length as you cut the miters on each end.

4 Assemble the frame. On a flat surface, glue and clamp the mirror frame

together and make sure that the frame is square. The frame is square if the diagonal corner-to-corner measurements are equal. To strengthen the miters, pre-drill and brad the miters together as shown in the *Front View.*

SPLINED MITER DETAIL

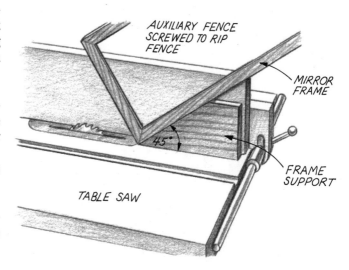

AUXILIARY FENCE SCREWED TO RIP FENCE

MIRROR FRAME

45°

FRAME SUPPORT

TABLE SAW

SHOP TIP: For extra-strong miter joints, glue splines in the corners instead of using nails. Cut the spline joints on the table saw after the frame has been glued and is completely dry.

First, lay out a spline on one corner of the frame as shown in the *Front View* and *Side View.* With the table saw miter gauge, cut a 45-degree angle on the end of a ¾ × 8 × 12-inch scrap of plywood. This is your frame support. Screw or clamp an auxiliary 12 × 24-inch plywood fence on the table saw fence. Raise the saw blade the depth of the spline cut. Put the frame support block against the auxiliary fence and put the mirror frame

against the support block as shown in the *Splined Miter Detail.* Adjust the saw fence until the spline layout aligns with the blade and lock the fence. Hold the frame firmly and push the frame and frame support piece completely through the blade to cut the spline slot. Turn the frame and cut the spline slot on each corner.

Next, rip a spline from some scrap wood to the thickness of the spline slot. The spline should slip snugly into the slot cut for it. Glue each spline in its slot and squeeze the frame against the spline with a C-clamp. When the glue has dried, trim the spline flush with the mirror frame with a sharp chisel or hand plane.

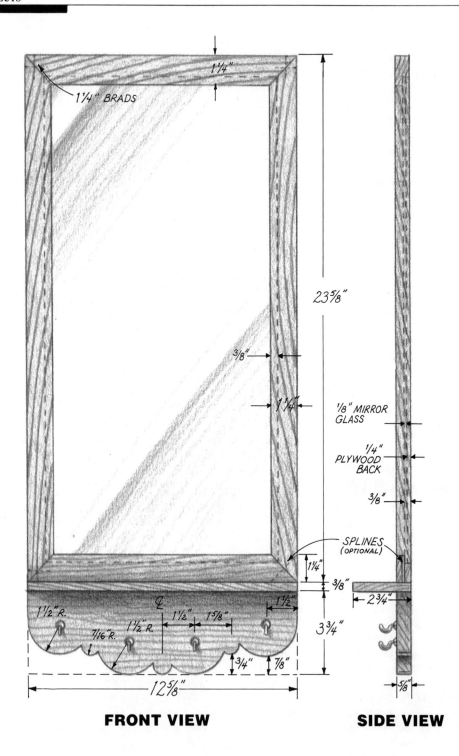

FRONT VIEW

SIDE VIEW

1¼"

1¼" BRADS

23⅝"

³⁄₈"

1¼"

⅛" MIRROR GLASS

¼" PLYWOOD BACK

³⁄₈"

SPLINES (OPTIONAL)

1¼"

³⁄₈"

2¾"

1½" R.

7⁄16" R.

1½" R.

C L

1½"

1⁵⁄₈"

1½"

3¾"

3¼"

¾"

⅞"

12⅝"

5⁄8"

5 **Attach the shelf to the frame.** Glue and clamp the shelf to the bottom of the frame. Clean up any excess glue.

6 **Cut the hanging board to shape.** With a compass, lay out the pattern on the bottom of the hanging board as shown in the *Front View*. Cut out the shape on the band saw. Clean up the sawed edge with files and sandpaper.

7 **Drill holes for the hanging hooks.** Lay out the hooks and drill holes for them that are slightly smaller than their threaded shank.

8 **Attach the hanging board.** Glue and clamp the hanging board to the bottom of the mirror shelf. Sand the mirror frame, frame back, shelf, and hanging board.

9 **Apply the finish and add the mirror glass and hooks.** After sanding, stain and varnish or paint the assembly to complement your decor. When the finish is dry, install the mirror glass. Cut your own mirror glass, or have a local glass shop cut it to size for you. Glue or nail the plywood backing in place. Screw four brass cup hooks into the predrilled holes.

10 **Hang your hall mirror.** Your local hardware store will have several options for hanging hardware. One of the simplest ways to hang the mirror is to screw two #8 × ¾-inch roundhead wood screws into the back of the frame, and stretch a stout wire between them. Then hang the mirror as you would a picture.

CUTTING LIST

Part	Quantity	Dimension	Comment
A. Sides	2	⅝″ × 1¼″ × 23⅝″	Cut top, bottom, and sides from one 80″ piece.
B. Top/bottom	2	⅝″ × 1¼″ × 12⅝″	
C. Mirror back	1	¼″ × 10⅞″ × 21⅞″	Plywood
D. Shelf	1	⅜″ × 2¾″ × 12⅝″	
E. Hanging board	1	⅝″ × 3¾″ × 12⅝″	
F. Mirror glass	1	⅛″ × 10¾″ × 21¾″	
G. Splines	4	⅛″ × 1¼″ × 1¼″	Optional

Hardware

4 ⅞-in.-long brass cup hooks
8 1¼-in. brads

DOVETAIL MIRROR

This mirror provides you with an interesting alternative to the usual mitered corner frame. Miters are attractive but must be reinforced with nails, splines, or other fasteners. Two dovetails and a single pin make up each joint of this frame, and the result is an extremely strong joint that easily holds a mirror or a picture.

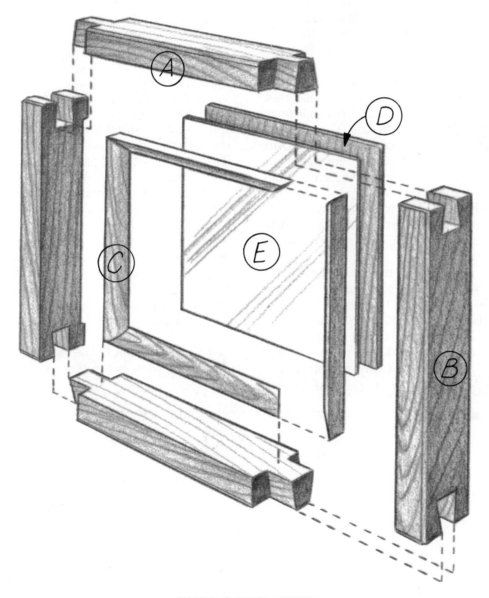

EXPLODED VIEW

1 **Select the stock and cut the parts.** Make your frame from any knot-free hardwood or softwood stock. Quarter-round molding is available from most lumber suppliers, but another ¾-inch molding could be substituted. Joint, plane, rip, and cut the parts to the sizes given in the Cutting List.

2 **Cut the dovetail joints.** Dovetail joints are made up of pins and tails. In the case of this frame, there is a single pin on each end of the rails. The pin slides between two tails on the stiles. If you are inexperienced at cutting dovetails, cut some practice dovetails before cutting them in the mirror frame.

First, set a marking gauge to the thickness of the rails and stiles and scribe a line around each end of the rails and stiles.

Next, lay out the pins, as shown in the *Side View,* on each end of the rails. Set a T-bevel to 80 degrees and lay out the pins on the end grain. Transfer the lines to the faces of the board with a square. Clearly mark the waste and cut it away with a dovetail saw or band saw.

When the pins have been cut, lay out the tails directly from the pins. Put the rails and stiles together as if to form a corner of the mirror. Trace around the pins to lay out one face of the tails. To lay out the second face, first transfer the lines across the end grain with a square and a sharp knife. Transfer the lines onto the second face with a sliding T-bevel set to the angles on the first face.

Put the stiles in a vise and cut down along the layout lines to the scribe lines with a dovetail saw. Stay to the outside of the layout lines. Chisel out the waste. Test fit the joints and pare the pins to fit, if necessary.

For more on cutting dovetails, see "Dovetailing" on page 42.

3 **Glue the frame together.** Glue and clamp the dovetail joints of the frame together on a flat surface. Measure across the corners to make sure the frame is square. Clean up any excess glue and allow the joints to dry.

4 **Cut the rabbet.** The mirror back fits within a rabbet routed in the back

CUTTING LIST

Part	Quantity	Dimension	Comment
A. Frame rails	2	1⅜″ × 2¾″ × 11¾″	
B. Frame stiles	2	1⅜″ × 2¾″ × 11¾″	
C. Quarter-round stock	1	¾″ × ¾″ × 40″	Miter to fit.
D. Mirror back	1	¼″ × 9¾″ × 9¾″	Plywood
E. Mirror glass	1	⅛″ × 8⅞″ × 8⅞″	

Hardware

8 #4 × ⅝-in. screws
1 mirror hanger

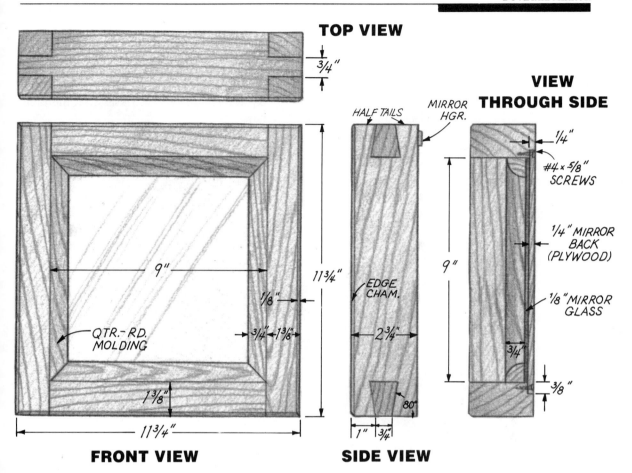

TOP VIEW

¾"

VIEW THROUGH SIDE

HALF TAILS

MIRROR HGR.

¼"

#4 x ⅝" SCREWS

¼" MIRROR BACK (PLYWOOD)

⅛" MIRROR GLASS

9"

11¾"

EDGE CHAM.

9"

QTR.-RD. MOLDING

⅛"

¾" 1⅜"

¾"

1⅜"

2¾"

80°

⅜"

11¾"

1" ¾"

FRONT VIEW

SIDE VIEW

inside edge of the frame as shown in the *View through Side*. Put a ⅜-inch rabbeting bit with a ball bearing guide in your router. Secure the router in a router table and adjust it to cut a ¼-inch-deep rabbet. Lay the frame flat on the router table over the bit and cut the rabbet by guiding the inside edge of the frame against the bit's bearing. Use a push stick and keep your hands well away from the cutter. Square the corners with a chisel.

5 **Chamfer the outside edges.** Put a chamfering bit in the router. Secure router in the router table and cut a ⅛-inch-wide chamfer on the outside edges of the mirror frame.

6 **Miter the quarter-round stock.** If you're not using ready-made quarter-round stock, you can make your own with a router and a router table. Guide the cut along a fence and shape the edge of a wide piece of stock with a ¾-inch-radius roundover bit. On the table saw, rip off the roundover stock. Set up the fence so the roundover edge is to the left of the blade rather than between the blade and the fence.

Once you have the stock, cut some test miters. Set your table saw blade to 45 degrees and cut the miters in some scrap. Put the test miters together and make sure that the resulting angle equals 90 degrees. Adjust the blade angle as necessary and miter the quarter-round stock to fit inside the mirror frame as shown in the *Front View*.

7 **Glue the quarter-round stock to the frame.** Adjust a marking gauge to scribe a line ⅛ inch from the rabbet on the inside of the frame. Scribe the line and glue and clamp the quarter-round stock just above the line. Clean up any excess glue with a damp cloth.

SHOP TIP: If you need to glue a small molding to an awkward spot, try clamping it with spring clamps. Spring clamps—which look something like large clothes pins—are available at most hardware stores and are an excellent help in an awkward situation. Open the clamp with one hand and set it in place. A plastic coating on the clamp helps protect the wood.

8 **Fit the back.** Depending on the accuracy of your dovetails, the back may need some adjustment. Test fit the back and trim it, if necessary, on the table saw.

9 **Apply the finish and install the mirror glass.** Finish sand the mirror frame. Stain and varnish or paint it to match your decor.

When the finish is dry, put the mirror glass in place in the back of the mirror frame. Set the back in its rabbet and screw it in place with #4 × ⅝-inch screws.

Attach a mirror hanger, which is available at most hardware stores, to the back of the mirror frame and hang your dovetail mirror.

WALL CLOCK

People have been fascinated with clocks ever since they were invented long ago in China. There is something very special about making a clock. Maybe it's the feeling that we have somehow captured time and controlled it.

This particular clock is unique in that its face, numerals, and hands are all made of wood. The wall clock shown is made from pine, but any type of wood will work fine.

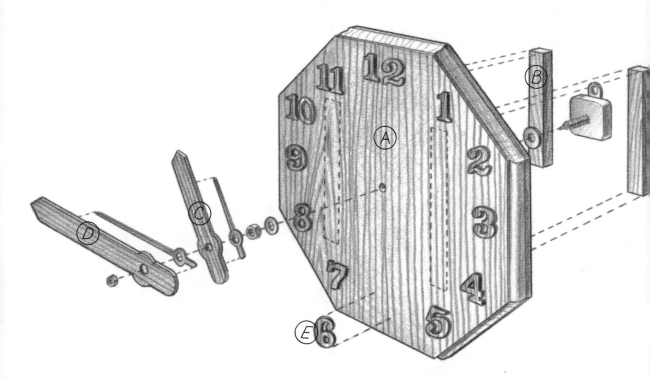

EXPLODED VIEW

CUTTING LIST

Part	Quantity	Dimension
A. Face	1	$\frac{3}{4}''$ × 14″ × 14″
B. Spacers	2	$\frac{3}{4}''$ × $\frac{11}{16}''$ × 7″
C. Hour hand	1	$\frac{3}{32}''$ × $\frac{3}{4}''$ × $5\frac{3}{4}''$
D. Minute hand	1	$\frac{3}{32}''$ × $\frac{3}{4}''$ × 7″
E. Numerals	15	$\frac{1}{8}''$ × $1\frac{1}{4}''$ × $1\frac{1}{4}''$

Hardware

6 $1\frac{1}{4}$-in. brads

$1\frac{5}{8}$ × $2\frac{1}{8}$ × $2\frac{1}{8}$-in. movement. Available from Precision Movements, 2024 Chestnut Street, Emmaus, PA 18049. Part #QC24US, extralong shaft.

1 Select the stock and cut the parts. Choose straight, flat stock for the face. Joint, plane, rip, and cut the parts to the sizes given in the Cutting List. If necessary, glue up stock to get a board wide enough for the face.

2 Cut the corners off the face to form an octagon. Mark and cut off the corners of the face on your band saw as shown in the *Front View.* Even up the cuts with a block plane or belt sander.

3 Rout the profile on the edge of the face. Put a ⁵⁄₃₂-inch-radius Roman ogee bit in your router. Secure the router in a router table and adjust the fence and router height to cut the profile shown in the *Side View.*

4 Attach the spacers to the back. Glue the spacers to the back of the face as shown. Nail them in place with 1¼-inch brads.

5 Drill the movement shaft hole. Lay out and drill a ⁵⁄₁₆-inch-diameter hole for the clock shaft in the center of the face. This hole must be drilled at exactly 90 degrees to the surface for the movement to seat correctly.

FRONT VIEW

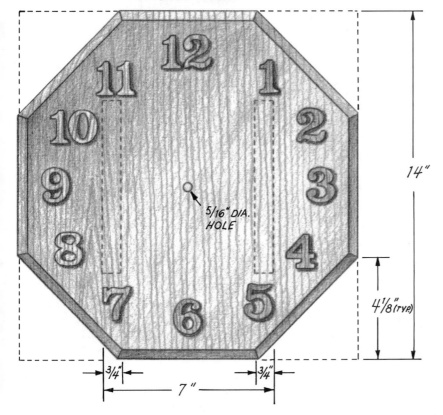

5/16" DIA. HOLE

14"

4¹⁄₈"(TYP.)

¾"   ¾"

7"

SIDE VIEW

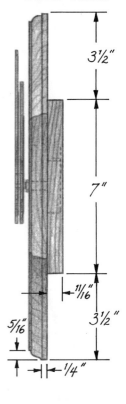

3½"

7"

¹¹⁄₁₆"

3½"

5/16"

¼"

ONE SQUARE = 1/4" (ACT. SIZE)

6 Cut the hands to shape and fasten them to the metal hands. Cut the hour and minute hands on the band saw to the dimensions shown. Sand the sawed edges and drill a 1/4-inch-diameter hole in each, as shown. Epoxy the metal hands included with the movement to the back of the wooden hands. Make sure that the shaft holes on the metal hands align with the holes in the wooden hands.

HOUR HAND LAYOUT

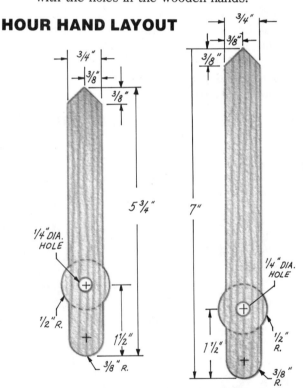

MINUTE HAND LAYOUT

7 Cut the numeral shapes and glue them to the face. Draw a 1/4-inch grid on a piece of paper and draw the numeral patterns onto it. Transfer the patterns to the wood. Note that you will need five "ones" and two "twos" for a complete set. Cut the numerals on a scroll saw, or by hand with a coping saw.

NUMERAL LAYOUT

Sand the sawed edges smooth and glue the numerals in place as shown in the *Front View.*

8 **Apply the finish.** Finish sand the clock. Because a completely wooden face makes this clock unique, give your clock a clear finish. An oil or a clear lacquer finish would work well.

9 **Install the movement.** Put the rubber washer over the movement shaft and insert the movement shaft through the shaft hole in the face. The shaft should protrude through the clock face. Put the brass washer over the shaft and lock it in place with the hex nut.

Slip the hour hand onto its shaft. The hour hand is held in place by friction.

Put the minute hand in place on its shaft and lock it in place with the nut provided. Because this nut drops below the surface of the wooden minute hand, you may have to do final tightening with tweezers or needle-nose pliers.

Install the battery, adjust the hands, and hang your clock on the wall.

BRACKET SHELF

Probably one of the quickest, easiest, most economical, and most useful projects you will ever build is a bracket shelf. These sturdy shelves can be adapted to fit any wasted wall space. Put them above a piece of furniture, base cabinet, or doorway.

These shelves can handle a lot of weight because they are attached directly to the frame of your house. You can load them up with your favorite books, or you can put breakables there that you want to keep out of little hands.

The shelf shown is made of pine. Hardwood will give the shelf a different look and provide strength for an extra-heavy load. Feel free to change the dimensions to fit your space.

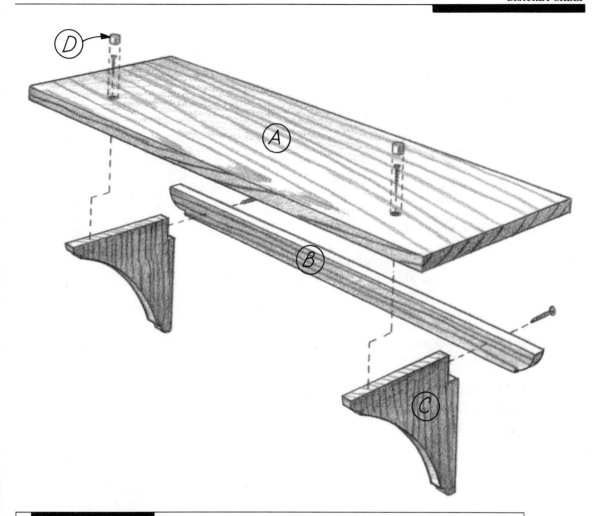

CUTTING LIST

Part	Quantity	Dimension
A. Shelf	1	$\frac{3}{4}'' \times 9\frac{1}{4}'' \times 24''$
B. Cleat	1	$\frac{3}{4}'' \times 1\frac{1}{2}'' \times 21\frac{1}{2}''$
C. Brackets	2	$1\frac{1}{8}'' \times 8'' \times 8''$
D. Plugs	6	$\frac{3}{8}''$ dia.

Hardware

2 #6 × 1½-in. flathead screws
2 #6 × 1-in. flathead screws
2 #8 × 2-in. flathead screws

1 **Select the stock and cut the parts.** Choose straight, flat stock. Joint, plane, rip, and cut the parts to the sizes given in the Cutting List. If you plan to make a longer-than-specified shelf, add an additional bracket for every 24 inches of additional length.

2 **Notch the brackets.** Cut a notch for the cleat in the corner of each bracket, as shown in the *Side View,* with a backsaw or dovetail saw.

3 **Cut the shape in the cleat ends and brackets.** Draw a ½-inch grid on a piece of paper and draw the cleat end and bracket patterns on to it. Transfer the patterns to the stock and cut the parts to shape with a band saw or jigsaw. Sand off the kerf marks left by the saw.

SHOP TIP: Because the brackets should have identical profiles, cut both at once. First stack the pieces together and secure by putting double-sided tape between them. Then cut both brackets in one operation.

4 **Glue the cleat to the bottom of the shelf.** Glue the top edge of the cleat to the bottom of the shelf. Secure with clamps and allow the glue to dry.

5 **Attach the brackets to the cleats and shelf.** Glue and screw the brackets to the cleat. Screw, but do not glue, the brackets to the shelf.

SHOP TIP: Test fit the shelf and drill the screw holes with a combination pilot hole bit. These bits drill a hole for the plug, a clearance hole for the screw shank, and a slightly smaller pilot hole for the screw threads all in one operation. Pilot hole bits are available at most hardware stores and are sold according to the screw size.

6 **Sand and finish the bracket shelf.** Plug the screw holes. Sand the shelf and remove excess glue. Sand the plugs flush. You can round the edges of the brackets and shelf with sandpaper to give the shelf an aged appearance.

Apply a finish that will complement your decor.

7 **Hang your bracket shelf.** Drill clearance and plug holes in the cleat so that you can drive screws through it and into the studs in your wall. (Normally studs are on 16- or 24-inch centers.) Screw the shelf in place. To cover the screws, tap some prefinished plugs into the plug holes.

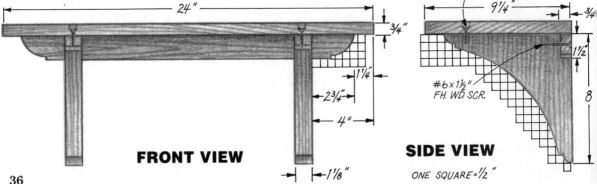

FRONT VIEW

SIDE VIEW

ONE SQUARE = ½"

BOOK-SHELF

In most homes, additional shelf space is always welcome. This bookshelf's dovetail construction, along with the thicker than normal shelves, provides ample support for heavy items like books. The drawer provides storage for loose or small items, like paper and pens. The playful design makes these shelves ideal for a child's room. At the same time, these straightforward shelves would be perfectly at home in the kitchen or den.

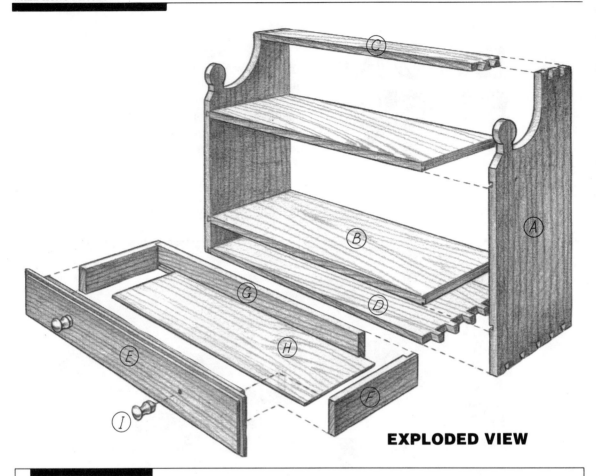

EXPLODED VIEW

CUTTING LIST

Part	Quantity	Dimension	Comment
A. Sides	2	$\frac{3}{4}'' \times 9\frac{1}{2}'' \times 25''$	
B. Shelves	2	$\frac{7}{8}'' \times 9\frac{1}{2}'' \times 26''$	
C. Top	1	$\frac{7}{8}'' \times 3\frac{1}{4}'' \times 26\frac{3}{4}''$	
D. Bottom	1	$\frac{7}{8}'' \times 9\frac{1}{2}'' \times 26\frac{3}{4}''$	
E. Drawer front	1	$1'' \times 4\frac{1}{2}'' \times 26\frac{3}{4}''$	
F. Drawer sides	2	$\frac{5}{8}'' \times 2\frac{11}{16}'' \times 9''$	
G. Drawer back	1	$\frac{5}{8}'' \times 2\frac{11}{16}'' \times 24\frac{5}{8}''$	
H. Drawer bottom	1	$\frac{1}{4}'' \times 8\frac{3}{8}'' \times 24\frac{3}{8}''$	Plywood
I. Drawer pulls	2	$2\frac{3}{4}'' \times \frac{13}{16}'' \times \frac{13}{16}''$	Cut to length after turning.

Hardware

As needed, 4d coated nails
$2\frac{1}{2} \times 2$-in. hangers. Available from The Woodworkers' Store, 21801 Industrial Boulevard, Rogers, MN 55374. Part #D3008.

1 Select the stock and cut the parts. You can build these shelves out of almost any wood. Softwoods such as pine or fir are fine. If you choose to build the bookcase out of hardwood, good choices are red or white oak, cherry, maple, walnut, or mahogany. Choose lumber that is relatively free of knots. If you wish, select a less-expensive wood such as poplar for the drawer sides and back.

Joint, plane, rip, and cut the parts to the sizes given in the Cutting List. If necessary, glue up boards to get the wider parts.

2 Rout sliding dovetail slots in the sides. The shelves are joined to the sides with sliding dovetails. Lay out the dovetail groove on the bookshelf sides. Put a ½-inch dovetail bit in your router. Clamp a straightedge across the side and rout the dovetail groove to the depth indicated. Repeat for each shelf groove.

SHOP TIP: Dovetail grooves must be routed in one pass, and this can strain the router and leave a ragged cut. Avoid this by first routing a narrow *dado* along the path of the dovetail. Rout the dado to slightly less than the full depth with a double-fluted straight bit no wider than the top of the dovetail bit's cut (about ⅜ inch). This removes most of the waste. Follow up the dado by routing with the dovetail bit.

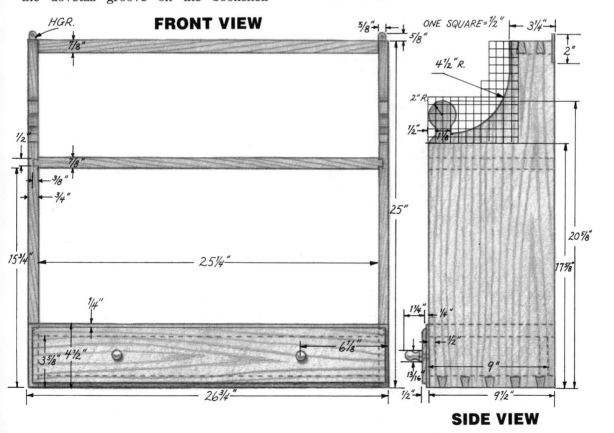

FRONT VIEW

SIDE VIEW

ONE SQUARE = ½"

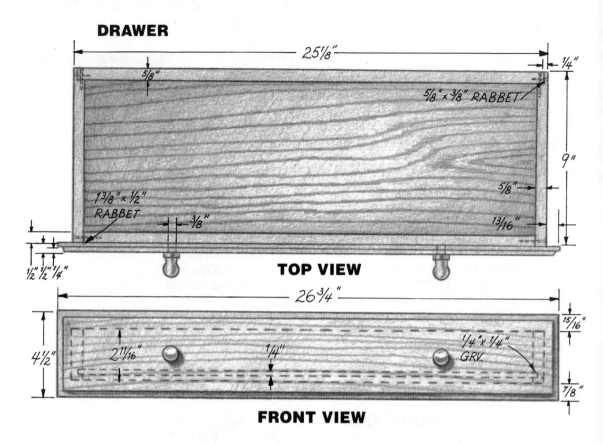

DRAWER

25⅛"

¼"

5/8"

5/8" x 3/8" RABBET

9"

1⅜" x ½" RABBET

3/8"

5/8"

13/16"

½" ½" ¼"

TOP VIEW

26¾"

15/16"

4½"

2 11/16"

¼"

¼" x ¼" GRV.

7/8"

FRONT VIEW

3 **Cut the sliding dovetails in the shelves.** Put a ½-inch dovetail bit in the router. Secure the router in your router table. Measure the depth of the dovetail groove in the bookshelf sides. Raise the router bit this amount above the table. Set the router table fence so most of the bit is partially buried in the fence. Stand the shelves upright on the table against the fence. Make one pass on each end of each shelf; flip the boards over and repeat. Test the fit in the grooves of the sides.

4 **Lay out and cut the profile in the sides.** Draw a ½-inch grid on a piece of paper and draw the profile shown in the *Side View* onto it. Transfer the pattern to the wood and cut the profile with a band saw, jigsaw, or coping saw. Clean up the cut with files and sandpaper.

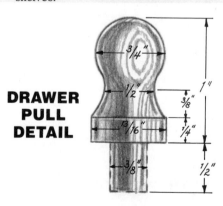

DRAWER PULL DETAIL

¾"

½"

1"

3/8"

13/16"

¼"

3/8"

½"

SHOP TIP: When cutting the profile on the band saw, do not try to cut the pattern in one pass. Make several relief cuts to remove the bulk of the waste material before making the final cuts to your line.

5 **Lay out and cut the dovetails.** The sides are connected to the top and bottom with dovetails. The joint is made up of tails and pins. Lay out the tails on the sides as shown in the *Side View.* After the tails have been cut, lay out and cut the pins on the top and bottom. If you haven't cut a lot of dovetails, practice on a piece of scrap. "Dovetailing" on page 42 shows you exactly how to cut the joint.

6 **Assemble the sides to the top, bottom, and shelves.** Be sure to glue up on a flat surface. Presand the interior of the bookcase. Put glue on the mating surfaces of the dovetails and clamp them together. Put glue in the sliding dovetail grooves and on the shelf dovetails. Push them together by hand. If they stick, pull them together with clamps. Put one shelf in at a time, until the front edges are flush with the bookcase sides.

Measure the bookcase across both diagonals, from corner to corner. If the bookcase is square, the measurements will be equal. If they aren't, run a clamp from corner to corner across the longer diagonal. Tighten it gently until the measurements are equal.

Sight across the front of the shelves to make sure the bookcase is not twisted. The front edges of the shelves should be parallel. If one corner of a shelf appears higher than the others, the cabinet is twisted. Push down gently on the high corner until it aligns with the others.

7 **Rout the drawer front.** Put a ¼-inch roundover bit in the router. Secure the router in the router table and adjust it as shown in the *Drawer Front Router Setup.* Stand the drawer front on edge and rout the detail on all four sides as shown. Rout the end grain first, to avoid tear out.

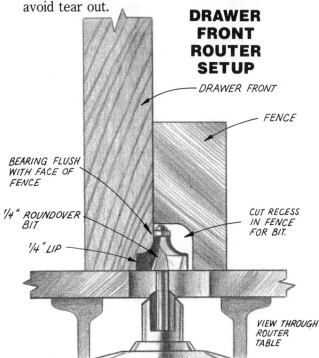

DRAWER FRONT ROUTER SETUP

DRAWER FRONT

FENCE

BEARING FLUSH WITH FACE OF FENCE

¼" ROUNDOVER BIT

¼" LIP

CUT RECESS IN FENCE FOR BIT.

VIEW THROUGH ROUTER TABLE

8 **Lay out the rabbets for the drawer sides.** Clamp the drawer front in place over the drawer opening on the bookcase and set the drawer sides in place on either side of the compartment. Reach into the drawer compartment from the rear and mark the outline of the opening on the back of the drawer front with a pencil.

9 **Rabbet for the drawer sides.** Put a ½-inch straight bit in the router. Secure the router in the router table. Raise the bit to a height of ½ inch and rout to the layout lines in several passes, adjusting the fence with each pass. Steady the drawer face with a miter gauge, if your router table has one, or with a 12 × 12 × ¾-inch scrap of plywood riding against the fence behind the drawer face.

10 Cut the rabbets in the drawer sides. Put a ¾-inch straight bit in the router. Secure the router in a router table and adjust the bit height and the fence to cut the rabbet on the back edge of the drawer sides. Support the drawer sides with a miter gauge or a scrap of plywood as before.

11 Rout the groove for the drawer bottom. Put a ¼-inch straight bit in the router. Secure the router in the router table. Rout a groove for the bottom ¼ inch from the bottom edge of the drawer sides and back, as shown in the *Drawer Front View*. Rout a groove in the drawer front to align with the groove in the drawer sides.

12 Make the drawer pulls. Turn the drawer pulls on your lathe to the profile shown in the *Drawer Pull Detail*. If you don't have a lathe, substitute ready-made pulls. Lay out and drill holes

DOVETAILING

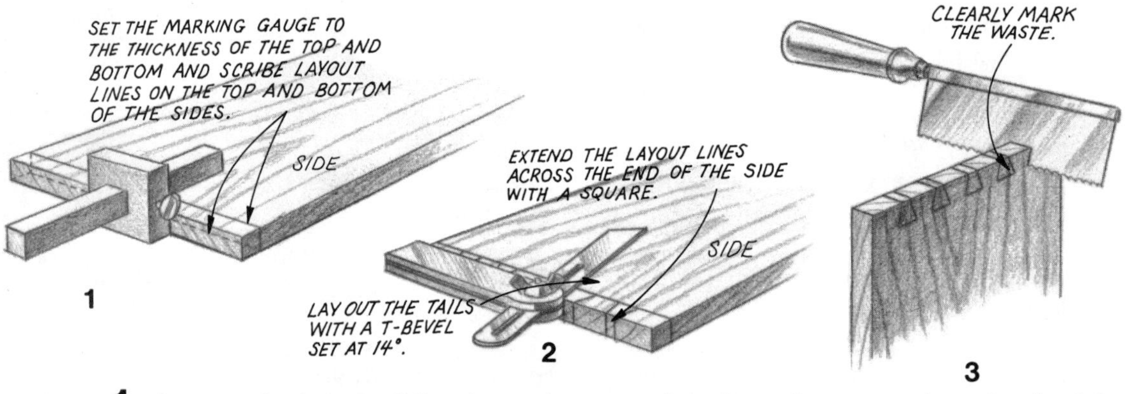

SET THE MARKING GAUGE TO THE THICKNESS OF THE TOP AND BOTTOM AND SCRIBE LAYOUT LINES ON THE TOP AND BOTTOM OF THE SIDES.

SIDE

EXTEND THE LAYOUT LINES ACROSS THE END OF THE SIDE WITH A SQUARE.

SIDE

CLEARLY MARK THE WASTE.

LAY OUT THE TAILS WITH A T-BEVEL SET AT 14°.

1   2   3

1 Lay out the length of the pins and tails. Set a marking gauge to the thickness of the top and bottom—⅞ inch, in this case. Scribe a line around the top and bottom of the sides. Then set the marking gauge to the thickness of the sides—¾ inch—and scribe a line around both ends of the top and bottom.

2 Lay out the tails. First, lay out the tails as shown in the *Side View* with a sliding T-bevel set at 14 degrees in this case. Then, ex-

tend the layout lines across the end grain of the side with a square. Next, lay out the angle of the tails on the back face of the board, so that they meet the lines you drew on the end grain.

3 Cut out the tails. Saw down to the scribe line, cutting on the waste side of the layout lines. A Japanese Dozuki saw, like the one shown here, is easy to control and cuts crisp lines. Watch your layout lines carefully: Follow the angle of tails and make sure you don't cut for the pulls in the drawer front as shown in the *Front View*.

13 **Assemble the drawer.** Presand the drawer interior and assemble the drawer on a flat surface. Glue and nail the sides into the rabbet you routed in the drawer face. Slip the drawer bottom into the grooves. Nail and glue the drawer back into the rabbets in the drawer sides. If you are making your drawer from hardwood, predrill all of the nail holes to avoid splitting. Make sure that the drawer is square.

14 **Apply the finish and attach the hangers.** Finish sand the bookshelf. Stain and varnish or paint your bookshelf to match your decor.

When the finish is dry, attach the hangers to the back of the bookshelf. You can buy hangers similar to the ones shown from most hardware stores, or you can order them from the source given in the Cutting List. Position the hangers as shown in the *Front View*. Trace around the hangers and rout recesses for the hangers. Screw the hangers in place.

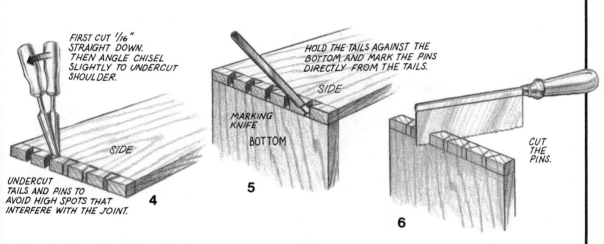

through either one of the scribe lines.

4 **Remove the waste between the tails.** Chisel halfway through the board from one side; turn the board over and chisel from the other side. Undercut slightly as shown to ease assembly of the joint.

5 **Lay out the pins.** For best results, lay out the pins by tracing around the tails. Hold the tails against the end grain of the top

and bottom and trace around the tails with a marking knife. Carry your layout lines down to the scribe lines and clearly mark the waste with a pencil.

6 **Cut out the pins.** Saw along the layout lines to the scribe lines, and chisel away the waste as before. Test fit the dovetails. Pare the pins to fit the tails if necessary. Do not glue them in place until you have finished the rest of the cabinet.

PEG SHELF

Here's a peg shelf that's more than just a board with some pegs pounded into it. There are two shelves, a towel bar, and mug pegs. A peg shelf like this is an attractive addition to any country kitchen or dining room.

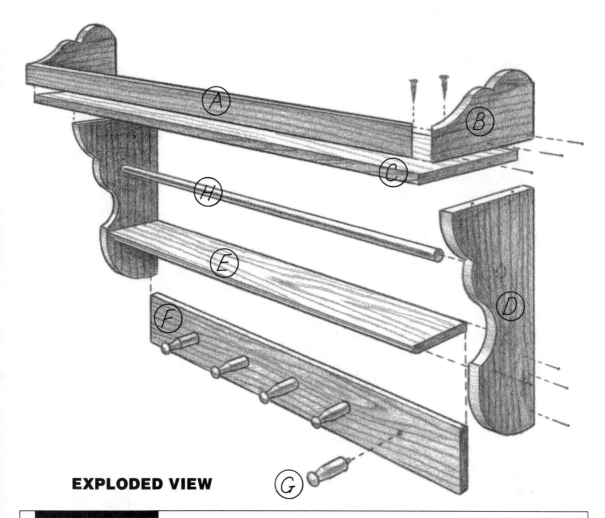

EXPLODED VIEW

CUTTING LIST

Part	Quantity	Dimension	Comment
A. Front rail	1	½″ × 2″ × 48″	Miter to fit.
B. Side rails	2	½″ × 5″ × 9″	Miter to fit.
C. Upper shelf	1	¾″ × 8″ × 45¾″	
D. Brackets	2	¾″ × 7″ × 17″	
E. Lower shelf	1	¾″ × 4″ × 37″	
F. Peg support	1	¾″ × 5″ × 37″	
G. Mug pegs*	5	¾″ dia. × 3⅜″	Overall dimension
H. Dowel	1	¾″ dia. × 37¾″	

*Mug pegs are available from Cherry Tree Toys, Inc., P.O. Box 369, Belmont, OH 43718. Part #143 (maple, oak, cherry, or walnut).

Hardware

As needed, 4d finishing nails
4 #8 × 1¼-in. flathead wood screws
2 brass hangers. Available from Cherry Tree Toys, Inc. Part #2710-A.

1 Select the stock and cut the parts. The shelf pictured is made from pine, but you can make yours from whatever wood you have. Choose straight, flat stock. Joint, plane, rip, and cut the parts to the sizes given in the Cutting List.

2 Cut the miters. Cut miters in the front rail and side rails to fit around the upper shelf. Test fit the rails.

3 Make a paper pattern and cut the parts to shape. Draw a 1-inch grid on a large sheet of paper and draw the bracket and side rail patterns onto it. Transfer the patterns to the wood. Cut the shapes using a band saw or jigsaw.

SHOP TIP: To get two pieces with identical curves, cut both at once. First stack the pieces together and secure by putting double-sided tape between them. Then cut both brackets in one operation.

4 Assemble the upper shelf. Glue and nail the front rail to the front edge of the top shelf. Make sure that the mitered ends are even with the corners of the upper shelf. Nail, but do not glue, the side rails to the upper shelf.

5 Chamfer the front edge of the lower shelf. Set your table saw blade to 45 degrees. Place the table saw

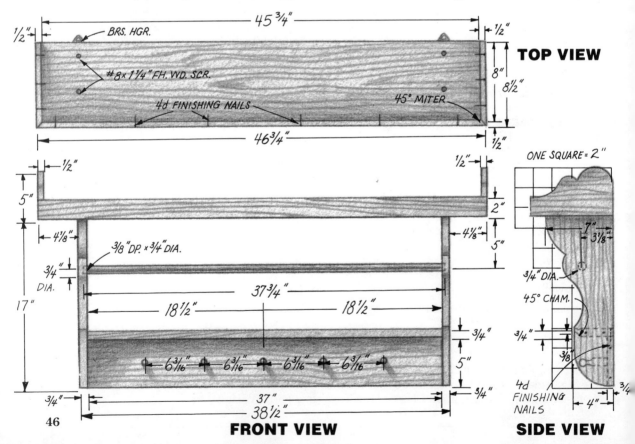

TOP VIEW

FRONT VIEW

SIDE VIEW

fence to the left of the blade and position the fence to cut the chamfer on the front edge of the lower shelf. Make sure that you leave a ⅜-inch unchamfered edge as shown in the *Side View*.

6 **Drill the peg holes and attach the lower shelf to the peg support.** The mug pegs for this shelf are commercially made, and the diameter of the shank sometimes varies slightly. To make sure the pegs will fit in the holes drilled for them, drill a sample ½-inch hole in a piece of scrap wood. The peg should fit snugly. If not, change drill bits as necessary. When you have found the proper drill bit, lay out and drill the peg holes in the peg support as shown in the *Front View*. Nail and glue the lower shelf to the top edge of the peg support as shown in the *Side View*, but don't attach the mug pegs yet.

7 **Mark and drill the dowel holes.** Mark the brackets for the dowel holes as shown in the *Side View*. Before you drill, make sure that your markings are both on the *inside* edge of the brackets. Drill a ⅜-inch-deep by ¾-inch-diameter hole into each bracket.

8 **Assemble the peg shelf.** On a flat surface, test fit the peg shelf and make any necessary adjustments. Put the dowel in place and glue and nail the lower shelf and peg support assembly to the brackets.

When you have assembled the lower section of the peg shelf, center the upper shelf on the brackets. Make sure that the back of the upper shelf is even with the back of the brackets. Screw and glue the upper shelf to the brackets.

SHOP TIP: Mark and drill recess and pilot holes through the top shelf and into the brackets with a combination pilot hole bit. These bits drill a hole for the plug, a clearance hole for the screw shank, and a slightly smaller pilot hole for the screw threads. Combination pilot hole bits are available at most hardware stores and are sold according to the screw size.

9 **Attach the mug pegs.** Apply a small amount of glue to the base of the mug pegs and insert them into the peg holes.

10 **Apply finish.** Countersink the nails and fill the nail holes with wood putty. Finish sand the peg shelf, rounding the edges slightly as you sand. Finish the peg shelf in any way you choose. The one pictured has a natural finish, which allows the wood grain to show through.

When the finish has dried, attach the brass hangers to the back edge of the top shelf.

PLATE RACK

Do you remember that assortment of unique old dinner plates stacked up in your grandmother's cupboard? Lovers of fine china have always lamented the fact that they have no place to display their collection. This pine plate rack offers an inexpensive and unique solution.

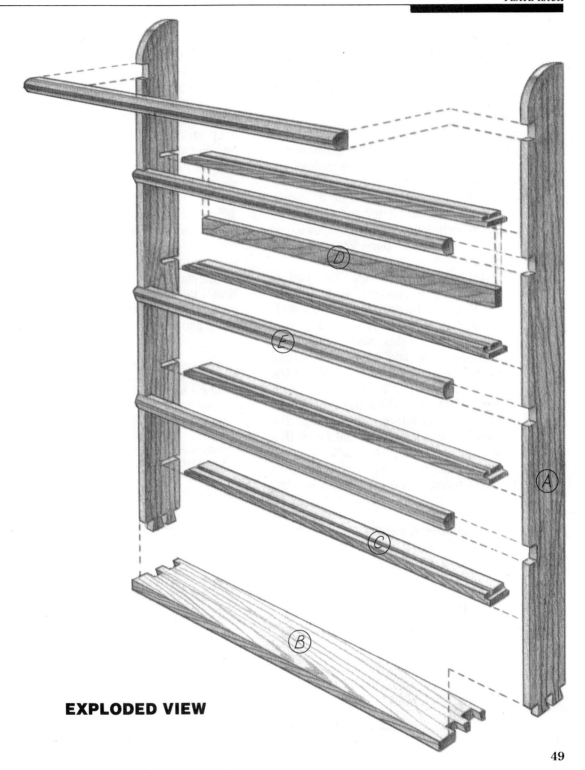

EXPLODED VIEW

1 **Select the stock and cut the parts.** Choose straight, flat stock without knots. Joint, plane, rip, and cut the parts to the sizes given in the Cutting List.

2 **Lay out and rout the dadoes in the sides.** Lay out the dadoes for the shelves on the sides as shown in the *Side View Joinery Detail*. Put a ½-inch straight bit in your router and set it up to cut a ⅜-inch-deep dado, as explained in "Routed Dadoes" on page 52.

3 **Rabbet the shelves.** The end of each shelf is rabbeted to fit the dadoes. Rout the rabbets in the shelf ends with the router and bit you used to rout the dadoes in the sides. Secure the router in a router table and adjust the bit and fence to cut a ¼ × ⅜-inch rabbet in the shelf ends as shown in the *Shelf Detail*. Check the fit by routing the rabbet in a scrap piece and fitting it into one of the dadoes in the sides. Guide the cut with a miter gauge, if your router table has one, or with a 12 × 12 × ¾-inch scrap of plywood riding against the fence and behind the shelf.

4 **Rout the plate groove in the shelves.** To rout a plate groove in each shelf, put a 45-degree "V" grooving bit in the router. Secure the router in a router table and set it up to cut a ¼-inch-deep groove as shown in the *Groove Detail*. Set up a fence and guide the shelves against it as you rout the plate groove shown in the *Groove Detail*.

5 **Notch the sides for the shelf rails.** Lay out ⅝-inch-deep by 1¼-inch-wide notches for the shelf rail as shown in the *Side View Joinery Detail*. Cut the notches with a dado blade in your table saw. Put the side on the table with the front edge down and guide the cut with a miter gauge set at 90 degrees.

SHOP TIP: To get two identical notches, cut both at once. Stack the pieces together with the shelf dadoes facing in and the front edges aligned with each other and secure by putting double-sided tape between them. Then cut both notches in one operation to ensure perfect notch alignment.

CUTTING LIST

Part	Quantity	Dimension
A. Sides	2	¾" × 4" × 50"
B. Bottom	1	¾" × 5" × 32½"
C. Shelves	4	¾" × 2" × 33¼"
D. Hanging strip	1	¾" × 1¼" × 32½"
E. Shelf rails	3	1" × 1¼" × 34"

Hardware		

8 4d finishing nails

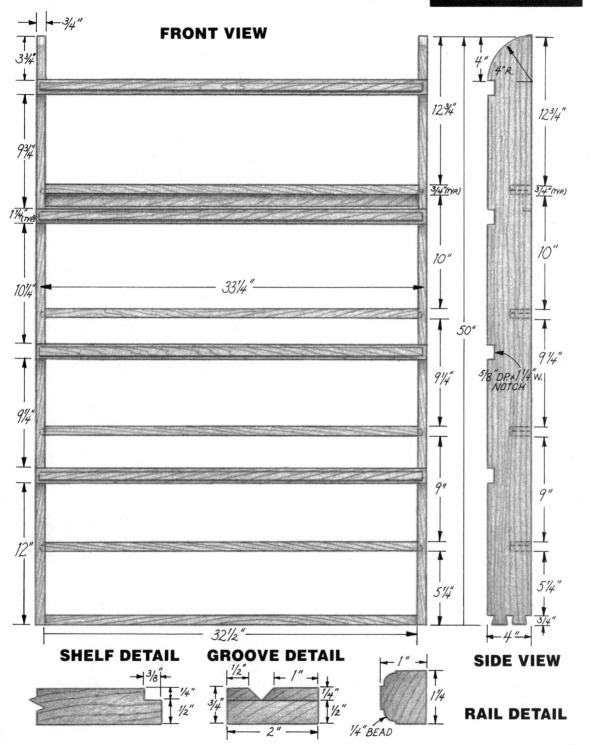

FRONT VIEW

SIDE VIEW

SHELF DETAIL

GROOVE DETAIL

RAIL DETAIL

ROUTED DADOES

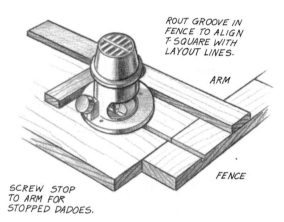

ROUT GROOVE IN
FENCE TO ALIGN
T-SQUARE WITH
LAYOUT LINES.

ARM

FENCE

SCREW STOP
TO ARM FOR
STOPPED DADOES.

1 **Make a T-square.** Screw together two pieces of hardwood at right angles, as shown. Make the square out of a durable hardwood.

2 **Rout an index groove.** To determine exactly where the router will cut, put the bit you plan to use in it and rout a shallow groove in the head of the T-square.

3 **Lay out dadoes on the stock.** Lay out the dadoes with a sharp pencil and align the index groove with the layout lines. Clamp the T-square in place.

4 **Rout the dadoes.** Set the router to cut a groove about ⅛ inch deep. Rout the dado by guiding the router along the arm of the T-square. Rout the dado in a series of passes, each about ⅛ inch deeper than the last.

If the dadoes stop at one end, as those on the plate rack do, attach a stop block to the fence so that each dado will be exactly the same length. Lay out and rout a test dado in a piece of scrap wood. When you have determined the length of the dado, screw a block to the T-square arm to keep the router from traveling any farther.

6 **Rout the front edges of the shelf rails.** Rout the rails to the profile shown in the *Rail Detail*. Put a ¼-inch beading bit in a router. Secure the router in a router table and rout all around the front edge, starting with the end grain to eliminate tear out. Guide the end grain cuts with a miter gauge or plywood scrap.

7 **Cut the curve on the top of the sides.** Lay out the curve on the top of the sides as shown in the *Side View Joinery Detail*. Cut the sides to shape with a jigsaw or band saw and sand away the saw marks.

8 **Cut the dovetails in the sides and the pins in the bottom.** Lay out and cut the dovetails on the side of the rack. Use the tails as a template to lay out the pins on the bottom of the rack. For more on cutting dovetails, see "Dovetailing" on page 42.

9 **Assemble the plate rack.** Sand any surfaces that will be difficult to reach once the rack is assembled. Be careful not to sand any of the joinery.

Assemble the plate rack beginning with the bottom. Coat the inside of the pins with glue and press the bottom into the sides. Put a small amount of glue in each dado and slide the shelves into place. Glue and clamp the hanging strip to the underside of the top shelf.

Next, put a little glue in the shelf rail dadoes in the sides, position the rails, and nail them in place with 4d finishing nails. If necessary, clamp across the sides to hold the dovetails tight while the glue sets.

10 **Finish the plate rack.** When the glue is dry, remove any excess glue and finish sand the plate rack. As you sand, round-over the edges of the plate rack slightly to give it a softer look. The plate rack shown has a clear varnish finish. You can do the same, but feel free to finish your plate rack in a way that will best fit your decor.

11 **Hang plate rack.** Select a spot on the wall for the rack and locate the studs in the wall. Drill clearance holes in the hanging strip that will align with the studs. Screw the shelf to the studs.

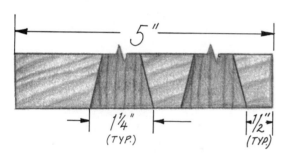

JOINERY DETAIL

PART TWO

CABINETS, BOXES, AND STORAGE

QUILT RACK

Is there a quilt lover in your house? With only two different parts, this quilt rack is nearly as easy to make as it is to assemble.

This project is designed to be easily built on the router table. Because you'll be setting up the router anyway, why not make several? The rack doesn't use much material and it makes a terrific gift.

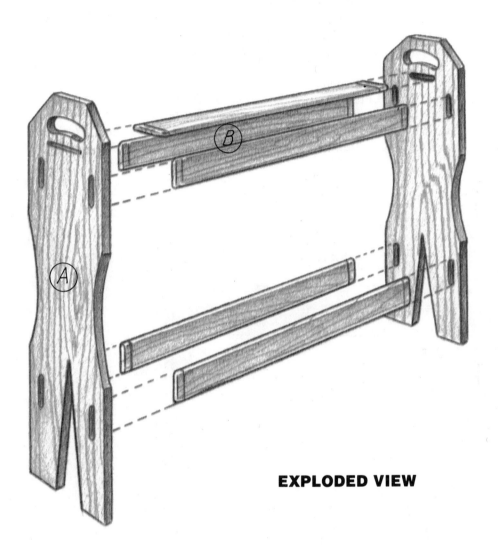

EXPLODED VIEW

CUTTING LIST

Part	Quantity	Dimension	Comment
A. Sides	2	¾″ × 9″ × 34″	Final length is 33″.
B. Slats	5	½″ × 2½″ × 29¾″	

1 Select the stock and cut the parts. Joint, plane, rip, and cut the parts to the sizes given in the Cutting List. You can cut the sides from 1 × 10s and the slats from ½-inch-thick stock that's usually used for doorjambs. The dimension given in the Cutting List for the sides is longer than necessary to make routing the mortises easier. You will cut the legs to the exact length later.

2 Cut vertical mortises in the sides. The eight vertical mortises are cut on a single router table setup. Put a ¼-inch straight bit in your router. Secure the router in a router table and adjust it to cut ¼ inch deep. Position the fence 1⅛ inches from the bit. Clamp stops to the fence at the positions illustrated in *Routing the Vertical Mortises*.

To rout the mortises, put a side

FRONT VIEW

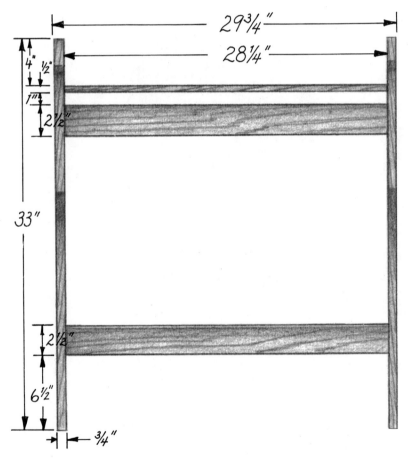

SIDE VIEW

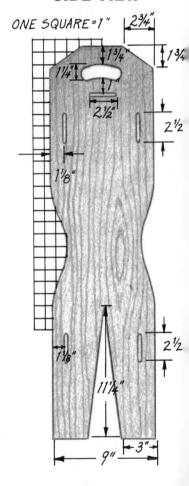

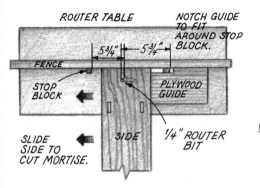

ROUTING THE
HORIZONTAL MORTISES

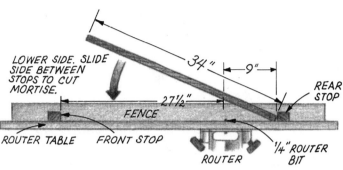

ROUTING THE
VERTICAL MORTISES

against the rear stop and lower the it into the bit, as shown in *Routing the Vertical Mortises*. Move the side forward until it hits the other stop. Raise one end of the side to remove it from the router table. Repeat for the remaining vertical mortises. Raise the bit another ¼ inch or so, repeat the process, and then raise the bit to a little over ¾ inch so it cuts through the side on the third round of cuts.

3 **Cut horizontal mortises in the sides.** Cut the extra length off one end of the sides. Rout the mortises with a two-stop router-table setup as before. This time, set the fence 4 inches from the router bit and set the blocks at the dimensions shown in *Routing the Horizontal Mortises*. Guide the freshly cut end along the fence with a miter gauge. Square the edges of each mortise with a ¼-inch chisel.

SHOP TIP: If your router table doesn't have a slot for a miter gauge, use a piece of plywood, as illustrated, to guide the stock along the fence. Cut a notch in the plywood to fit around the stop block.

4 **Shape the sides.** Draw a ½-inch grid on a piece of paper and draw the curve in the sides onto it. Transfer the pattern to the wood. Lay out the angled cuts on the top of one side as shown in the *Side View*. Clamp the sides together, align them carefully. Cut the curves on a band saw or jigsaw. Cut the angles with a jigsaw or circular saw. Sand the sawed edges.

5 **Cut the handholds.** With the sides still clamped together, lay out the handholds as shown in the *Handhold De-*

tail. Use a compass to draw two ⅝-inch-radius circles with their centers 2⅝ inches apart. Connect the circles with lines at top and bottom, both curving slightly upward. Drill out the circles with a 1¼-inch bit and complete the cuts with a jigsaw.

6 **Make the slats.** To round-over the slats to the profile shown in the *Tenon Detail* put a ¼-inch roundover bit in the router. Secure the router in the router table and make the cut, guiding the slat against a fence.

Set up a dado blade in your table saw to cut the tenons in the end of the slats. Test the cut on a piece of scrap and adjust the height of the blade to get a tenon that fits snugly in the mortise. Cut tenons on both ends of each slat.

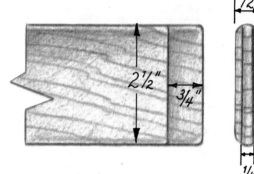

TENON DETAIL

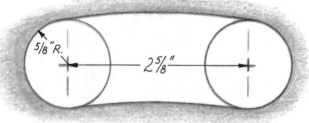

HANDHOLD DETAIL

SHOP TIP: To get perfectly aligned shoulders on the tenons, guide the cut against the table saw fence. First, screw a straight, surfaced length of wood to the fence to protect it. Set the fence so the ¾-inch-wide dado blade just touches it. Guide the stock over the cutter with the miter gauge. Turn the stock over and repeat.

7 **Apply finish.** Finish sand the parts. The quilt rack shown has a light brown stain and is finished with shellac.

MAGAZINE RACK

Originally built as a garden tool tote, this piece now serves its owner as a magazine rack. The same tote could hold woodworking tools, household cleaning supplies, or even freshly harvested vegetables and fruits as originally intended.

A wonderful aspect of the country style is that it doesn't require flawless materials and craftsmanship. As you look at the original, pictured here, every bevel and miter is just a tad different than all the others in the tote. The divider is far from symmetrical. Yet the piece works, both functionally and visually.

EXPLODED VIEW

CUTTING LIST

Part	Quantity	Dimension	Comment
A. Divider	1	$\frac{3}{4}'' \times 9\frac{5}{8}'' \times 27''$	Cut to pattern.
B. Ends	2	$\frac{3}{4}'' \times 4\frac{1}{2}'' \times 15''$	Cut to pattern.
C. Sides	2	$\frac{1}{2}'' \times 4\frac{1}{2}'' \times 27''$	Cut to fit.
D. Bottom	3	$\frac{1}{2}'' \times 12\frac{5}{8}'' \times 26''$	

Hardware

As needed, 4d square-cut nails

1 **Select the stock and cut the parts.** The tote is made up of four basic parts: divider, ends, sides, and bottom. Joint, plane, rip, and cut the parts to the sizes given in the Cutting List. The dimensions for the divider, end, and sides are all slightly long. You will cut them to size as you make the rack.

2 **Cut out the divider.** Lay out the shape of the divider directly on the wood. First, draw a 23½-inch-long line along the bottom. Draw 98-degree angles on each end of the line, as shown in the *Divider Pattern*. Mark where they end on the board. Draw the 6-inch straight section along the top of the divider. Connect the end of the angles with the end of the straight section to lay out the long slope of the divider.

Cut out the ends of the divider on your table saw with the miter gauge set to 8 degrees. Cut the long slope with a saber saw, hand saw, or circular saw. Drill 1-inch-diameter holes for the handle, as shown in the pattern. Sketch a curve that approximates that shown on the grid. Cut

out the rest of the handle with a saber saw or coping saw. Sand away any saw marks that will be visible when the rack is assembled.

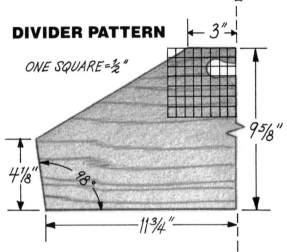

DIVIDER PATTERN

ONE SQUARE = ½"

3"

9⅝"

4⅛"

98°

11¾"

3 **Bevel the ends and sides.** Rip the end and side pieces to the profile shown in the *End Pattern, End View* and *Side Pattern, End View*. Cut two 105-degree angles on each end, as shown in the *Front View*, cutting the ends to length in the process.

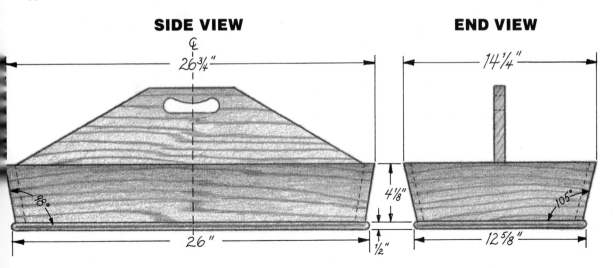

SIDE VIEW

26¾"

26"

8°

½"

4⅛"

END VIEW

14¼"

12⅝"

105°

END PATTERN

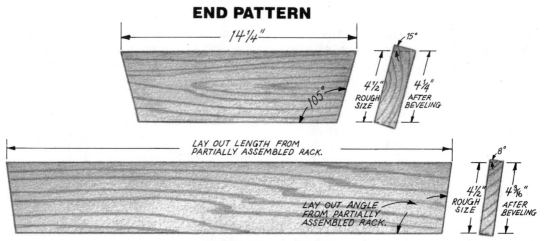

SIDE PATTERN

4 **Nail the ends to the divider.** Mark a centerline on the end grain of the divider and the inside face of each end. Put the divider in a vise, align the centerlines, and nail the ends in place.

5 **Cut the sides to fit.** Butt the sides in place against the ends and trace the angle of the ends on them. Set the miter gauge on the table saw to cut along the lines, then nail the sides in place. With a file or coarse sandpaper, round the top edges of the frame and the outer edge of the corners of the tote to simulate wear. There may be a slight gap at the seam between the sides and end. Don't worry; the gap's on the original, too.

6 **Attach the bottom.** The bottom is made of three boards nailed in place. Before you nail the boards in place, round-over what will be the exposed edges of the bottom. Put a ¼-inch-radius round-over bit in your router. Secure the router in a router table. Adjust the height of the bit and position the fence to rout the pro-

file shown. Rout the appropriate edges. Nail the boards in place with a single nail at each end; allow a ⅛-inch gap between the boards. The gap isn't mere country sloppiness; it allows the bottom to expand and contract without pushing the sides apart.

SHOP TIP: End grain tends to splinter when routed. To prevent this, guide the cut with a square piece of plywood that measures at least 12 × 12 inches. Put one edge of the plywood against the board and an adjoining edge against the fence. Keep the end of the board against the fence as you rout. The plywood will support the edge of the board and keep it from splintering.

7 **Apply finish.** The original magazine rack has a painted interior and a varnished exterior. After sanding the whole piece, finish your rack however you desire.

CRADLE

Grandparents and expectant parents, this is a weekend project that will bring you great satisfaction. A cradle you make for your own child or grandchild has special significance. It quickly becomes an heirloom.

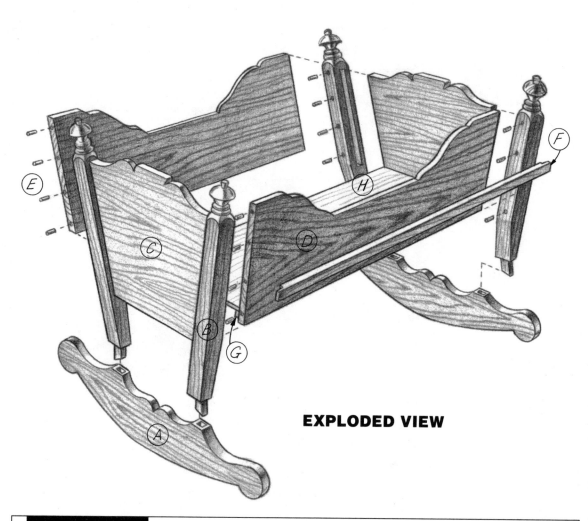

EXPLODED VIEW

CUTTING LIST

Part	Quantity	Dimension	Comment
A. Rockers	2	$1\frac{1}{4}'' \times 5\frac{3}{4}'' \times 28\frac{1}{4}''$	
B. Corner posts	4	$1\frac{3}{4}'' \times 1\frac{3}{4}'' \times 24''$	Cut to 22" after turning.
C. End panels	2	$\frac{7}{8}'' \times 13\frac{3}{8}'' \times 16\frac{5}{8}''$	
D. Sides	2	$\frac{7}{8}'' \times 11\frac{5}{8}'' \times 28\frac{1}{8}''$	
E. Dowel stock	1	$\frac{1}{2}''$ dia. $\times 20''$	Cut to fit.
F. Side strips	2	$\frac{5}{8}'' \times 1\frac{1}{4}'' \times 30\frac{3}{4}''$	
G. Floor support	2	$\frac{7}{16}'' \times \frac{7}{8}'' \times 28\frac{1}{8}''$	
H. Floor boards	9	$\frac{3}{8}'' \times 3\frac{3}{16}'' \times 13\frac{5}{8}''$	Cut to fit.

Hardware

As needed, #4 × ¾-in. flathead wood screws

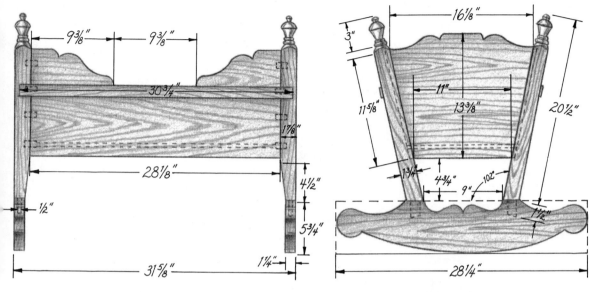

SIDE VIEW

END VIEW

1 **Select the stock and cut the parts.** You can build this cradle out of pine, but an heirloom like this really deserves a hardwood like mahogany, walnut, or cherry. Choose straight, flat stock. Joint, plane, rip, and cut the parts to the sizes given in the Cutting List. If necessary, glue up stock to make the sides and end panels.

2 **Drill the mortises in the rockers.** Lay out the mortises on the rocker blanks as shown in the *End View* and *Side View*. Put a ½-inch drill bit in the drill press and set the depth stop to drill a hole 1½ inches deep. Drill a series of holes inside the layout lines. Then cut up to the layout lines with a sharp chisel.

3 **Turn the knobs on the corner posts.** Put a corner post in your lathe and turn the "knob" on its end to the dimensions shown in the *Corner Post Detail*. Remove the corner post from the

lathe and trim off the waste. Turn the remaining posts, then crosscut the corner posts to the finished length.

If you don't have a lathe, you can either purchase knobs or finials separately and attach them, or make decorative top details with the table saw or band saw as shown in the *Alternate Table Saw/Band Saw Corner Post Detail.*

CORNER POST DETAIL

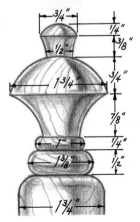

4 **Cut the corner post tenons.** The tenons at the bottom of the corner posts are angled as shown in the *End View.* Lay out tenons according to the dimensions shown in the *Tenon Detail.* Cut the tenons by hand with a dovetail saw or backsaw, constantly checking the tenons for proper fit in their mortises. For step-by-step directions on cutting angled tenons, refer to "Angled Tenons" on page 138.

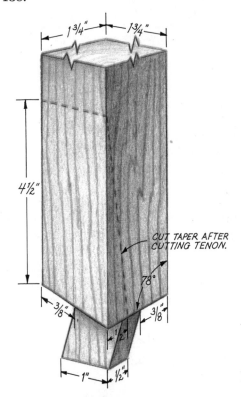

TENON DETAIL

5 **Rout grooves for the end panels.** The end panels are housed in grooves in the corner posts. Put a ⅜-inch straight bit in your router. Secure the router in a router table and adjust the height to cut a groove ¼ inch deep and adjust the fence to cut the groove down the middle of the corner post. Rout an 11⅝-inch-long groove, beginning just below the finial. Square off the ends of the groove with a chisel.

6 **Taper the corner posts.** Lay out the taper shown in the *Side View* on the bottom of the corner posts. The taper begins 4½ inches from the shoulder of the tenon. Cut the taper on the band saw, staying 1/16 inch to the waste side of the layout lines. Complete the taper on each post by sanding down to the layout lines.

7 **Cut the end panels to size.** Lay out the angle on the ends of the panels to the dimensions shown in the *End View.* Cut along the layout lines with a band saw or jigsaw.

Both ends of the panels are rabbeted on both sides, creating a tongue that fits in the corner post groove. Cut the rabbets on the table saw or router so that they leave a tongue ⅜ inch thick. If necessary, put a wooden auxiliary fence over the tool's fence to protect it from the cutter. Guide the cut along the auxiliary fence.

8 **Cut the curves on the end panels, rockers, and sides.** To cut the curves on the end panels, first draw a ½-inch grid on a piece of paper and draw the *End Panel Detail* onto it. Transfer the pattern to the stock. To ensure that the panel fits snugly in the groove, cut 1/16 inch wide of the layout lines. Shave the excess away with a round-bottom spokeshave or file until the panel fits in the groove. Smooth the rest of the curve with the spokeshave or file and sandpaper.

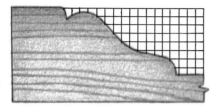

SIDE DETAIL

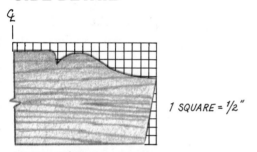

1 SQUARE = ½"

END PANEL DETAIL

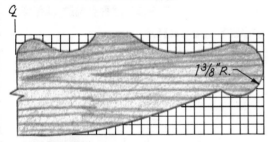

1⅜" R.

ROCKER DETAIL

Lay out and cut the curves on the sides and rockers following the patterns shown in the *Side Detail* and *Rocker Detail*. Smooth the curves as before.

9 **Assemble the cradle ends.** Assemble the ends one at a time. Put glue in the corner post grooves and rocker mortises. Slip the panel in its grooves and the corner post tenons in the rocker mortises. Clamp the assembly together and allow it to dry.

SHOP TIP: Clamping nonparallel surfaces, like those of the corner posts, can be tricky. To provide parallel surfaces, cut 3-inch blocks from a scrap 2 × 4. Cut one long face of the wedge at 78 degrees to the short face. Put the wedges between the clamp heads and the corner posts when clamping to provide parallel surfaces.

10 **Glue the sides to the end units.** Lay out the dowel holes shown in the *Side View* along the center of the corner posts. The holes should be evenly spaced, but their exact locations aren't critical. Drill the holes. To transfer their locations to the cradle sides, put dowel centers in the holes and press the cradle lightly together. The points on the dowel centers will mark the cradle sides, showing you exactly where to drill the dowel holes. Drill the holes, then glue, dowel, and clamp the cradle sides to the assembled end units. After you've clamped the sides in place, measure diagonally from corner to corner to make sure the cradle is square. If one diagonal is longer, clamp gently across it until the diagonals are equal.

SHOP TIP: When you rock a rocking cradle or a rocking chair, it will scoot across the floor if it was twisted when it was assembled. To ensure that this cradle is assembled properly, glue the sides with the cradle upside down on a flat surface. The tops of the four corner posts should touch evenly to ensure a true assembly.

11 **Attach the side strips.** Set the side strips in place against the side of the cradle and mark the position of the corner posts. On the band saw, notch each end of the side strips to fit around the posts. Lightly clean up the rough-sawed surface with a chisel. Thin and slightly round-over the end of each side strip on the stationary belt sander, then glue and clamp them onto the sides of the cradle.

12 **Make the floor support strips.** Set the table saw blade to 12 degrees and rip this angle on one edge of each of the floor support strips. Lightly joint the strips, then glue and clamp them to the inside bottom edge of the cradle sides as shown in the *End View.*

13 **Cut the floorboards to fit into the cradle.** With the table saw blade set at 12 degrees, crosscut the ends of each floorboard so the board just fits within the sides. Cut notches in the appropriate floorboards to fit around the corner posts. Sand the floorboards and attach them to the floor supports with #4 × ³⁄₄-inch flathead wood screws.

14 **Sand and apply the finish.** Finish sand the cradle. Remove any excess glue and round the sharp edges as you sand. When choosing the finish for your cradle, make sure that you choose a nontoxic formula. Stain and varnish or paint the cradle, and add the baby.

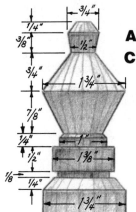

ALTERNATIVE TABLE SAW/BAND SAW CORNER POST DETAIL

LITTLE BOXES

Everyone can find a use for a little box. A deck of cards, some jewelry, your reading glasses, or some loose change could all find a happy home in a little wooden box. The little boxes shown here aren't made of ticky-tacky. They're cherry, bird's-eye maple, Honduras mahogany, and rosewood—all of it scraps from other projects.

The joinery is simple, yet effective: The box is rabbeted together, and then the lid is cut off after the box has been sanded.

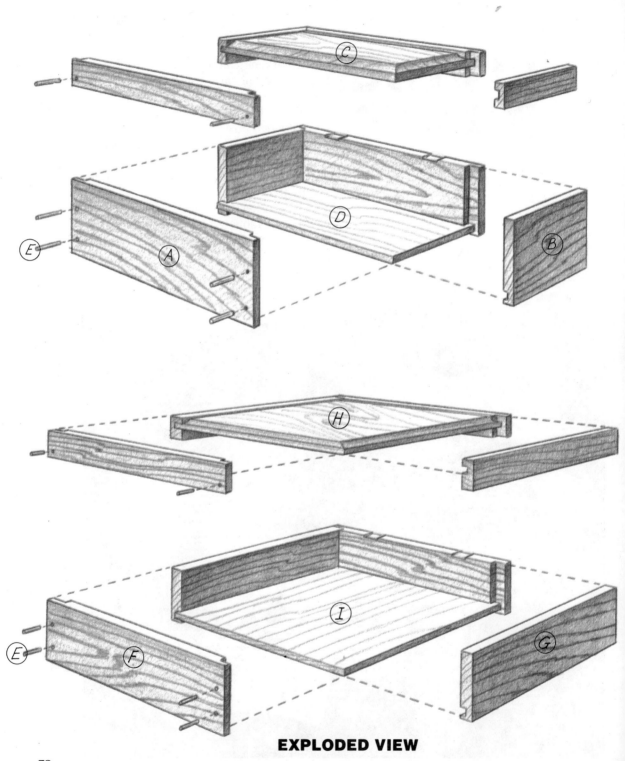

EXPLODED VIEW

CUTTING LIST

Part	Quantity	Dimension	Comment
Rectangular Box			
A. Front/back	2	$3/8'' \times 3\,1/16'' \times 6\,1/4''$	Removing lid makes box $1/16''$ narrower.
B. Sides	2	$3/8'' \times 3\,1/16'' \times 3\,1/4''$	Removing lid makes box $1/16''$ narrower.
C. Top	1	$7/16'' \times 3\,1/4'' \times 5\,7/8''$	Trim to allow for expansion.
D. Bottom	1	$1/4'' \times 3\,1/4'' \times 5\,7/8''$	Trim to allow for expansion.
E. Pegs	12	$1/8''$ dia. $\times 3/4''$	
Square Box			
F. Front/back	2	$3/8'' \times 2\,9/16'' \times 6''$	Removing lid makes box $1/16''$ narrower.
G. Sides	2	$3/8'' \times 2\,9/16'' \times 5\,5/8''$	Removing lid makes box $1/16''$ narrower.
H. Top	1	$7/16'' \times 5\,5/8'' \times 5\,5/8''$	Trim to allow for expansion.
I. Bottom	1	$1/4'' \times 5\,5/8'' \times 5\,5/8''$	Trim to allow for expansion.
E. Pegs	12	$1/8''$ dia. $\times 3/4''$	

Hardware

2 $13/16 \times 1\,3/16$-in. hinges per box. Available from Meisel Hardware Specialties, P.O. Box 70, Mound, MN 55364. Part #1632.

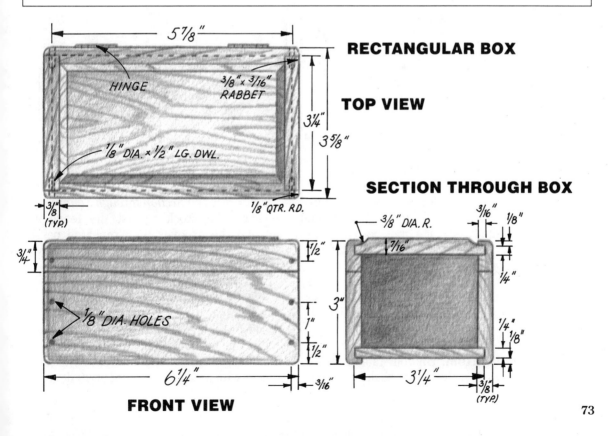

RECTANGULAR BOX

TOP VIEW

HINGE
$3/8'' \times 3/16''$ RABBET
$1/8''$ DIA. $\times 1/2''$ LG. DWL.
$3/4''$
$3/8''$ (TYP.)
$5/8''$
$5\,7/8''$
$3\,1/4''$
$3\,5/8''$
$1/8''$ QTR. RD.

SECTION THROUGH BOX

$3/8''$ DIA. R.
$7/16''$
$3/16''$
$1/8''$
$1/4''$
$1/4''$
$1/8''$
$3''$
$3\,1/4''$
$3/8''$ (TYP.)

FRONT VIEW

$3/4''$
$1/8''$ DIA. HOLES
$1/2''$
$1''$
$1/2''$
$6\,1/4''$
$3/16''$

73

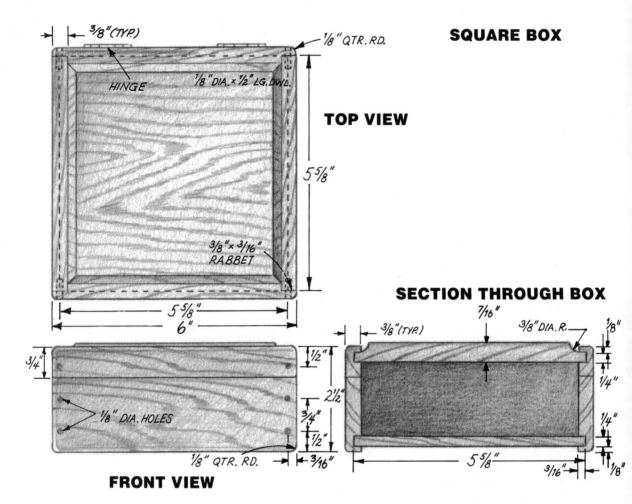

SQUARE BOX

TOP VIEW

3/8"(TYP)

1/8" QTR. RD.

HINGE

1/8" DIA. x 1/2" LG. DWL.

5 5/8"

3/8" x 3/16" RABBET

5 5/8"

6"

SECTION THROUGH BOX

7/16"

3/8" (TYP.)

3/8" DIA. R.

1/8"

1/4"

1/4"

5 5/8"

3/16"

1/8"

1/2"

2 1/2"

3/4"

3/4"

1/2"

1/8" DIA. HOLES

1/8" QTR. RD.

3/16"

FRONT VIEW

1 **Select the stock and cut the parts.** Look for straight, flat hardwood stock without knots. Try to find scraps with interesting grain patterns. Mix and match different wood types. Choose a tight-grained wood like walnut, maple, or rosewood for the pegs. Joint, plane, rip, and cut the parts, except for the pegs, to the sizes given in the Cutting List.

2 **Cut grooves to receive the top and bottom.** On your table saw, cut the grooves in the front, back, and sides as shown in the *Section through Rectangular Box* and *Section through Square Box*. Guide the stock against the fence and make the grooves with repeated passes over the blade, adjusting the fence with each cut.

3 **Cut rabbets in the front and back.** Cut the rabbets in the front and back as shown in the *Top View.* Cut the rabbets with repeated passes over a standard blade on the table saw. Guide the cuts with a miter gauge set at 90 degrees.

4 **Shape the top.** To shape the raised-panel top put a ⅜-inch-radius cove bit in your router. Remove the bearing from the bit so that you can make a cut wider than normal. Secure the router in a router table. Cut a notch in a wooden fence that fits around the bit. Adjust the fence and bit height to cut the profile shown in the *Top View*.

SHOP TIP: When routing a profile around all four sides of the face of a piece of wood, rout the end grain first. Because of the nature of end grain, the wood tends to splinter at the corner when routing across the end of a board. You can't really avoid this splintering, but if you rout the end grain first, any splintering is cut away when you rout the sides.

---

5 **Trim the top and bottom for expansion.** When fitting a lid like this into a box, always leave room for the wood to expand. On the table saw, trim ¹⁄₃₂ inch from an edge parallel to the grain on the top and bottom panels to allow for this expansion.

6 **Assemble the box.** Test fit the sides, front, back, top, and bottom. Make sure that everything fits correctly and adjust as necessary.

When everything fits properly, lay the back on a flat surface and glue the sides into the rabbets. Then slide the top and bottom in place *without glue*. The bottom and top must be free to float in their grooves. Apply glue to the rabbets in the front of the box and put the front in place. Clamp the box together. Make sure that the sides are seated snugly in the rabbets.

Allow the glue to dry.

7 **Drill and peg the rabbet joints.** When the glue has dried, lay out and drill the ⅛-inch-diameter peg holes in the front and back as shown in the *Front View*.

With a block plane or spokeshave, shape the pegs to the size given in the Cutting List from ³⁄₁₆-inch square stock. Tap the pegs into the peg holes and cut off any excess.

8 **Round-over the edges and sand the box.** Even up all the joints with sandpaper. Put a ⅛-inch roundover bit in the router. Secure the router in a router table and round all the edges of the box.

Finish sand the box.

9 **Cut and hinge the top.** To cut the lid from the rest of the box, set the box on edge on your band saw. Clamp a straightedge to the band saw to guide the cut, then cut slowly and carefully. Use push sticks to keep your hands away from the blade.

Sand away the kerf marks by rubbing the box lid and body over a piece of 180-grit sandpaper taped to a flat surface. Sand the cut edge as little as possible. Oversanding will produce an uneven fit.

The top is hinged to the body. The hinge is mortised between the back and top. With the hinge as your guide, mark and cut the hinge mortises. Cut the mortises by hand as explained in "Hinge Mortises" on page 7.

Mark and predrill holes for the hinge screws and attach the top to the back.

10 **Finish the box.** The boxes shown have an oil finish. If you have chosen a nice mix of hardwoods, you should show off the wood with an oil finish that brings out the grain and color.

JEWELRY CABINET

Furniture making has a long history of miniature work. This cabinet falls somewhere between full-size and doll-house furniture. Traditionally, such pieces have several purposes. To an experienced cabinetmaker, they provide a means of viewing a design without investing a great deal of labor and materials. For an apprentice, they provided practice without undue risk and demonstrated the level of skill.

Most of these small pieces can still be quite functional. Small chairs, for example, were given to children. This small cabinet and mirror are perfect for jewelry.

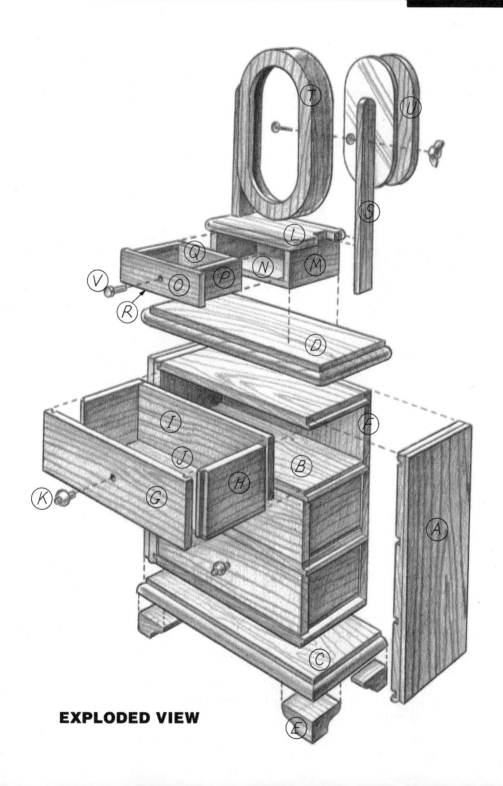

EXPLODED VIEW

CUTTING LIST

Part	Quantity	Dimension	Comment
Lower Cabinet			
A. Cabinet sides	2	$\frac{5}{8}'' \times 3\frac{3}{8}'' \times 8\frac{5}{8}''$	
B. Drawer shelves	4	$\frac{3}{8}'' \times 3'' \times 7\frac{1}{4}''$	
C. Cabinet bottom	1	$\frac{13}{16}'' \times 3\frac{1}{2}'' \times 8\frac{5}{8}''$	
D. Cabinet top	1	$\frac{13}{16}'' \times 4'' \times 8\frac{5}{8}''$	
E. Foot stock	1	$1\frac{1}{2}'' \times 1\frac{1}{2}'' \times 20''$	Shape and cut to length.
F. Back	1	$\frac{1}{4}'' \times 7\frac{1}{4}'' \times 8\frac{1}{2}''$	Cut to fit.
G. Drawer faces	3	$\frac{1}{4}'' \times 2\frac{3}{8}'' \times 7\frac{1}{4}''$	Cut to fit.
H. Drawer sides	6	$\frac{1}{4}'' \times 2\frac{3}{8}'' \times 3''$	Cut to fit.
I. Drawer backs	3	$\frac{1}{4}'' \times 2\frac{3}{8}'' \times 7\frac{1}{4}''$	Cut to fit.
J. Drawer bottoms	3	$\frac{1}{8}'' \times 3'' \times 7\frac{1}{4}''$	Cut to fit.
K. Drawer knobs	3	$\frac{5}{8}'' \times \frac{5}{8}'' \times 3''$	Cut after turning.
Upper Cabinet and Mirror			
L. Top	1	$\frac{3}{8}'' \times 3\frac{1}{8}'' \times 4\frac{3}{4}''$	
M. Sides	2	$\frac{3}{8}'' \times 2\frac{3}{4}'' \times 1\frac{1}{2}''$	
N. Bottom	1	$\frac{1}{4}'' \times 2\frac{3}{4}'' \times 3\frac{1}{4}''$	
O. Drawer face	1	$\frac{1}{4}'' \times 1\frac{3}{4}'' \times 4''$	Cut to fit.
P. Drawer sides	2	$\frac{1}{4}'' \times 1\frac{1}{4}'' \times 3\frac{1}{8}''$	Cut to fit.
Q. Drawer back	1	$\frac{1}{4}'' \times 1\frac{1}{4}'' \times 3''$	Cut to fit.
R. Drawer bottom	1	$\frac{1}{8}'' \times 3'' \times 3''$	Cut to fit.
S. Mirror supports	2	$\frac{1}{4}'' \times \frac{3}{4}'' \times 7\frac{1}{2}''$	
T. Mirror frame	1	$1'' \times 3\frac{7}{8}'' \times 7\frac{1}{4}''$	
U. Mirror back	1	$\frac{1}{4}'' \times 3\frac{7}{8}'' \times 7\frac{1}{4}''$	Cut to fit.
V. Drawer knob	1	$\frac{5}{8}'' \times \frac{5}{8}'' \times 3''$	Cut after turning.

Hardware

As needed, $\frac{3}{4}$-in. brads
$2\ \frac{1}{8} \times 2$-in. bolts with wing nuts and washers
As needed, $\frac{1}{2}$-in. brads
$1\ \frac{1}{8} \times 3\frac{3}{8} \times 6\frac{5}{8}$-in. oval mirror glass
6 pushpins

1 Select the stock and cut the parts. Choose a close-grained wood such as cherry for this cabinet. The open grain of a wood such as oak would seem coarse in a project this size. One board should provide all the material you need.

Because this project requires thin pieces of stock, resaw thicker material on your band saw or table saw where necessary. Joint, plane, rip, and cut the parts to the sizes given in the Cutting List.

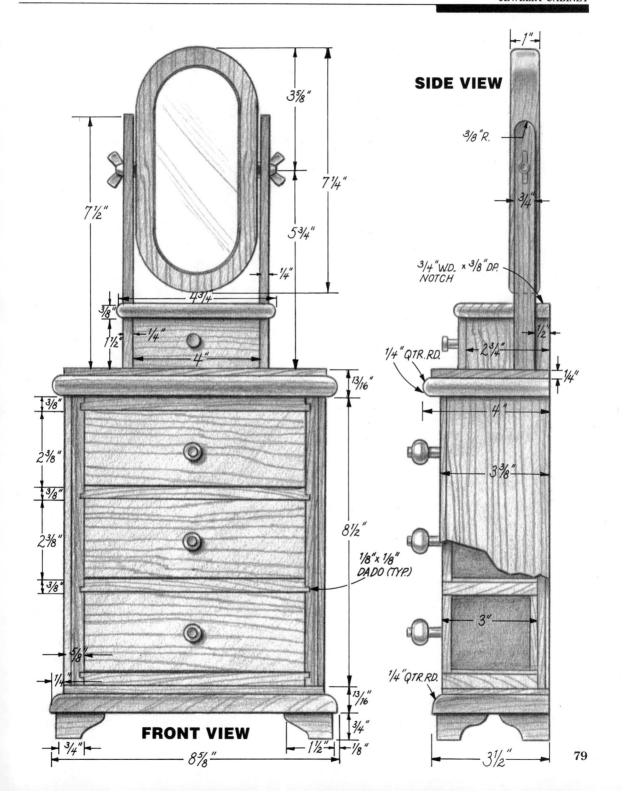

SIDE VIEW

1"

3/8"R.

3/4"

3/4"WD. x 3/8"DP.
NOTCH

1/4" QTR.RD.

2 3/4"

1/2"

1/4"

4"

3 3/8"

3"

1/4" QTR. RD.

3 1/2"

3 5/8"

7 1/4"

5 3/4"

1/4"

4 3/4"

3/8"

1 1/2"

1/4"

4"

7 1/2"

13/16"

3/8"

2 3/8"

3/8"

2 3/8"

3/8"

8 1/2"

1/8" x 1/8"
DADO (TYP.)

5/8"

1/4"

13/16"

3/4"

FRONT VIEW

3/4"

8 5/8"

1 1/2"

1/8"

2 Cut the shelf dadoes in the sides. The shelves fit into the sides with dado joints the width of the table saw blade. Adjust the height of the blade to cut a ⅛-inch-deep dado. Lay out the dado spacing on one of the sides.

Screw a long wooden extension to your miter gauge. Position the cabinet side against the extension to cut one of the dadoes. Clamp a stop block to the fence at the end of the side farthest from the blade.

Cut the first dado. Put the other cabinet side against the stop block and cut a dado on the second side. The stop block ensures perfectly matching dadoes.

Cut all the dadoes in both sides.

3 Rout the front edge of the sides. This detail is easily made. Put a ¼-inch roundover bit in your router. Secure the router in a router table and adjust the height of the bit so there is a step with the roundover as shown in the *Edge Detail.* Set up a fence to guide the side as you rout. If you don't use a fence, the bit's bearing will fall into the dadoes.

EDGE DETAIL

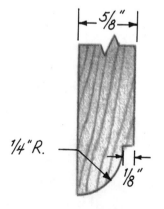

4 Cut the tongue in the ends of the shelves. Each shelf has a ⅛-inch-long tongue on each end that fits into the dadoes cut in the cabinet sides. You can cut these tongues on the table saw with the miter gauge as a guide. Before you do, cut a sample tongue in a piece of scrap. The scrap should be the thickness of the actual shelves. Adjust the fence and the blade height, until the sample fits snugly in the dadoes. Clamp a stop block to the miter gauge fence to ensure that all tongues are the same length. Cut the tongues. Sand the shelves and sides.

5 Assemble the sides and shelves. On a flat surface, glue and clamp the shelves into the dadoes. Make sure the front of the shelves are flush with the front of the sides. Check to make sure the cabinet is square.

6 Rout the profile in the bottom and top. Put a ¼-inch roundover bit in the router. Secure the router in a router table. Raise the bit to cut a step the same size as the one on the cabinet sides. Set up a fence and guide the bottom and top against it as you cut. Rout the front and sides of each piece.

After you cut the stepped profile, lower the bit to round-over the bottom edge of the top.

7 Attach the top and bottom to the side and shelf assembly. Sand the top and bottom cabinet pieces. Position them as shown in the *Front View* and *Side View,* then glue and clamp them in place.

8 Shape and attach the feet. Because the feet are small, the Cutting List calls for extralong stock so you can work safely. Cut the end of the stock on a band saw to the shape shown in the *Foot Detail*. Sand or file the cut smooth. Cut the foot to its finished length on the table saw.

Repeat the process with each foot. Then glue and clamp the feet in place to the cabinet bottom.

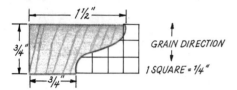

FOOT DETAIL

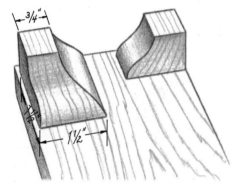

9 **Attach the cabinet back.** The cabinet back is attached to the cabinet with ½-inch brads. Measure the opening for the back and cut the back to fit. Predrill holes for the brads through the back pieces and into the shelves. Drill the holes with a bit that matches the size of your brads and then tap the brads in place.

SHOP TIP: Predrill brad holes by putting a brad in your drill instead of a regular drill bit. Drill the holes as you normally would for a hole the exact diameter of the brad.

10 **Notch the upper cabinet top.** Round-over the front and sides of the upper cabinet top to the profile shown with a ³⁄₁₆-inch-radius roundover bit. Lay out the ⅜-inch-deep notch on each side of the top for the mirror support and cut the notches on a band saw.

11 **Assemble the upper cabinet.** Sand the top, sides, and bottom of the upper cabinet. Assemble the upper cabinet with glue and ¾-inch brads. First, set the sides against the bottom and drill brad holes through the sides into the bottom. Apply glue to the mating surfaces and tap the brads in place. Next, center the top over the sides, as shown in the *Front View* and *Side View,* and drill brad holes through the top and into the sides. Again, apply some glue and tap in the brads.

When the glue has dried, glue and clamp the upper cabinet in position on the top of the lower cabinet and clean up any excess glue.

12 **Cut and assemble the drawers.** Whenever you build a cabinet with drawers, it's a good idea to fit the drawer parts to the actual cabinet. The dimensions in the Cutting List yield parts about ¼ inch larger than needed. Measure the opening for the drawers and cut the parts to make drawers that are ¹⁄₁₆ inch smaller than the actual openings.

The upper drawer face overlaps the cabinet sides, while the lower drawers do not. Although this means the joints are spaced differently, construction of the joints is identical. The sides of the drawers are attached to the drawer fronts with small tongue-and-groove joints. Cut the joints on the table saw, the same way you cut the joints for the shelves.

Sand all the drawer parts. Attach the sides to the back with glue and ½-inch brads as shown in the *Upper Cabinet Drawer, Top View* and *Lower Cabinet Drawer, Top View.* Predrill through the sides into the back for the brads, then glue and brad the sides to the back. Glue and clamp the side tongues into the dadoes in the drawer face. Glue and clamp the drawer bottom to the underside of each drawer. Keep each drawer flat and square.

13 **Turn or purchase the drawer knobs.** Turn the knobs to the profile shown in the *Upper Drawer Knob Detail* and *Lower Drawer Knob Detail* or purchase similar knobs at a hardware store.

Drill a hole in each drawer face for the knob shaft and glue the knobs in place.

UPPER DRAWER KNOB DETAIL

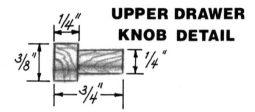

LOWER DRAWER KNOB DETAIL

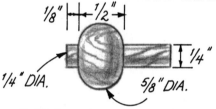

UPPER CABINET DRAWER

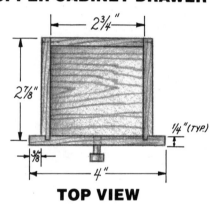

TOP VIEW

LOWER CABINET DRAWER

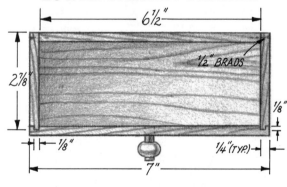

TOP VIEW

14 **Cut the mirror supports to shape.** Lay out the ⅜-inch-radius curve at the top of each mirror support. Cut the curve on the band saw and sand away the saw marks.

Lay out and drill holes for the bolts and wing nuts shown in the *Front View.* Sand the supports, then attach them to the upper cabinet sides with glue and ½-inch brads.

15 **Make the mirror frame.** First, draw a ¼-inch grid on a piece of paper and draw the *Mirror Frame Detail* onto it. Transfer the pattern to the stock, drill a ⅜-inch hole in the center section, and cut out the center shape with a jigsaw or scroll saw. Sand the sawed edge smooth.

Put ¼-inch roundover bit in a router. Secure the router in a router table and adjust the bit to cut the profile shown in the *View through Mirror Frame.*

Next, rout a ¼ × ⅝-inch rabbet in the back of the mirror frame to accept the mirror glass and back. You can rout this rabbet with a normal ⅜-inch rabbeting bit, but you must first add a larger bearing. Replace the bearing on your ⅜-inch rabbeting bit so that you can cut a ¼-inch-wide rabbet. Cut the ⅝-inch-deep rabbet in two passes. Cut the back to fit in the rabbet.

After you've rabbeted for the back, cut the outside of the mirror frame to shape with a jigsaw or band saw and sand the sawed edge smooth. Round-over the outside edges of the mirror frame with a ¼-inch roundover bit.

MIRROR FRAME DETAIL

1 SQUARE = ¼″

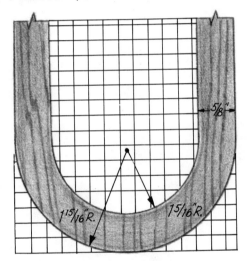

VIEW THROUGH MIRROR FRAME

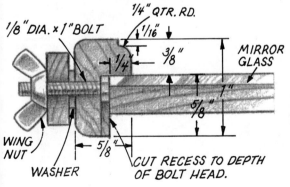

16 **Attach the mirror frame to the mirror supports.** The mirror frame attaches to the mirror supports with ⅛-inch bolts and wing nuts. Drill ⅛-inch-diameter holes for the bolts centered in each side of the mirror frame as shown in the *Front View.*

Next, chisel out a recess in the mirror frame rabbet for the bolt head as shown in the *View through Mirror Frame.* Cut the recess deep enough so that the bolt head is flush with the surface of the wood.

Finally, put the mirror frame between the mirror supports and insert the bolts into their holes. Put small washers between the mirror frame and support and turn the wing nuts in place.

17 **Apply the finish.** Remove the mirror frame from its supports and finish sand the jewelry cabinet. The cabinet shown has an oil finish. Heavy varnishes could interfere with the movement of the little drawers. When the finish is dry, put the mirror frame back in its supports and install the mirror glass and back. Hold the mirror glass and back in place with push pins.

DRESSING MIRROR

This mirror is patterned after an antique dressing mirror, yet the design is so clean and practical it could be mistaken for a contemporary piece. It is small enough to fit easily on a dresser, a vanity, or a shelf. The mirror swivels for convenience, and the drawer can hold makeup, jewelry, or pocket items.

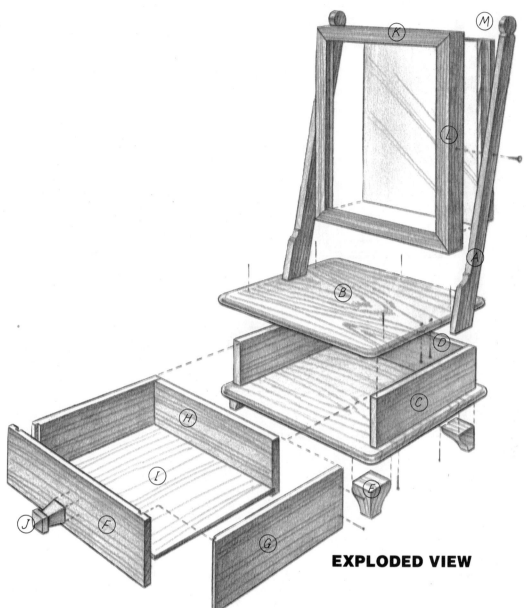

EXPLODED VIEW

1 Select the stock and cut the parts. The dressing mirror shown is made from pine, but a project this size could also be made inexpensively from a fine hardwood. Because people tend to get close to mirrors, they'll see any defects in the wood. Take extra care to select wood free of knots or defects. Joint, plane, rip, and cut the parts to the sizes given in the Cutting List. Miter the mirror frame rails and stiles as you cut them to length.

2 Cut the mirror supports to shape. Lay out the mirror supports, as shown in the *Mirror Support Detail*. Cut the bottom bevel on the table saw and cut the rest of the support on the band saw. Sand away any saw marks.

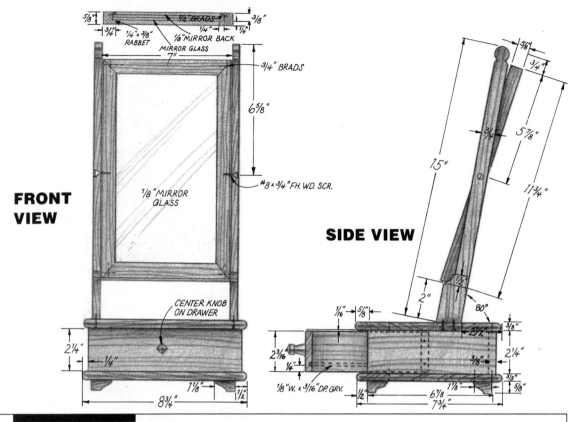

FRONT VIEW

SIDE VIEW

5/8"
3/4"
1/4" x 3/8" RABBET
1/2" BRADS
1/8" MIRROR BACK
MIRROR GLASS
3/8"
1/4"
1/8"
7"
3/4" BRADS
6 5/8"
#8 x 3/4" F.H. WD. SCR.
1/8" MIRROR GLASS
CENTER KNOB ON DRAWER
2 1/4"
1/4"
1 1/8"
1 1/2"
8 3/4"

5/8"
3/4"
3/4"
5 7/8"
15"
11 3/4"
1/2"
2"
80°
1/16"
5 1/8"
2 3/16"
1/4"
1/8" W. x 3/16" DP. GRV.
1/2"
6 7/8"
7 3/4"
2 1/2"
3/8"
3/8"
2 1/4"
3/8"
5/8"
1 1/8"
3/8"

CUTTING LIST

Part	Quantity	Dimension	Comment
A. Mirror support	2	3/8" × 1 1/4" × 15"	Bevel one end 80 degrees.
B. Top/bottom	2	3/8" × 7 3/4" × 8 3/4"	
C. Sides	2	3/8" × 2 1/4" × 6 7/8"	Miter to fit.
D. Back	1	3/8" × 2 1/4" × 8 1/4"	Miter to fit.
E. Feet	1	1 1/8" × 1 1/8" × 8"	Makes 4
F. Drawer face	1	3/8" × 2 3/16" × 8 1/4"	
G. Drawer sides	2	3/8" × 2 3/16" × 6 3/8"	
H. Drawer back	1	3/8" × 2 3/16" × 7"	Cut to fit.
I. Drawer bottom	1	1/8" × 6 3/16" × 7 1/16"	Plywood or Masonite
J. Drawer knob	1	9/16" × 9/16" × 6"	Cut to length after shaping.
K. Mirror rails	2	5/8" × 3/4" × 7"	Miter to fit.
L. Mirror stiles	2	5/8" × 3/4" × 11 3/4"	Miter to fit.
M. Mirror back	1	1/8" × 6" × 10 3/4"	

Hardware

1 1/8 × 6 × 10 3/4-in. mirror glass
1 #8 × 1-in. brass flathead wood screw
4 #6 × 1-in. brass flathead wood screws
2 #8 × 3/4-in. brass flathead wood screws
As needed, 3/4-in. brads
10 1/2-in. brads

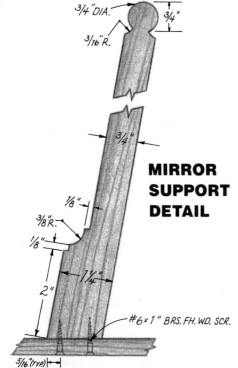

3/4" DIA.

3/4"

3/16" R.

3/4"

**MIRROR
SUPPORT
DETAIL**

1/8"

3/8" R.

1/8"

1 1/4"

2"

#6 × 1" BRS. FH. WD. SCR.

5/16" (TYP.)

3 **Round-over the edges of the top and bottom.** Put a 3/16-inch round-over bit in your router. Secure the router in a router table and adjust it to rout the top and bottom to the profile shown in the *Front View.* Set up a fence on the router table and guide the top and bottom against it as you rout.

4 **Lay out and drill the screw holes for the mirror support.** Lay out holes for the screws that attach the mirror support to the top. Drill the 1/8-inch clearance holes perpendicular to the top, as shown in the *Mirror Support Detail.* Put the mirror supports in place on the top and push an awl up through the screw holes to mark the location of the screw holes on the bottom of the supports. Drill 3/32-inch-diameter pilot holes for the #6 × 1-inch brass flathead wood screws at the marks left by the awl and screw the supports to the top.

5 **Miter the sides and back.** Miter the back edge of the sides and both ends of the back. Put glue on the miters and clamp them together with corner clamps. When the glue is dry, reinforce the miters with 1/2-inch brads.

SHOP TIP: To get accurate miters, check your setup on some pieces of scrap. Set the table saw blade to the 45-degree position. Set the miter gauge to 90 degrees and use it to cut miters in two pieces of scrap wood. Put the miters together and make sure that the resulting angle equals 90 degrees. Adjust the blade as necessary.

6 **Glue the top and bottom to the sides and back.** Attach the top and bottom to the sides with glue and 3/4-inch brads. Make sure that the top overhangs the sides and back by 1/4 inch and that it overhangs the front of the sides by 5/8 inch, as shown in the *Side View.*

7 **Shape the feet.** Because the feet are small, it's best to cut them on an oversize piece of stock and then cut the stock to length. Begin with a piece the size given in the Cutting List. On the band saw, cut the profile shown in the *Foot Detail* on one side of the stock. Rotate the stock and cut the profile on an adjoining face. Sand or file the saw cut smooth and then cut the feet to their finished lengths.

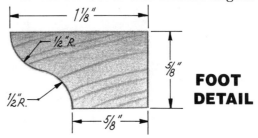

1 1/8"

1/2" R.

5/8"

1/2" R.

5/8"

**FOOT
DETAIL**

8 **Cut the drawer joints.** The drawer sides have tongues that fit into dadoes in the drawer face. Measure the front of the cabinet from edge to edge and cut the drawer face to this length. Lay out the dadoes on the drawer face, as shown in the *Drawer, Top View*. The distance between the outside of the dadoes should be $\frac{1}{16}$ inch less than the opening for the drawer.

Both the dadoes and the tongues can be cut on a table saw with the normal blade—the dado is a single saw kerf wide. Adjust the height of the blade to cut a $\frac{1}{8}$-inch-deep dado. Guide the stock with a miter gauge as you cut the dadoes.

Lay out the $\frac{1}{8}$-inch-long tongue on the front end of the sides, as shown in the *Drawer, Top View*.

Before you cut the joint, cut a few samples on a piece of scrap the exact thickness as the drawer side. Lay the scrap flat on the table saw and guide it over the blade with the miter gauge. Adjust the blade height so the tongue fits snugly in the dadoes in the drawer face. Cut the

tongues on the drawer sides.

Cut the back to fit between the sides.

9 **Rout the groove for the drawer bottom.** Put a $\frac{1}{8}$-inch straight bit in your router. Adjust the router's fence attachment to cut a groove $\frac{1}{4}$ inch from the drawer face's bottom edge. Rout the groove, beginning at one dado and stopping at the other.

Rout a groove with the same setup $\frac{1}{4}$ inch from the bottom edges of the sides and back. Rout these grooves along the entire piece.

SHOP TIP: Small pieces can be difficult to clamp in place while routing. Hold them to the bench with doubled-sided tape or buy a commercially available foam rubber mat designed to hold pieces while routing.

10 **Drill for the drawer knob hole.** Measure and mark the drawer face for the drawer knob screw. Drill and countersink a $\frac{1}{8}$-inch hole for the screw.

11 **Assemble the drawer.** Glue the tongues on the drawer sides into the dadoes in the drawer face. Trim the plywood bottom to fit, if necessary, and slide it in place. Attach the sides to the back with glue and $\frac{1}{2}$-inch brads. Clamp the drawer face tightly against the sides and check to make sure the drawer is square.

12 **Shape the drawer knob.** The knob, like the feet, should be cut on a piece of long stock and then cut to length. Begin with a piece the size given in the Cutting List. On the band saw, cut

DRAWER

3/8"

13/32"

3/16"

PLYWOOD BOTTOM
6 3/16" x 7 1/16"

6 11/16"

8 1/4"

3/8"

3/8"

1/8" W. x 3/16" DP. DADO

6 3/8"

TOP VIEW

the profile shown in the *Knob Detail* on one side of the stock. Rotate the stock and cut the profile on an adjoining face. Sand or file the saw cut smooth and then cut the knob to its finished length.

Drill a hole for the screw in the knob and use a #8 × 1-inch brass flathead wood screw to secure the knob to the drawer face.

KNOB DETAIL

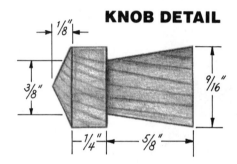

13 **Rabbet and assemble the mirror frame.** To rabbet the parts of the mirror frame to the profile shown, put a ¼-inch rabbeting bit in a router. Secure the router in a router table and use a fence while cutting the rabbets.

Put glue on all the miters and clamp the mirror frame together with corner clamps. When the glue dries, reinforce the mitered corners with ¾-inch brads, as shown in the *Front View*. If your dressing mirror is made from hardwood, predrill holes for the brads before you drive them in place.

14 **Attach the mirror frame to the supports.** Lay out and drill a pilot hole in each side of the mirror frame for the #8 × ¾-inch supporting screws. Screw the mirror frame to the mirror supports.

15 **Apply the finish.** Remove the mirror frame from the supports and finish sand all of the parts. Stain and varnish or paint the dressing mirror to match your decor. Don't apply a thick finish to the drawer sides and the box interior, because the drawer may bind.

When the finish is dry, install the mirror glass and back, and hold them in place with ½-inch brads. Reattach the mirror frame to the supports.

CASSETTE BOX

If you're a music lover, you've probably run into this problem. A mountain of cassettes begins to cover your sound system. Every time you hit the power button there's an avalanche; the cassettes shatter on the floor.

Before you drop-kick your tape deck, bring some harmony back into your entertainment area by building this cassette storage box.

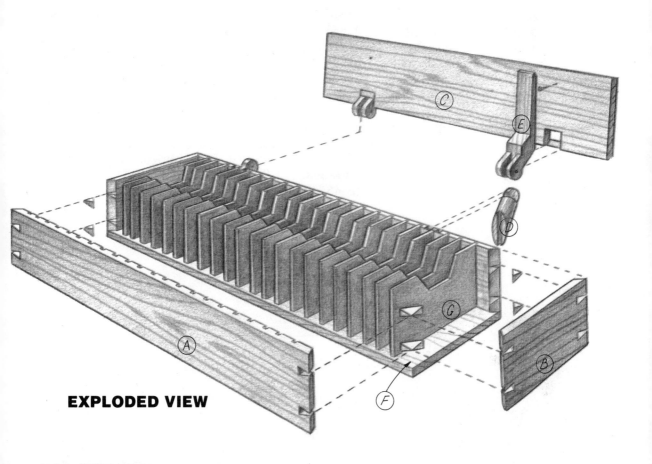

EXPLODED VIEW

CUTTING LIST

Part	Quantity	Dimension	Comment
A. Front/back	2	⅜″ × 3″ × 21¾″	Miter to 20¾″.
B. Sides	2	⅜″ × 3″ × 6¼″	Miter to 5¼″.
C. Top/bottom	2	⅜″ × 5¼″ × 20¾″	
D. Hinge dowels	2	⅝″ dia. × 2½″	
E. Hinge leaves	2	¾″ × 1¼″ × 6″	Shape to length.
F. Insert stock	1	½″ × ½″ × 15″	Makes 8
G. Dividers	21	⅛″ × 3″ × 4¾″	

Hardware

As needed, 1-in. brads
2 #5 × ½-in. flathead wood screws
1 1/16-in. dia. brass braising rod

1 Select the stock and cut the parts. The cassette box shown has a poplar body, cedar top and bottom, and purpleheart dovetail inserts. For your box, mix and match woods that complement each other and highlight the construction. Choose straight, flat stock. Joint, plane, rip, and cut the parts to the sizes given in the Cutting List.

2 Miter the front, back, and sides. Set your table saw blade to 45 de-

grees. Set your table saw miter gauge to 90 degrees and guide the miter cuts with it. Because the sides are short, you'll need to screw an extension fence to the miter gauge.

Miter one end each of the front, back, and sides. When these miters have been cut, clamp a stop block to the miter gauge extension fence. Position the stop block so that when you cut the second miters the parts will also be cut to length.

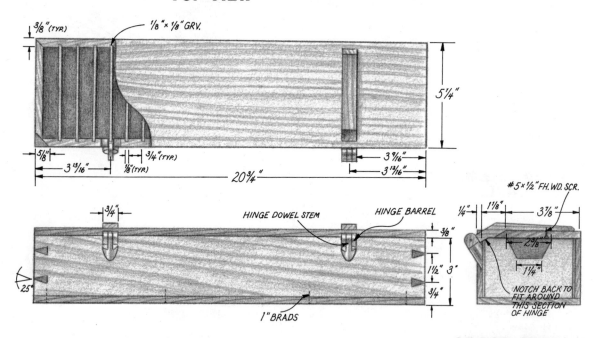

TOP VIEW

BACK VIEW

CROSS SECTION THROUGH BOX

3 Drill the hinge-dowel holes. Lay out the location of hinge dowel on the back of the box. Put a ⅝-inch drill bit in your drill press and adjust the table to drill the 30-degree holes in the back. Sandwich the back between two pieces of scrap to prevent the back from splintering as the drill enters and exits. Clamp a fence to the drill press table to support the back and adjust it so that when drilling, the edge of the hole just meets the top edge of the back as shown in the *Cross Section through Box.*

4 Cut the divider grooves. Stack the front and back together with inside surfaces touching. Make sure that the ends are even and secure with clamps. Lay out for the dividers across the top edges of the front and back. Remove the clamps.

Cut ⅛ × ⅛-inch grooves to hold the dividers. Most table saw blades cut a ⅛-inch kerf. Guide the cuts with a miter gauge at set 90 degrees.

5 Assemble the sides to the front and back. When the grooves have been cut, spread glue on the mitered ends of the front, back, and sides. Clamp them together with corner clamps and make sure the box is square. Allow glue to dry.

6 Attach the bottom. Glue the bottom to the underside of the front, back, and side assembly. Secure with 1-inch brads. When the glue has dried, plane or sand the edges of the bottom even with the front, back, and sides.

7 Glue the hinge dowels in place. The hinges are made from two pieces: a dowel mounted in the back of the box and a hinge leaf, which slips through a hole in the box lid.

Mount the hinge dowels before cutting them to the profile shown. To mount the dowels, spread glue in the hinge-dowel holes and slide the dowels in place. Slide each dowel in until its base is completely through the hole. When the glue has dried, saw and sand the dowel flush with the inside of the box.

8 Cut the hinge leaves to shape. Carefully lay out the hinge leaves, as shown in the *Hinge Leaf Detail,* on the hinge leaf stock. With a band saw, cut the wood to the shape shown. Cut the slot in the hinge barrel as shown.

HINGE LEAF DETAIL

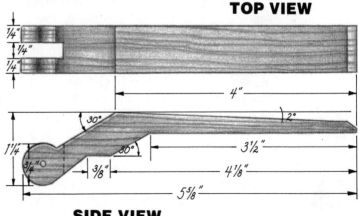

TOP VIEW

SIDE VIEW

9 **Attach the hinge leaves to the top.** The hinge leaves fit through a slot in the lid. Lay out the slot, as shown in the *Cross Section through Box*. Use a ¼-inch drill bit to drill a hole through the lid that follows the angle of the slot.

Next, slip your coping saw blade through the hole and carefully cut the slot. Try to approximate the angle of the front and back of the slot as you cut.

Finally, test fit the hinge leaves and trim the slot as necessary with a sharp chisel. Screw the hinge leaves to the top with #5 × ½-inch screws as shown.

10 **Complete the hinge assembly.** With a backsaw or dovetail saw, cut stems on the hinge dowels that fit in the hinge barrel. As you cut the stems, you must also cut small notches in the box on either side of the stems. These notches, shown in the *Cross Section through Box*, provide clearance for the hinge barrel. Without the notches, the lid will not close.

When the top sits flat on the box, cut the hinge-dowel stem flush with the top edge of the hinge leaves. Round the corners of the stems with sandpaper.

Make hinge pins from 1/16-inch brass braising rod. With the lid in place, use a 1/16-inch drill bit to drill through the hinge barrel and dowel. Remove the top and redrill the hole in the hinge dowel with a 3/32-inch drill bit to provide clearance. Put the top back in place and tap the hinge pins into their holes. Cut the hinge pins even with the hinge leaf sides.

11 **Cut the mock dovetails.** Scribe lines ⅝ inch from each corner. Lay out the dovetails, as shown in the *Back View*. Cut and chisel them out, as shown in *Cutting Mock Dovetails*.

Cut the dovetail inserts on the table saw. Set the blade to approximately 30 degrees. Guide some scrap stock against the fence to make a number of sample inserts, adjusting the blade angle until one of the samples fits the cutout. Cut the inserts with that same setup.

Glue the dovetail inserts in place and allow to dry.

When the glue has dried, trim the inserts and sand flush.

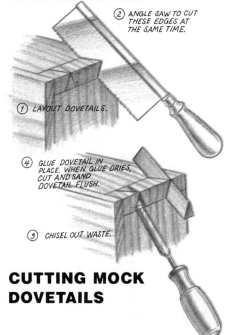

① LAYOUT DOVETAILS.

② ANGLE SAW TO CUT THESE EDGES AT THE SAME TIME.

③ CHISEL OUT WASTE.

④ GLUE DOVETAIL IN PLACE. WHEN GLUE DRIES, CUT AND SAND DOVETAIL FLUSH.

CUTTING MOCK DOVETAILS

12 **Cut out the dividers.** Lay out the notch shown in the *Cross Section through Box*. Cut out the notch on the band saw and sand the sawed edges smooth.

13 **Apply finish.** Finish sand the assembled cassette box. The cassette box shown has an oil finish, which highlights the grain and shows off the mock dovetails. When the finish is dry, slip the dividers into their grooves.

SEWING BOX

While this was originally designed as a sewing box, it can be a jewelry box, a cassette box, or a box for your stationery. The nice thing about a handsome wooden box such as this is that there are always many uses for it.

The long wooden hinges give this box charm. Before everyday metal products were common, and each object had to be individually handmade by a smith, wood often served as the material of choice. These hinges also serve as battens that keep the lid flat.

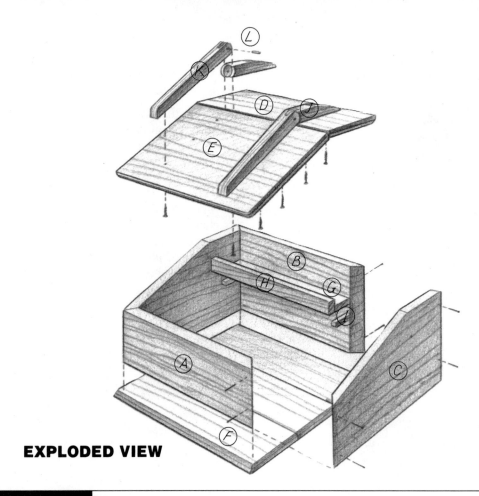

EXPLODED VIEW

CUTTING LIST

Part	Quantity	Dimension	Comment
A. Front	1	$\frac{5}{8}'' \times 3\frac{3}{4}'' \times 10\frac{1}{4}''$	
B. Back	1	$\frac{5}{8}'' \times 6\frac{1}{2}'' \times 10\frac{1}{4}''$	
C. Sides	2	$\frac{5}{8}'' \times 6\frac{1}{2}'' \times 10\frac{1}{4}''$	
D. Top	1	$\frac{5}{8}'' \times 3\frac{3}{4}'' \times 11\frac{1}{4}''$	
E. Lid	1	$\frac{5}{8}'' \times 8\frac{3}{8}'' \times 11\frac{1}{4}''$	
F. Bottom	1	$\frac{5}{8}'' \times 11\frac{1}{4}'' \times 11\frac{1}{4}''$	
G. Shelf	1	$\frac{3}{8}'' \times 1\frac{3}{4}'' \times 10''$	Cut to fit.
H. Shelf front	1	$\frac{3}{8}'' \times \frac{7}{8}'' \times 10''$	Cut to fit.
I. Shelf supports	2	$\frac{1}{4}'' \times \frac{1}{4}'' \times 1\frac{3}{4}''$	
J. Top hinges	2	$\frac{5}{8}'' \times \frac{7}{8}'' \times 4\frac{1}{4}''$	
K. Lid hinges	2	$\frac{5}{8}'' \times \frac{7}{8}'' \times 8\frac{5}{8}''$	
L. Hinge pins	2	$\frac{1}{4}''$ dia. $\times 2''$	Dowel

Hardware

10 #6 × 1-in. brass flathead wood screws
As needed, 3d finishing nails

1 Select the stock and cut the parts. Choose wood free of knots or defects. Almost any kind of wood is appropriate. Small-size projects like this encourage a fine quality hardwood since the cost of the material is not great. Joint, plane, rip, and cut the parts to the sizes given in the Cutting List. If necessary, glue up boards to make the wider parts.

Bevel the top edge of the front and lid 21 degrees as you rip them to the sizes given.

2 Miter the ends of the front, back, and sides. Set your table saw blade to 45 degrees and cut a couple of test miters in some scrap. Put the test miters together and make sure that the resulting angle equals 90 degrees. Adjust the blade angle as necessary and miter the ends of the front, back, and sides. Guide the stock with a miter gauge set at 90 degrees as you cut the miters.

3 Cut the angle in the sides. Set the box sides, front, and back upright together on a flat surface. Trace the bevel of the front onto the sides. Continue the line to lay out the angle of the sides.

When you have laid out the angle, tape the sides together and cut the angle in both sides in one operation on the band saw. Sand or hand plane any saw marks smooth.

4 Assemble the front, back, and sides. Sand the front, back, and sides. Put glue on the mitered corners and clamp the parts together. A commercially available band clamp works best for a mitered box like this one, because it produces clamping pressure from all directions. Make sure that the box is square.

SHOP TIP: Gluing a mitered box can be a nightmare, because the parts keep slipping around. Prevent this slippage with good old-fashioned masking tape. First, stretch masking tape with the sticky side up across your workbench and put the mitered pieces on the tape end to end (front-side-back-side) with the miters touching. Next, simply fold the miters closed so that the box forms a square. Then, clamp the box with a band clamp, and the tape will keep the miters from sliding around.

5 Chamfer the edges of the top, lid, and bottom boards. Put a chamfering bit in your router. Secure the router in a router table and rout a chamfer on the top, lid, and bottom, as shown in the *Front View* and *Side View*. Guide the stock against a fence as you rout. Note that only three edges of the lid and top are chamfered. Chamfer all four edges of the bottom board.

6 Attach the bottom to the box frame. Position the bottom as shown in the *Front View* and *Side View* and attach it with 3d finishing nails. If you are working with hardwood, predrill holes for the nails. Set the nails and fill the holes with wood putty.

7 Attach the shelf. Glue the shelf and shelf front together to form an *L,* as shown in the *Side View.* Lay out the shelf support positions in the box, then glue and clamp the supports to the box sides.

When the glue dries on both assemblies, glue and clamp the shelf to the shelf supports and to the back of the box.

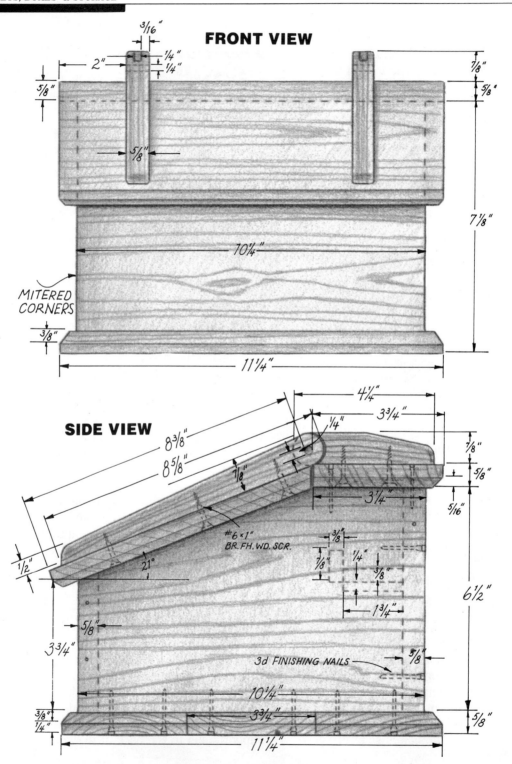

FRONT VIEW

3/16"

2"

1/4"

1/4"

5/8"

5/8"

7/8"

5/8"

7/8"

10¼"

MITERED CORNERS

3/8"

11¼"

SIDE VIEW

4¼"

3¾"

8⅜"

8⅝"

1/4"

7/8"

5/8"

1/8"

3¼"

5/16"

#6 × 1"
BR. FH. WD. SCR.

3/8"

1/4"

21°

7/8"

3/8"

6½"

1/2"

1¾"

5/8"

3¾"

3d FINISHING NAILS

5/8"

10¼"

3/8"

3¾"

5/8"

1/4"

11¼"

8 **Cut the hinge joint.** Draw a ¼-inch grid on a piece of paper and draw the lid hinge and top hinge patterns onto it. Transfer the patterns to the stock and cut the lid hinges and top hinges to shape on a band saw. Sand smooth any saw marks.

Next, cut the notch shown in the *Lid Hinge, Top View* and the tongue shown in the *Top Hinge, Top View* on the band saw. Cut the notch first, and then cut the tongue to fit the notch.

Lay out and carve the curves shown on both sides of the tongue in the *Top Hinge, Side View*. Do not cut into the tongue. Check the fit and trim any excess.

9 **Drill the hinge-pin holes through the lid hinges and top hinges.** Lay out the hinge-pin holes on the lid hinges, as shown. Put the hinge tongue into the hinge notch and clamp them to the bench. Drill a ¼-inch dowel hole through both for the hinge pin. Drill both hinges.

Chamfer one end of the each hinge pin in a pencil sharpener and insert the dowel into the hinge-pin hole. Check to see that the assembly can move freely and make any necessary adjustments. Repeat the test with the other hinge assembly.

When both hinge assemblies work properly, tap the hinge dowels into their holes until they are about ⅛ inch from

coming through the opposite side. Put a drop of glue in the dowel-pin hole and then tap the dowel in the rest of the way. Trim the dowel flush with the sides of the lid hinge.

10 **Attach the hinge assemblies to the top and lid.** Temporarily hinge the box top and lid with masking tape and set them in place on the box. Position the hinges on the box and mark their location. Make sure the lid opens freely.

Drill pilot, clearance, and countersink holes for brass screws through the top and lid into the hinges, as shown in the *Side View*. Remove the masking tape and screw the hinges to the top and lid. Do not glue the hinges.

11 **Attach the top to the box.** Glue and clamp the box top to the sides and back of the box. Drive 3d finishing nails through the top and into the sides. Predrill for the nails if your box is made from hardwood. Set the nails and fill the nail holes with putty. Clean up any excess glue.

12 **Sand and apply the finish.** Finish sand the sewing box. Stain and varnish or paint to match your decor.

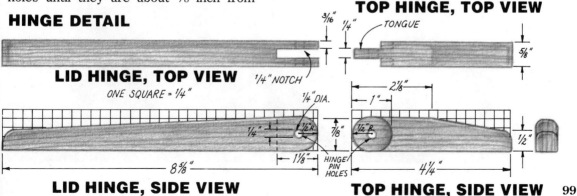

HINGE DETAIL

TOP HINGE, TOP VIEW

³⁄₁₆"   ¼"   TONGUE

⁵⁄₈"

LID HINGE, TOP VIEW

ONE SQUARE = ¼"

¼" NOTCH

¼" DIA.

2⅛"

1"

¼"   1½ R.   ½ R.

⅞"

1⅛"   HINGE PIN HOLES

8⅝"

4¼"

½"

LID HINGE, SIDE VIEW   **TOP HINGE, SIDE VIEW**   **99**

BLANKET CHEST

This blanket chest can provide extra household storage for more than just blankets. It would be a great place to store bulky winter jackets and boots, toys and games, or those sentimental treasures that you can't bring yourself to throw away.

But it's more than just another storage project. This chest also doubles as an attractive seat that would look great in a bedroom or under a sunny window.

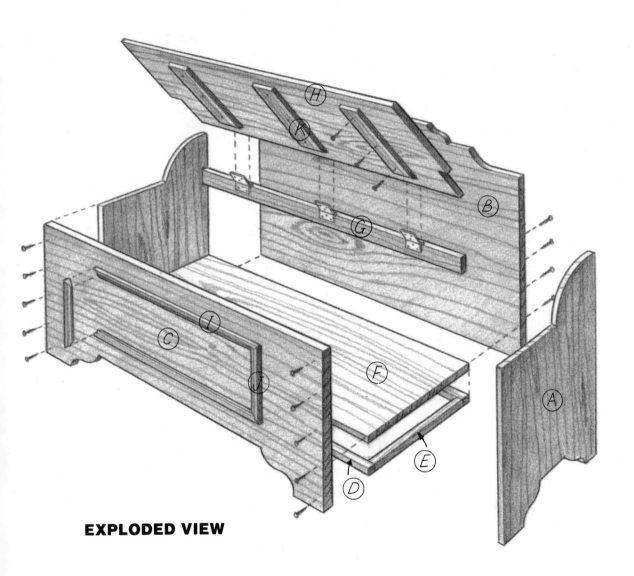

EXPLODED VIEW

1 Select the stock and cut the parts. The blanket chest shown is made from pine, but various hardwoods will also work fine. You will have to glue several boards together to make up the width of the sides, front, back, bottom, and lid. Choosing flat and straight stock will make assembly easier and more precise. Joint, plane, rip, and cut all of the parts except for the molding to the sizes given in the Cutting List.

SHOP TIP: The bottom of this blanket chest could be made of aromatic cedar. Not only will the cedar make the chest smell good, it will also repel fabric-eating moths.

2 Cut the sides, back, and feet to shape. First, lay out the radius on each side, as shown in the *Side View*. Next, draw a ½-inch grid on a piece of

BACK DETAIL

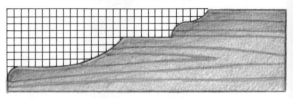

ONE SQUARE = ½"

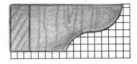

FOOT DETAIL

CUTTING LIST

Part	Quantity	Dimension
A. Sides	2	¾" × 17½" × 23½"
B. Back	1	¾" × 28¾" × 43"
C. Front	1	¾" × 17¼" × 43"
D. Long supports	2	¾" × ¾" × 41½"
E. Short supports	2	¾" × ¾" × 16"
F. Bottom	1	¾" × 17½" × 41½"
G. Hinge cleat	1	¾" × 1" × 41½"
H. Lid	1	¾" × 18" × 44"
I. Horizontal moldings	2	¾" × ⅞" × 26"
J. Vertical moldings	2	¾" × ⅞" × 9½"
K. Lid battens	3	¾" × 3" × 15"

Hardware

As needed, #8 × 2-in. flathead wood screws
As needed, #8 × 1¼-in. flathead wood screws
3 2 × 1½-in. hinges (approx. size)
As needed, ⅜-in.-dia. plugs
As needed, 3d finishing nails
2 self-balanced lid supports. Available from The Woodworker's Store, 21801 Industrial Boulevard, Rogers, MN 55374. Part #D7611.

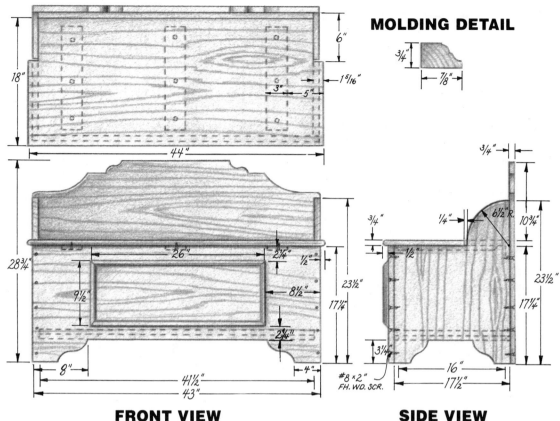

TOP VIEW

MOLDING DETAIL

FRONT VIEW

SIDE VIEW

paper and draw the *Back Detail* and *Foot Detail* onto it. Transfer the patterns to the stock. Notice that the side feet are narrower than the front and back feet.

When you've drawn the radii and shapes on the stock, cut the parts to shape with a jigsaw or band saw. Sand the sawed edges smooth.

3 Assemble the sides, front, and back. The sides are butted to the front and back, then screwed in place. Although this joinery is simple, it can be quite a trick holding everything in position while you drill for and drive the screws. The best way to position the parts is by getting someone to help you clamp the sides between the front and back. Make sure your parts are set up on a flat surface, or the assembly may twist. The surface of the sides should be even with the ends of the front and back.

When everything is clamped up properly, lay out and drill evenly spaced plug, clearance, and pilot holes for #8 × 2-inch flathead wood screws, as shown in the *Front View.* Drill the holes with a hand held drill and a combination pilot hole bit. A combination pilot hole bit drills a hole for the plug, a clearance hole for the screw shank, and a slightly smaller pilot hole for the screw threads all in one operation. Combination pilot hole bits are available at most hardware stores and are sold according to the screw size. Drill for five screws along each front corner and six screws along each back corner.

When the holes have been drilled, drive the screws and glue the plugs in place.

4 Attach the bottom. First, attach
the long and short supports along the
top of the foot cutouts on the front, back,
and sides, as shown in the *Front View* and
Side View. Clamp the long supports in
place along the front and back, as shown.
Next, drill pilot and clearance holes for #8
× 1¼-inch flathead wood screws along
the length of the long supports. Remove
the clamps and glue and screw the long
supports in place, as shown in the *Bottom*

BOTTOM JOINERY DETAIL

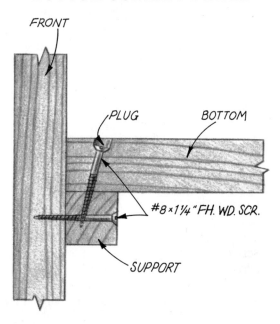

FRONT

PLUG   BOTTOM

#8×1¼"FH. WD. SCR.

SUPPORT

Joinery Detail. Repeat the process with
the short supports, but omit the glue.

Next, measure the opening and check
these measurements against those of the
bottom. You may have to remove a little
stock from the edges of the bottom for it
to fit easily in the opening. Drop the bottom in place on top of the supports, as
shown in the *Front View, Side View,* and
Bottom Joinery Detail, and drill several pilot, clearance, and plug holes for #8 ×
1¼" flathead wood screws through the
bottom and into the supports. Drive the
screws and glue the plugs in place.

5 Attach the hinge cleat. Position
the hinge cleat, as shown in the *Side
View,* and drill pilot, clearance, and recess
holes for #8 × 1¼-inch flathead wood
screws at 6-inch centers along its length.
Glue and screw the hinge cleat in place.

6 Cut the notches in the lid. Lay
out and cut the side clearance notches
in the ends of the lid, as shown in the *Top
View.* Cut the notch with a jigsaw or band
saw and sand the sawed edges smooth.

When the notches have been cut, attach the battens to the underside of the
lid with #8 × 1¼-inch flathead wood
screws as shown in the *Top View.*

7 Hinge the lid. Put the lid in position
over the opening. Make sure that the
notches in the lid provide enough clearance, both from side to side and when the
lid will swing up on its hinges. Make any
necessary adjustments by widening the lid
notches or by sanding the side radii.

After making any necessary adjustments, lay out the hinge placement on the
back of the lid. Center one hinge along the
back of the lid and place the remaining two

hinges 4 inches from each end, as shown in the *Top View.* Carry your hinge layout lines across to the hinge cleat. Lay out the hinge mortises directly from the hinges and cut them with a dovetail saw and chisel. For more information on hinging, see "Hinge Mortises" on page 7.

Once you've cut the hinge mortises, screw the hinges in place on the back of the lid. Have a helper hold the lid open while you screw the hinges to the hinge cleat.

SHOP TIP: Predrill the hinge screw holes with a special bit called a Vix bit. The Vix bit uses the hinge as a template and automatically centers the screw hole. A stop on the bit lets you set it to drill any depth hole.

---

8 **Mill and attach the molding.** Make or buy an 84-inch long piece of molding. The profile of the molding really isn't that important, so it's your choice. The profile shown in the *Molding Detail* is the molding that was chosen for the blanket chest pictured here. The profile shown can be cut with a Bosch classical bit (number 85581M). Put the bit of your choice in your router. Secure the router in a router table and adjust it to cut your desired profile.

When the profile has been cut, miter the horizontal and vertical moldings as you cut them to length. Cut the horizontal and vertical pieces to the lengths given in the Cutting List.

Attach the molding to the front, as shown in the *Front View,* with 3d finishing nails. Set the nails and fill the holes with wood putty.

9 **Sand and apply the finish.** Sand the plugs even with the surface of the wood and sand away any excess glue. Paint or stain and varnish your blanket chest. If you wish, add some stenciled ornaments to the chest.

When the finish is dry, add a pair of heavy-duty lid supports to the blanket chest. You can usually find a variety of lid supports at a hardware store. Self-balanced lid supports, available from the source given in the Cutting List, help keep the lid from crashing down unexpectedly.

ARMOIRE

Storage has been a problem around the house for ages. Early homes did not have built-in closets, and as a result, linen presses, wardrobes, and armoires kept cabinetmakers busy. The armoire shown here is a country antique that could solve the storage problem in the modern home.

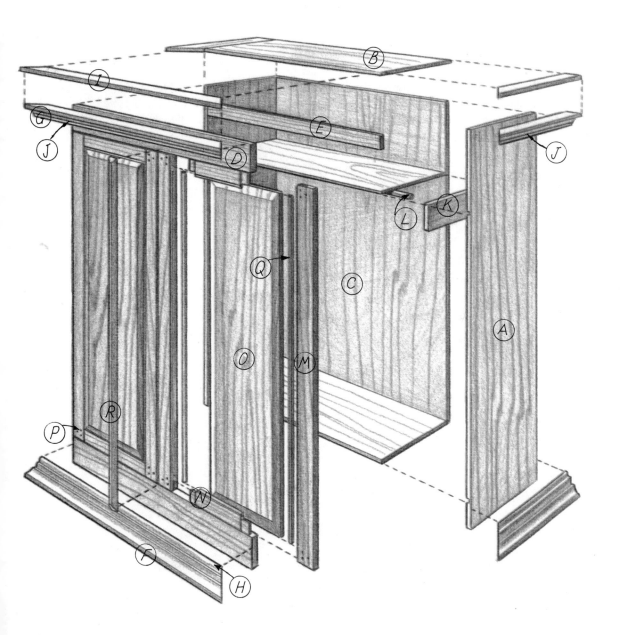

EXPLODED VIEW

1 **Select the stock and cut the parts.** Joint, plane, rip, and cut the parts to the sizes given in the Cutting List. If necessary, glue up boards to make the wider parts.

If you have access to a shaper, you can make the moldings yourself. Otherwise, purchase the moldings through a local lumber yard. Because the the types of wood available in ready-made moldings are usually limited, you may have to stain the stock to match the rest of the armoire. The plywood back is a modern addition. If you wish to be true to the original, nail random-width boards across the back instead.

2 **Dado the sides.** Lay out the dadoes, as shown in the *Front View* and *Side View*. Rout the dadoes as explained in "Routed Dadoes" on page 52.

CUTTING LIST

Part	Quantity	Dimension	Comment
A. Sides	2	$\frac{3}{4}'' \times 19\frac{1}{2}'' \times 83\frac{1}{4}''$	
B. Top/bottom/shelf	3	$\frac{3}{4}'' \times 18\frac{3}{4}'' \times 47\frac{1}{4}''$	
C. Back	1	$\frac{3}{4}'' \times 48'' \times 78''$	Plywood; cut to fit.
D. Front rails	2	$\frac{3}{4}'' \times 6'' \times 49''$	Cut to fit.
E. Stop rail	1	$\frac{3}{4}'' \times 2\frac{1}{2}'' \times 48''$	Cut to fit.
F. Baseboard	1	$\frac{3}{4}'' \times 3\frac{1}{2}'' \times 96''$	Cut to fit.
G. Cove molding	1	$\frac{3}{4}'' \times 2\frac{1}{4}'' \times 17'$	Cut to fit.
H. Quarter-round lower bead molding	1	$\frac{5}{8}'' \times \frac{5}{8}'' \times 96''$	Cut to fit.
I. Top frame	1	$\frac{3}{4}'' \times 4'' \times 120''$	Miter to fit.
J. Quarter-round upper bead molding	1	$\frac{3}{8}'' \times \frac{3}{8}'' \times 96''$	Cut to fit.
K. Clothes rod supports	2	$\frac{3}{4}'' \times 5\frac{1}{2}'' \times 18\frac{1}{2}''$	
L. Clothes rod	1	$1\frac{1}{8}''$ dia. $\times 48''$	Cut to fit.
M. Door stiles	4	$\frac{3}{4}'' \times 3'' \times 72''$	Cut to fit.
N. Door rails	4	$\frac{3}{4}'' \times 3'' \times 22''$	Cut to fit.
O. Raised panels	2	$\frac{3}{4}'' \times 18\frac{3}{4}'' \times 65\frac{11}{16}''$	
P. Door pegs	24	$\frac{1}{4}'' \times \frac{1}{4}'' \times 1''$	
Q. Door bead	1	$\frac{1}{4}'' \times \frac{1}{4}'' \times 32'$	Cut to fit.
R. Door lip	1	$\frac{7}{8}'' \times 1\frac{3}{8}'' \times 72''$	Flat astragal molding; cut to fit.

Hardware

As needed, #8 $\times$ 1¾-in. flathead wood screws
As needed, ⅜-in.-dia. wooden plugs
As needed, #8 $\times$ 1¼-in. flathead wood screws
6 ¾ $\times$ ½-in. butt hinges

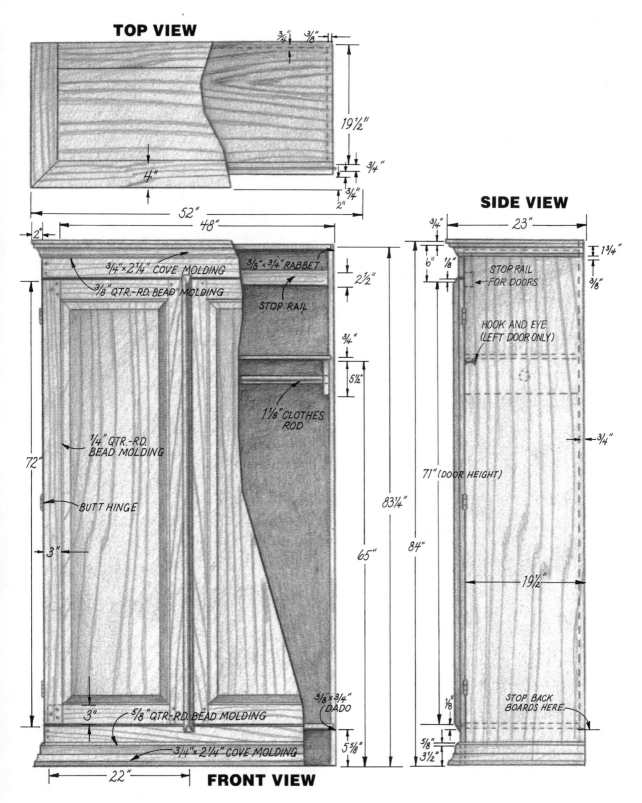

TOP VIEW

3/4" 3/8"

19 1/2"

4"

3/4"

3/4"
2"

52"

48"

2"

3/4" × 2 1/4" COVE MOLDING

3/8" QTR.-RD. BEAD MOLDING

3/8" × 3/4" RABBET

STOP RAIL

2 1/2"

3/4"

5 1/2"

1 1/8" CLOTHES ROD

1/4" QTR.-RD. BEAD MOLDING

72"

BUTT HINGE

3"

83 1/4"

65"

3/8" × 3/4" DADO

3"

5/8" QTR.-RD. BEAD MOLDING

3/4" × 2 1/4" COVE MOLDING

5 5/8"

22"

FRONT VIEW

SIDE VIEW

3/4"

23"

6" 1/8"

1 3/4"

STOP RAIL FOR DOORS

3/8"

HOOK AND EYE
(LEFT DOOR ONLY)

71" (DOOR HEIGHT)

3/4"

84"

19 1/2"

1/8"

STOP BACK
BOARDS HERE.

5/8"
3 1/2"

3 **Rabbet the sides for the back.** To rout the rabbet for the back, put a ¾-inch straight bit in your router. Set the router and router fence attachment to cut a ⅜ × ¾-inch rabbet.

4 **Assemble the carcase.** On a flat surface, clamp the carcase together without glue, so that the rabbet faces up. Predrill through the cabinet sides into the shelf, top, and bottom for #8 × 1¾-inch flathead wood screws. Use a commercially available combination pilot hole bit when drilling. This bit drills a hole for the plug, a clearance hole for the screw shank, and a slightly smaller pilot hole for the screw threads all in one operation. Pilot hole bits are available at most hardware stores and are sold according to the screw size. Screw the cabinet together. Plug the holes with wooden plugs, which you can either cut with a plug cutter or buy at the lumberyard.

Once the case is assembled, check to make sure it is square. Measure diagonally from corner to corner. The cabinet is square when the measurements are equal. If they are not equal, push the corners of the long diagonal gently together until the measurements match.

When the cabinet is square, cut the back to fit and put it in place. Predrill, as before, for #8 × 1¼-inch flathead wood screws.

5 **Attach the rails on the front.** With a helper, turn the case onto its back. Cut the front rails to fit across the top and bottom of the case. Position the top and bottom rails on the case. Drill through the rails into the top and sides, but not into the bottom shelf. Attach the rails with glue and #8 × 1-¼-inch flathead wood screws. Moldings, attached later, will cover the screws. Glue and screw the door stop to the back of the top rail, from inside the cabinet. Leave these screws exposed—they're in the cabinet where no one will see them.

6 **Attach the moldings.** The moldings on the top and bottom are built up from several moldings, as shown in the *Front View.* As you work, miter each piece to fit the cabinet.

Work from the bottom up. Miter the baseboard to fit and nail it in place. Cut the cove molding to fit over it and nail it in place. Miter and attach the quarter-round lower bead molding.

To install the top moldings, first miter and attach the top frame, as shown in the *Top View.* Miter the cove molding to fit around the front and sides of the cabinet and nail it in place. Miter and nail the quarter-round upper bead molding in place.

7 **Install the rod.** Drill a 1¼-inch diameter hole in each rod support with a hole saw. Snug a support board up against the shelf, even with the front of the case. Predrill for #8 × 1¼-inch flathead wood screws and screw the supports in place. Put the clothes rod in place, slip the other support in place, and screw the support to the side.

8 **Cut the door parts to fit.** The stiles and rails in the Cutting List are 1 inch longer than necessary. Cut them to fit the actual cabinet. Cut the stiles to ¼ inch less than the actual opening. Cut the rails to leave a ¼-inch gap between the doors.

9 **Cut a groove for the raised panels.** Put a ¼-inch dado cutter in the table saw and cut a groove ⅜ inch deep along the middle of one edge of the rails and stiles. Guide the cut along the rip fence. To ensure that the grooves will align on assembly, keep the outside face of the door against the fence for each cut.

10 Mortise and tenon the rails and stiles. Lay out the mortises and tenons, as shown in the *Joinery Detail*.

To cut the mortises, drill a series of adjoining ¼-inch-diameter holes, 2 inches deep, inside the layout lines. Cut out the remaining waste with a sharp chisel.

Lay out the tenons, as shown. Cut the tenons by repeatedly passing the stock over a dado blade. Set up the cut with a test piece of scrap the exact thickness of the rail. Raise the blade to remove ¼ inch of wood. Guide the test piece over the blade with the miter gauge; turn the board over and repeat. Check to see how the resulting tenon fits in the mortise. Adjust the height of the blade, as necessary, for a snug-fitting joint.

Use the fence to control the length of the tenon. Position the fence so that when you guide the end of the stock along it, the blade cuts a shoulder 2 inches from the end of the board. Remove the rest of the wood by repositioning the stock in the miter gauge. Leave the fence where it is to help with subsequent tenons.

SHOP TIP: Lay out the joinery so that any bow in the stock faces what will be the front of the door. Closing the doors on the finished cabinet will temporarily flatten the bow, and the doors will close tightly against the cabinet.

DOOR DETAIL

JOINERY DETAIL

11 Raise the panels. Raise the panels on the shaper, if you have one. If not, cut them on the table saw, as explained in "Raised Panels" on the opposite page.

SHOP TIP: Sand the panels and put a coat of finish or stain on the panels so that any subsequent movement once the panel is framed will not reveal unfinished wood.

12 Assemble the doors. First, test fit the rails and stiles around the raised panels and make sure all the joints close snugly when lightly clamped. Make any necessary adjustments. Apply glue sparingly to the cheeks of the mortise and tenons, and clamp the door together. Check to make sure the door is square by measuring across the diagonals. If one diagonal is long, loosen the clamps. Angle the clamps in the direction of the long diagonal and gently retighten. Check again to make sure the door is square and readjust the clamps, if necessary.

Do not glue the panel in place. It must be allowed to expand and contract with changes in humidity.

SHOP TIP: Rub paraffin on the corners of the panel before assembling the door. The paraffin will keep any glue that squeezes out of the mortise from sticking to the panel.

13 Peg the joints. Drill three ¼-inch holes through each mortise and tenon, as shown in the *Front View* and *Door Detail*. The exact spacing of the holes isn't critical. Clamp a piece of scrap behind the joint before you drill to prevent the bit from tearing out wood when it exits the stock. Drive square door pegs through the holes. Square pins are traditional on pegged mortises.

14 Install the door molding. Miter the bead molding to fit around the inside of the door frame and glue it to the edge of the door.

Test fit the doors. Plane the doors to create an equal reveal top and bottom. When satisfied with the fit, lay out and cut the hinge mortises and hang the door, as explained in "Hinge Mortises" on page 7.

Cut the door lip to fit across the gap between the doors. Attach it to the right-hand door.

15 Apply the finish and install the remaining hardware. Remove the doors and apply your favorite finish, being sure to apply equal amounts on all the surfaces. When completed, make sure the case is standing plumb and level and rehang the doors. When the doors are back in place, add handles, a hook and eye set, and a wardrobe lock of your choice.

RAISED PANELS

1 **Cut the bevels.** Raising panels on the saw requires running stock through the saw on edge. To keep the panel from wobbling, screw or clamp a tall auxiliary fence to your table saw fence, as shown. Hold the panel against the auxiliary fence as you cut.

To set up the cut, put the table saw fence with the attached tall auxiliary fence to the left of the blade, and set the saw blade to 15 degrees. The saw blade should tilt away from the fence. Adjust the rip fence to cut a bevel that at its narrowest is as wide as the groove for the panel—⅜ inch in this case. Raise the blade until it just cuts through the face of the panel as shown. Cut a bevel on all four edges of the panel.

2 **Cut the tongue.** Set the blade to 90 degrees. Adjust the blade height and fences to cut a tongue that fits snugly in the door groove.

3 **Cut the shoulder.** This cut creates a step between the bevel and the face or "field" of the panel. Remove the tall auxiliary fence and adjust the height of the blade to cut a ⅛-inch step between the field and the bevel. Cut the step with the field flat on the table saw, as shown.

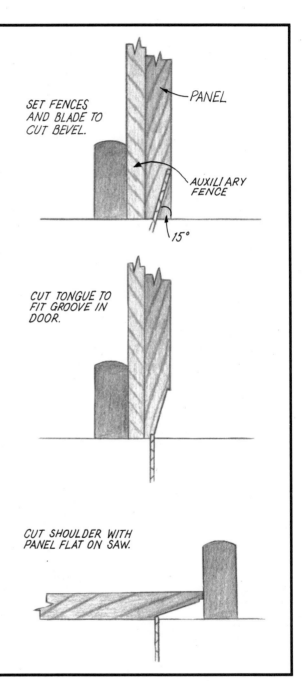

SET FENCES AND BLADE TO CUT BEVEL.

PANEL

AUXILIARY FENCE

15°

CUT TONGUE TO FIT GROOVE IN DOOR.

CUT SHOULDER WITH PANEL FLAT ON SAW.

PART THREE

TABLES AND SEATING

LAMP STAND

The lamp stand, or candle stand, is a small lightweight table that can be easily moved around the house. In the past, when light sources were limited to candles and lamps, you either moved closer to the candle for more light or moved it closer to you. Lamp stands could be easily carried from the chair side to the bedside for some bedtime reading.

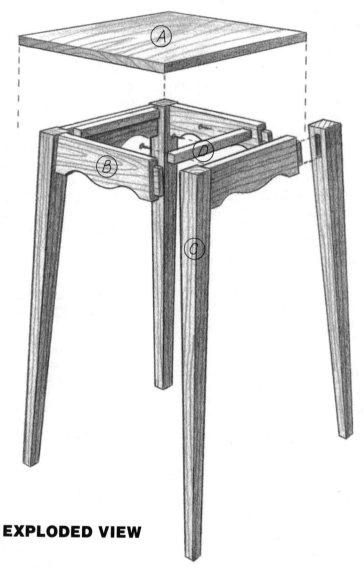

EXPLODED VIEW

CUTTING LIST

Part	Quantity	Dimension
A. Top	1	$\frac{3}{4}'' \times 14'' \times 14''$
B. Aprons	4	$\frac{3}{4}'' \times 3'' \times 10\frac{1}{2}''$
C. Legs	4	$1\frac{1}{4}'' \times 1\frac{1}{4}'' \times 28\frac{1}{4}''$
D. Cleats	2	$\frac{3}{4}'' \times \frac{3}{4}'' \times 9''$

Hardware

12 #8 × 1¼-in. roundhead wood screws and washers

1 Select the stock and cut the parts. The lamp stand shown is made of pine. You might consider making yours out of a hardwood like cherry, which was often used in the construction of small, thin-legged tables. Maple, walnut, or mahogany would also be suited to this project. Joint, plane, rip, and cut the parts to the sizes given in the Cutting List. If necessary, glue up boards to make the top.

2 Bevel the aprons. Because legs on this table angle outward, the ends of the apron are also angled. Set your miter gauge to 2 degrees. Put an apron flat on the table saw with the top edge against the miter gauge. Miter both ends of each apron.

3 Cut the tenons in the aprons. To set up the cut, put a dado blade in the table saw and clamp a wooden fence along the length of the saw's rip fence. Position the fence so that you can slowly crank the dado blade into it and leave ½ inch of blade exposed. Be careful not to hit the permanent fence.

With the miter gauge still set at 2 degrees, guide the aprons along the fence and over the blade to cut the cheeks of the tenon.

Cut ½ inch off the top and bottom of each tenon with a dovetail saw or other precision-cut hand saw. Take care not to damage the outside face of the apron.

4 Cut the shape in the aprons. Draw a ¼-inch grid on a piece of paper and draw the apron pattern onto it. Transfer the pattern to the wood and cut the shape with a band saw or jigsaw.

To get aprons with identical curves, cut them all at once. First stack the pieces together and secure by putting double-sided tape between them. Then cut the aprons in one operation.

5 Taper the legs. Lay out and cut the leg tapers, as shown in the *Leg Taper Detail*. Mark the tapers on two adjacent edges of the legs. Cut the tapers on the band saw. Make the cuts about ⅟₁₆ inch to the outside of the taper lines. Cut away the last ⅟₁₆ inch with a hand plane or jointer.

SHOP TIP: You can also cut tapers on a table saw with a commercially available taper jig. These jigs allow you to cut a taper that requires much less cleanup. The taper jig should be adjusted so that when guided against the table saw fence, the taper layout lines on the leg are parallel to the table saw blade. Adjust the fence to cut the taper along the layout lines.

6 Cut the mortises. Cut mortises on the inside faces (tapered edges) of the legs to accept the apron tenons. Lay out 2-inch-long mortises on the legs beginning ½ inch from the top, as shown in the *Top Joinery Detail*. To cut the mortises, first drill out a series of ⅜-inch holes inside the layout lines. Then cut up to the layout lines with a sharp chisel. Test fit the tenons and make sure that the top edges of the aprons are even with the top of the legs. Make adjustments as necessary.

7 Assemble the base. Glue the apron tenons into the leg mortises. The top edge of the aprons should be even with the top of the legs. Clamp the table base

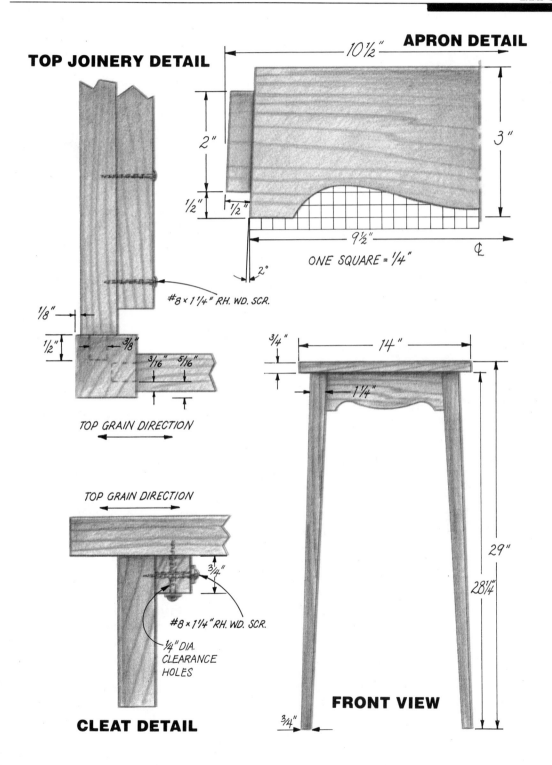

TOP JOINERY DETAIL

APRON DETAIL

10½"

2"

3"

½"

½"

9½"

2°

ONE SQUARE = ¼"

#8 × 1¼" RH. WD. SCR.

⅛"

½"

⅜"

3/16"   5/16"

TOP GRAIN DIRECTION

TOP GRAIN DIRECTION

¾"

14"

¾"

1¼"

#8 × 1¼" RH. WD. SCR.

¼" DIA.
CLEARANCE
HOLES

29"

28¼"

FRONT VIEW

CLEAT DETAIL

¾"

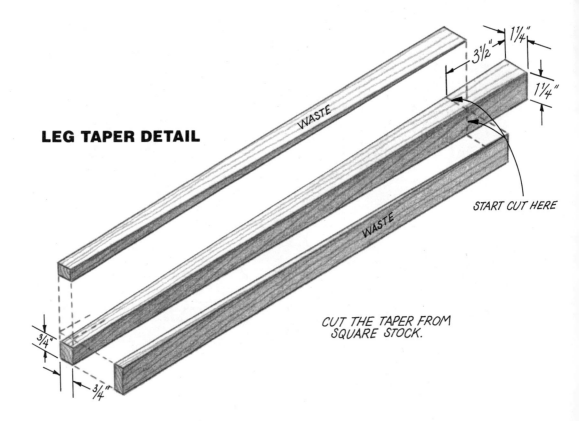

LEG TAPER DETAIL

WASTE

WASTE

START CUT HERE

CUT THE TAPER FROM
SQUARE STOCK.

together. Make sure that the base is square by measuring diagonally from corner to corner. If the measurements are equal, the table is square. If the measurements are unequal, clamp lightly across the long diagonal until the diagonals are the same length.

8 Attach the top. Drill three evenly spaced holes in two adjacent faces of the cleats, as shown in the *Cleat Detail*. Glue and screw the cleats to two parallel aprons. Center the top on the legs, so

that the grain runs perpendicular to the cleats. Screw, but do not glue, the top to the cleats. The oversize holes in the cleats will allow the top to expand and contract with changes in humidity.

9 Apply finish. Sand the table and slightly round all of the edges. The table shown has been stained, but you can finish your table in a way that best fits your decor. If your table is made from cherry or other hardwood, you may want to highlight the grain with an oil finish.

LIAR'S BENCH

How did this bench get its name? Well, it's just long enough for two people to sit on comfortably and swap tall tales on a warm summer's evening.

This is a simple bench with simple joinery. You simply glue and screw it together. It is unpretentious and practical. To ensure proper alignment of the parts, however, pay close attention to the layout when building this bench.

EXPLODED VIEW

CUTTING LIST

Part	Quantity	Dimension
A. Long legs	2	$1\frac{3}{8}'' \times 2\frac{3}{4}'' \times 33\frac{7}{8}''$
B. Short legs	2	$1\frac{3}{8}'' \times 2\frac{3}{4}'' \times 23\frac{5}{8}''$
C. Seat supports	2	$1\frac{3}{8}'' \times 2\frac{3}{4}'' \times 17''$
D. Seat boards	3	$\frac{15}{16}'' \times 5\frac{3}{4}'' \times 48''$
E. Back	1	$\frac{15}{16}'' \times 5\frac{3}{4}'' \times 51\frac{1}{8}''$
F. Bottom support	1	$\frac{3}{4}'' \times 2\frac{3}{4}'' \times 45\frac{3}{8}''$

Hardware

4 #12 × 3-in. drywall screws
16 #12 × 2¼-in. drywall screws
20 #12 × 2-in. drywall screws

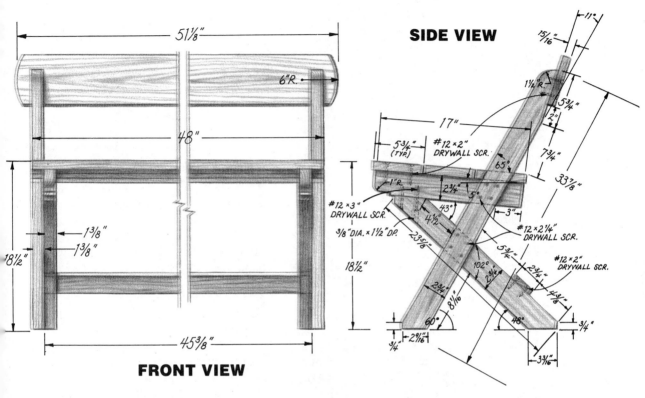

SIDE VIEW

FRONT VIEW

1 **Select the stock and cut the parts.** Almost any clear hardwood or softwood is suitable for this bench. If you plan to use this outdoors, cedar or mahogany would be good choices. Choose straight, flat stock. A few small knots are acceptable in this piece. Joint, plane, rip, and cut the parts to the sizes given in the Cutting List.

2 **Cut the long and short legs and the seat supports to shape.** Lay out the angles on the leg, as shown in the *Side View*. The easiest way to cut the sharp angles in the legs is with a good old-fashioned, muscle-powered crosscut saw. Hold the stock down on some sawhorses or a low bench and make the cut to the waste side of your layout lines. Sand away any saw marks.

Cut the curve in the front edge of seat supports and top of the long legs with a jigsaw or band saw, as shown in the *Seat Support Detail* and the *Side View*. Stay to the waste side of your layout lines as you cut. Clean up the sawed edges with sandpaper.

3 **Lay out and assemble the legs and seat supports.** Arrange the legs and seat supports on top of each other as they will be when assembled. Use a protractor to set a sliding T-bevel to the angles shown in the *Side View* and align the parts with it.

Clamp the legs and seat supports in position with C-clamps. Compare the two end assemblies by standing them next to each other with their seat supports side by side. Make sure that everything is po-

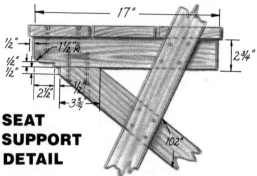

SEAT SUPPORT DETAIL

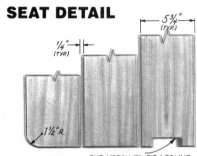

SEAT DETAIL

TOP VIEW *CUT NOTCH TO FIT AROUND LONG LEG.*

sitioned correctly. The angle of the seat supports and legs should match, and the long legs should be on the opposite sides of their seat supports. Make any necessary adjustments.

With the legs and seat supports still clamped, predrill and screw together each end assembly. Attach the long legs to the short legs and seat supports with four #12 × 2¼-inch drywall screws, as shown in the *Side View.* Attach the short legs to the seat supports with two #12 × 3-inch drywall screws angled up through the short legs and into the seat supports, as shown. Because of the angles involved, you must counterbore 1½ inches in each short leg for one of the screws, as shown.

4 Notch the rear seat board. The rear seat board is notched to fit around the long legs, as shown in the *Seat Detail, Top View.* To lay out the notch, put the seat board on one of the seat supports so that the end grain is against the long leg. Trace the location of the leg onto the end grain. Set a marking gauge to the thickness of the leg and lay out the depth of the notch on the top and bottom of the seat board. Repeat on the other end of the board.

Cut along the angled lines with a dovetail saw or back saw, until you reach the scribe line. Cut along the scribe line with a jigsaw to remove the waste.

5 Cut curves in the back board and front seat board. With a jigsaw cut the front seat board and the ends of the back board to the profiles shown in the *Front View* and *Seat Detail, Top View.* Sand away any saw marks or roughness.

6 Assemble the bench. Sand the end assemblies, seat boards, back, and bottom support.

On a flat surface, position the seat boards on the end assemblies, as shown in *Side View* and *Front View.* Clamp the seat in place. Next, clamp the back to the long legs. Clamp the bottom support to the short legs, as shown in the *Side View.* When everything is positioned correctly, predrill and countersink holes for #12 × 2-inch screws, as shown in the *Side View.* Drive the screws and remove the clamps.

SHOP TIP: To keep the ends from falling over while you position the other parts, clamp two 51-inch lengths of scrap between them. Position the ends the proper distance apart and begin assembly.

7 Sand and apply the finish. Give the assembled bench a final sanding. If your bench will be outside, protect it with a weather-resistant finish like spar varnish.

GATELEG TABLE

Where does your family gather? Jobs, school, and play keep us up and running all day and all evening. Often the only place we consistently gather as a family is around the supper table. Make that gathering place special for your family by building your own gateleg table.

EXPLODED VIEW

1 **Select the stock and cut the parts.** The gateleg table shown is made from pine, but it can be made from almost any kind of wood. Choose straight, flat stock. Joint, plane, rip, and cut the stock to the sizes given in the Cutting List.

You'll have to glue several boards together to create the top and leaves. When the leaves and top are glued, hand plane or sand the glue joints even.

SHOP TIP: When you need to create a wide, flat surface, it is better to glue together several narrow boards than to create the width with a few wide boards. Wide boards often cup, warp, or split as humidity changes. If you want the appearance of wide boards, rip wide boards down the middle, then carefully joint and glue them back together.

2 **Lay out and rout the rule joint between the top and leaves.** A rule joint is made by routing a roundover in the long edges of the tabletop and a cove in the adjoining edge of each leaf.

Start by making the roundover to the dimensions shown in the *Rule Joint Detail*. Clamp the top, with its bottom down, to a workbench or other stable work surface. Let one of the long edges of the top hang over the edge of the work surface and cut the roundover in a series of passes with a router and ½-inch-radius roundover bit. Lower the bit with each pass until you match the profile shown. Then rotate the tabletop and rout the remaining edge.

Next, rout the cove in the leaves. Clamp one of the leaves face down on a stable work surface with one of the long edges hanging over the side. Rout the cove in the leaf with a few passes of a router and ½-inch-radius cove bit. Again,

CUTTING LIST

Part	Quantity	Dimension
A. Top	1	1⅛″ × 17″ × 56″
B. Leaves	2	1⅛″ × 20″ × 56″
C. Feet	2	1⅛″ × 3¼″ × 14″
D. Top supports	2	1⅛″ × 3¼″ × 14″
E. Gate rails	4	1⅛″ × 3¼″ × 29¾″
F. Legs	2	1⅛″ × 7″ × 24″
G. Gate stiles	4	1⅛″ × 3½″ × 24″
H. Top/middle/bottom crosspieces	3	1⅛″ × 7″ × 48″
I. Pivot dowels	4	½″ dia. × 2⅛″

Hardware

4 #8 × 2-in. flathead wood screws
As needed, #10 × 2-in. roundhead wood screws
6 drop leaf table hinges

VIEW THROUGH TOP

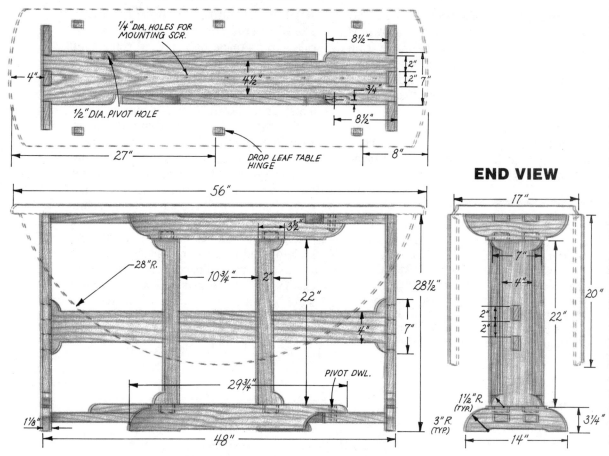

1/4" DIA. HOLES FOR MOUNTING SCR.

8 1/2"

2"
2"
7"

3/4"

4"

4 1/2"

1/2" DIA. PIVOT HOLE

8 1/2"

27"

DROP LEAF TABLE HINGE

8"

END VIEW

17"

56"

3 1/2"

7"

28" R.

10 3/4"

2"

4"

22"

28 1/2"

2"
2"

22"

20"

7"

4"

29 3/4"

PIVOT DWL.

3" R.
(TYP.)

1 1/2" R.
(TYP.)

1 1/8"

48"

3 1/4"

14"

VIEW THROUGH LEAF

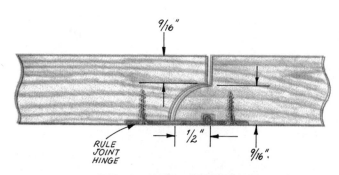

9/16"

9/16"

1/2"

9/16"

RULE JOINT HINGE

RULE JOINT DETAIL

lower the bit with each pass until you match the profile shown in the *Rule Joint Detail*. Repeat the process with the second leaf.

3 Hinge the leaves to the top. The leaves are hinged to the top with drop leaf table hinges. There are three hinges for each leaf, and mortises need to be cut for each. Each mortise also has a recess cut in it for the hinge barrels.

First, lay the top and leaves face down on a flat surface with the rule joints together. Separate the leaves from the top along the rule joint by 1/16 inch.

Next, lay out the hinges along each rule joint, as shown in the *View through Top*. Position the hinges across the joint with the hinge barrel underneath the top, as shown in the *Rule Joint Detail*.

When all the hinges are in position, trace around each one with a marking knife and mark the position of the hinge barrel. Cut a mortise for each hinge to the depth of the hinge leaf. Remove most of the wood with a router and straight bit; clean up to the layout lines with a chisel.

After you cut the mortises, use a ¼-inch gouge to cut deeper mortises for the hinge barrels. The cuts need not be perfect: They will be hidden by the hinges.

When all of the hinge mortises have been cut, hinge the leaves to the top.

4 Lay out and cut the circular top. Plot the center point on the underside of the tabletop by drawing diagonal lines from corner to corner. The point at which the lines intersect should be the exact center of the tabletop. Lay out the 28-inch-radius circle on the top and leaves from the center point. Cut out the top with a jigsaw and sand the edge smooth.

SHOP TIP: Lay out the top with the help of a circle-marking stick. Make the stick from a 29-inch-long piece of scrap. Drill a ¼-inch hole at one end and a ⅛-inch hole 28 inches from the first hole at the other end. Drive a 6d finishing nail about ½ inch into the center point that you plotted on the underside of the table. Put the ⅛-inch hole at the end of the stick over the finishing nail and put a pencil in the ¼-inch hole at the other end. Swing the stick in an arc to make a perfect 28-inch-radius circle.

5 Cut out and mortise the feet, top supports, and gate rails. When you build the base of this table, you first build a trestle, and then add the gates that support the leaves. It's more efficient, however, to cut the joints for both trestle and gate at the same time.

First, lay out the foot, top support, and gate rail shapes on the stock, as shown in the *Foot Detail, Side View; Top Support Detail, Side View;* and *Gate Detail,* with a compass and straightedge. Notice that the rails on the top and bottom of the gate do not have the same shape.

Lay out the leg mortises on the top supports and feet. To cut the mortises, drill a series of adjoining holes inside the layout lines with a ½-inch drill bit. Cut up to the layout lines and square the mortise corners with a chisel.

Next, lay out and cut the through mortises in the feet for the crosspiece. Cut the mortises as before. When you clean up to the layout lines, work from both sides of the feet.

Notch the top supports to hold the top crosspiece. Lay out the notches and cut them in a series of cuts on the table saw.

Cut the foot, top support, and gate rail to shape with a band saw or jigsaw and sand off the marks left by the saw.

6 Tenon the legs and gate stiles and cut them to shape. Lay out the tenons on the legs and gate stiles, as shown in the *Tenon Details*.

Before you cut the tenons, set up the cut by putting a dado blade in the table saw. Adjust the dado blade so that it protrudes about ¼ inch above the surface of the table saw. Clamp a stop block to the fence to set the length of the tenons and

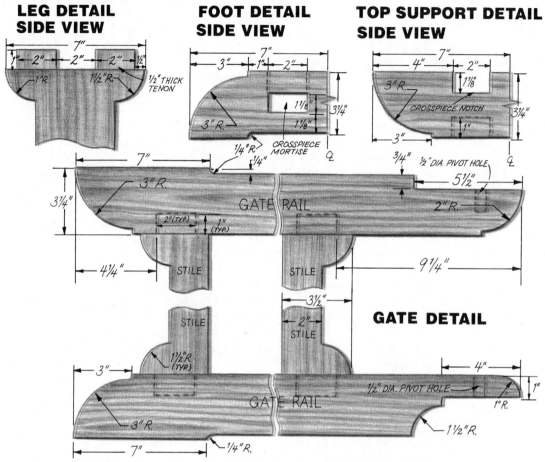

LEG DETAIL
SIDE VIEW

7"
2" 2" 2" ½"
1"R. 1½"R.
½" THICK TENON

FOOT DETAIL
SIDE VIEW

7"
3" 1½" 2"
3"R. 1⅛"
1⅛"
3¼"
¼"R. CROSSPIECE MORTISE
¼" ℄

TOP SUPPORT DETAIL
SIDE VIEW

7"
4" 2"
3"R. 1⅛"
CROSSPIECE NOTCH
3¼"
1"
3" ¾" ℄

7"
3"R.
3¼"
GATE RAIL
2"(TYP.) 1"(TYP.)
STILE STILE
4¼"
¾" ½" DIA. PIVOT HOLE
5½"
2"R.
9⅞"

STILE
3½"
2" STILE

GATE DETAIL

STILE
1½"R. (TYP.)
3"
GATE RAIL
3"R.
7" ¼"R.

4"
½" DIA. PIVOT HOLE
1"
1"R.
1½"R.

make the cut, as shown in *Tenoning on the Table Saw*. Test the setup on a piece of scrap the same thickness as the actual stock. Because the tenon is 1 inch long, you will have to cut each side of the tenon in two passes.

When you have cut one side of the tenon, flip the test piece over and make the cut on the other side. Then turn off the saw and test fit a corner of the tenon into a mortise. If it is too tight, raise the dado blade slightly and remove a little more stock from both sides of the tenon. When the test piece fits snugly, cut the thickness of the tenons in the legs and gate stiles with the same setup.

Cut the short face of the tenons by raising the dado blade ½ inch above the table and putting the stock on edge. Make the cuts as before.

Each leg has twin tenons on the top and bottom. Cut away a 2-inch section in the middle of the tenon you just cut, to create the twin tenons shown in the *Tenon Details*. Make the cuts that go with the grain with a backsaw. Cut across the grain with a coping saw. Keep the coping saw about 1/16 inch on the waste side of the layout line. Cut up to the line with a chisel.

When the tenons have been cut, cut the legs and gate stiles to shape. Sand away any saw marks.

TENON DETAILS

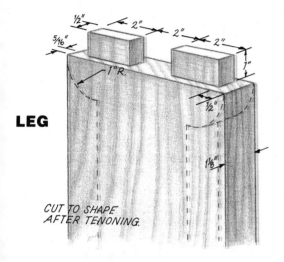

LEG

CUT TO SHAPE AFTER TENONING.

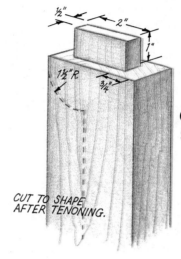

GATE STILE

CUT TO SHAPE AFTER TENONING.

TENONING ON THE TABLE SAW

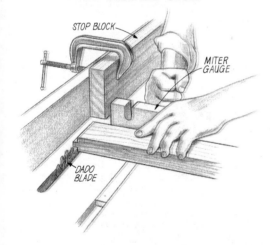

STOP BLOCK

MITER GAUGE

DADO BLADE

waste side of the layout lines with the coping saw as before. Clean up the cut with a chisel. Test the fit of the tenons in their mortises and make any necessary adjustments.

Cut the crosspieces to shape after you cut the tenons. Sand away any saw marks.

7 **Tenon the crosspieces and cut them to shape.** Lay out the crosspiece tenons, as shown in the *Crosspiece Detail.* Cut the tenons with a backsaw and remove the waste between them with a coping saw. Cut about ¹⁄₁₆ inch on the

CROSSPIECE DETAIL

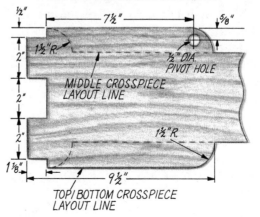

MIDDLE CROSSPIECE LAYOUT LINE

½" DIA. PIVOT HOLE

1½"R.

TOP/BOTTOM CROSSPIECE LAYOUT LINE

8 **Drill pivot holes in the gate rails and crosspieces.** Lay out the pivot holes in the crosspieces, as shown in the *View through Top*. To ensure that the holes align, clamp the top and bottom crosspieces together and drill the holes in one operation.

Drill the holes in the gate rails, as shown in the *Gate Detail*.

9 **Assemble the trestle.** Coat the leg tenons with glue and put them in their mortises in the feet and top supports. Clamp the assemblies together and make sure that the assemblies are square. Allow the glue to dry.

When the glue is dry, add the crosspieces. Spread some glue on the crosspiece tenons and put them in their mortises. Make sure that you position the crosspieces so that the pivot holes are positioned as shown in the *View through Leaf*. Reinforce the joint in the top crosspiece by driving #8 × 2-inch screws through the tenons and into the top supports.

Clamp the crosspieces in place and allow the glue to dry.

10 **Assemble the gates and attach them to the top and bottom supports.** First, spread glue on the gate tenons and insert them into their mortises. Make sure the curves on the legs are positioned as shown in the *Gate Detail*. Clamp the gates together and make sure that they are square. Make any necessary adjustments and allow the glue to dry.

Next, position the gates on the base so that the pivot holes in the gates line up with those in the base. Insert the pivot dowels into the top crosspiece and tap them down into the top gate rails with a mallet.

Tap the remaining pivot dowels through the bottom gate rails and about halfway into the bottom crosspieces. This should leave about ½ inch of the pivot dowels exposed above the bottom gate rails. Spread a little glue on the exposed portion of the pivot dowels and tap them the rest of the way into the bottom crosspiece. Clean up any excess glue.

11 **Attach the top to the completed base.** Drill a series of evenly spaced holes in the crosspiece, as shown in the *View through Top*. Center the top on the base. Attach the top to the base by driving #10 × 2-inch roundhead wood screws through the holes and into the top.

12 **Rout the profile around the top.** When the top has been screwed to the base, pull up the leaves and swing out the gates to hold them. Rout the profile around the full circle of the top with a router and a ½-inch-radius roundover bit. As you cross the rule joint, be careful not to let the router bit bearing fall into the joint. Float from one edge of the joint to the other.

13 **Apply the finish.** Finish sand your gateleg table. Apply stain or a clear wood finishing oil to your table to bring out the beauty of the wood grain. Follow the stain or oil with a tough polyurethane to protect your table from everyday wear.

COUNTRY CHAIR

Comfort has its price. On this chair, the price is low. The legs, rails, and seat supports are joined with mortises and tenons, and the seat is simply screwed in place. Part of what makes the chair comfortable, however, is that it is wider in front than in back. The price, of course, is a set of angled tenons. Don't worry. They're not hard, and it's a good chance to hone up on your hand skills.

EXPLODED VIEW

CUTTING LIST

Part	Quantity	Dimension	Comment
A. Front legs	2	1⅞″ × 1⅞″ × 15″	
B. Back legs	2	1¾″ × 3″ × 33½″	Cut to shape.
C. Front rail	1	⅞″ × 1⅜″ × 13³⁄₁₆″	
D. Side/back rails	3	⅞″ × 1⅜″ × 12⅞″	
E. Front support	1	⅞″ × 1¾″ × 13³⁄₁₆″	
F. Side supports	2	⅞″ × 1¾″ × 12⅞″	
G. Top rail	1	⅞″ × 2″ × 12⅞″	
H. Shaped rail	1	½″ × 2½″ × 12⅞″	
I. Seat	1	⁹⁄₁₆″ × 16½″ × 13¼″	
J. Cleats	2	¾″ × ¾″ × 10¾″	

Hardware

6 #8 × 1-in. flathead wood screws

1 Select the stock and cut the parts.

The chair shown is made from poplar. You could make your chair from other hardwoods like maple, cherry, or oak. Choose good straight stock that is free of knots and cut the parts to the sizes given in the Cutting List.

2 Cut the legs to shape.

Draw a ½-inch grid on a 36-inch-long piece of paper and draw the back leg pattern onto it. Transfer the pattern to the stock and cut the back legs to shape on a band saw. Sand away any saw marks.

Each of the legs is tapered on two adjacent sides, as shown in the *Front View* and *Side View*. Cutting the back legs created one of the back leg's two tapers. Lay out the remaining taper on the back legs and lay out the tapers on the front legs. Cut the tapers on the band saw. Stay about 1⁄16 inch to the waste side of the layout lines as you cut and then trim down to the layout lines on a jointer or with a hand plane. Use a push stick on the jointer and keep your hands well away from the cutter.

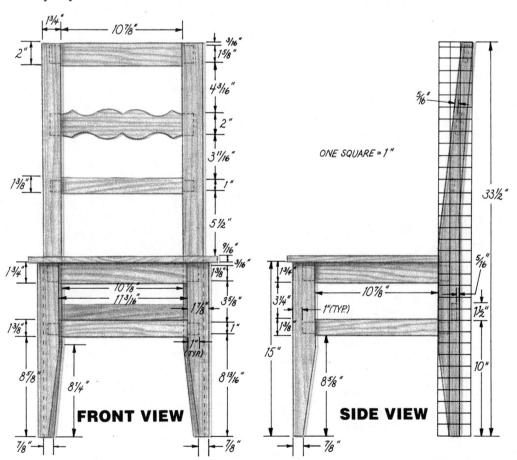

FRONT VIEW

SIDE VIEW

ONE SQUARE = 1"

JOINERY DETAIL

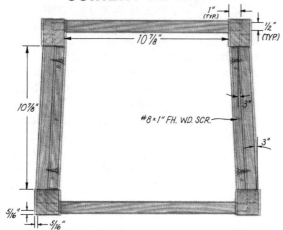

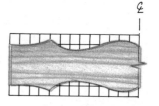

3 **Cut the mortises in the legs.** All of the legs are mortised to accept the tenons in the rails and supports. Lay out the mortises shown in the *Joinery Detail, Front View,* and *Side View.* Cut the mortises by drilling a series of adjacent ½-inch holes between the layout lines. Cut the mortise sides and corners square with a chisel.

4 **Cut the tenons.** Making this chair requires both straight and angled tenons. Cut the straight tenons first.

All of the straight tenons are 1 inch long and have ³⁄₁₆-inch shoulders. Cut the tenons in repeated passes over the dado blade. To set up the cut, raise the dado blade ³⁄₁₆ inch above the table. Test the setup on a piece of scrap the exact thickness of the rail. Cut one face of the test piece. Turn it over and cut the other face. Test fit the resulting tenon in the mortise. Adjust the blade height as necessary.

Adjust the fence so that guiding the end of the rail along it with the miter gauge cuts the tenon shoulder 1 inch from the end of the rail. To remove the remaining waste, reposition the rail in the miter gauge. Do not reset the fence. Cut the straight tenons.

5 **Cut the angled tenons.** Because the back of the chair frame is narrower than the front of the frame, the side rails and side supports run from front to back at an angle. To do this, you cut angled tenons on the pieces.

Lay out the tenons as shown in the *Joinery Detail.* Cut them as explained in "Angled Tenons" on page 138.

SHAPED RAIL PATTERN

ONE SQUARE = ½ "

SEAT PATTERN

6 **Cut the shaped rail.** The full thickness of this rail fits into the mortises you cut earlier. Slip a corner of the stock into the mortise to check the fit. Plane the stock to fit, if necessary. Draw a ¼-inch grid on a piece of paper and draw the *Shaped Rail Pattern* onto it. Transfer the pattern to the wood and cut out the shaped rail on a band saw. Sand away any saw marks.

7 **Assemble the chair frame.** First, assemble the two sides. Put some glue in the mortises for the side supports and side rails. Apply enough glue to coat the sides of the mortises, but don't apply so much that it squeezes out when you put the tenon in place. Put the rails and supports in the mortises, as shown in the *Exploded View.* Clamp each side together.

When the glue dries, test fit the rest of the chair and clamp it lightly together. If there are gaps between the front or back parts and the legs, you can correct them by trimming the rails and supports.

If the gaps are in front, correct them by trimming the rear rails and supports. If they are in the back, trim the front rails and supports. Trim the shoulders of one end of the appropriate rail and support by the amount of the gap.

To trim the shoulder on the table saw, put the piece in the miter gauge. Adjust the fence so that when you run the end of the stock against it, the blade will trim the necessary amount. Adjust the blade so that it won't cut into the tenon.

After you've done any necessary trimming, put glue in the remaining mortises, assemble the chair, and clamp it gently together.

8 **Cut the seat to shape.** Draw a ¼-inch grid on a piece of paper and draw the seat shape onto it, as grid in the *Seat Pattern.* Transfer the pattern to the wood and cut the seat to shape with a jigsaw or band saw. Sand the sawed edges smooth.

9 **Attach the seat to the chair frame.** The chair is attached to the frame with wooden cleats, as shown in the *Joinery Detail.* First, predrill clearance holes in the cleats that are slightly larger than the screw shank. Spacing of the holes isn't critical. Countersink the clearance holes. Screw and glue the cleats to the side supports, as shown. Then, center the seat on the frame and screw it in place. Do not glue the seat to the cleats or frame.

SHOP TIP: Drill the holes through the cleats with a combination pilot hole bit. These bits drill a countersink hole, a clearance hole for the screw shank, and a pilot hole for the screw threads in one operation. Pilot hole bits are available at most hardware stores and are sold according to the screw size.

10 **Sand and apply the finish.** Finish sand your chair. Paint or stain and varnish your chair to match your decor. Tack a colorful quilted pad to the seat for a homey, country look.

ANGLED TENONS

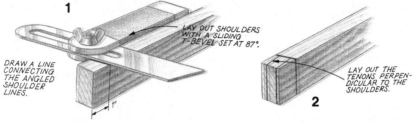

1

LAY OUT SHOULDERS WITH A SLIDING T-BEVEL SET AT 87°.

DRAW A LINE CONNECTING THE ANGLED SHOULDER LINES.

1"

LAY OUT THE TENONS PERPEN-DICULAR TO THE SHOULDERS.

2

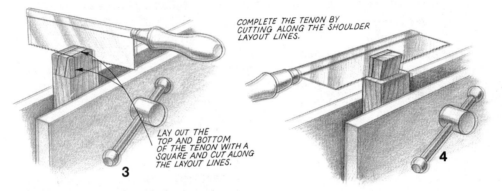

COMPLETE THE TENON BY CUTTING ALONG THE SHOULDER LAYOUT LINES.

LAY OUT THE TOP AND BOTTOM OF THE TENON WITH A SQUARE AND CUT ALONG THE LAYOUT LINES.

3

4

1 **Lay out the shoulders.** Set a sliding T-bevel to the angle of the tenon shoulders— 87 degrees in this case. Guide a pencil along the blade of the T-bevel to mark the shoulders on the top and bottom of the stock. These lines are directly above one another and parallel. With a square as a guide, draw lines connecting the shoulder lines.

2 **Lay out the angled tenons.** With the T-bevel still set at 87 degrees, lay out the tenon. First mark the base of the tenon along the shoulder lines—3/16 inch from the edges in this case. Use the T-bevel to draw lines from the base of the tenon to the end of the rail, as shown. The tenons are perpendicular to the angled shoulder lines.

3 **Lay out the top and bottom of the tenon and cut along the layout lines.** Lay out the top and bottom of the tenon—3/16 inch from the top and bottom edges of the board in this case. Cut along the layout lines down to the shoulder lines on all four sides of the tenon. A backsaw or dovetail saw will work best for these precise cuts. Be careful to follow the angles while cutting.

4 **Complete the tenon.** Cut carefully along the shoulder lines and remove the waste. Test fit the tenon and adjust the tenon width and thickness with a chisel if necessary.

FARM TABLE

Based on an old Scandinavian piece, this table is an example of country elegance. While it has a Shaker-like spareness, it also has a few uncharacteristic embellishments, like a beaded table edge and chamfered legs. The foot on the bottom of the leg appears at first glance to be lathe turned. In fact, it's merely a decorative detail sawn into the already-tapered leg.

EXPLODED VIEW

CUTTING LIST

Part	Quantity	Dimension	Comment
A. Legs	4	1½″ × 1½″ × 29″	
B. Side aprons	2	¾″ × 4½″ × 46½″	
C. End aprons	2	¾″ × 4½″ × 22″	
D. Dowel pins	16	¼″ dia. × ¾″	
E. Tabletop	1	¾″ × 27″ × 51½″	Glue up from narrower boards.
F. Clip	1	¾″ × 2″ × 25″	Makes 14

Hardware

14 #10 × 1¼-in. flathead wood screws

1 **Select the stock and cut the parts.** Look for straight, flat hardwood stock, without knots. Try to find lengths with interesting grain patterns. Joint, plane, rip, and cut the legs and aprons to the sizes given in the Cutting List.

2 **Cut the mortises in the legs.** The legs and aprons are joined by mortise and tenons, as shown in the *Joinery Detail.* One end of the mortise is open—it comes through the top of the leg. You can make these mortises with a table-mounted router. If you use a router, make sure your bit is long enough to cut a 1-inch-deep groove.

To cut the mortises, you must use two different fence settings. First, put a ¼-inch straight bit in the router. Set up the router to cut a 1-inch-deep groove, ¼ inch from the fence. Cut one mortise in each leg. Then reset the fence so it is 1 inch from the bit. Cut the second mortise on each leg.

SHOP TIP: Clamp a block of wood to the fence 4¼ inches beyond the cutter. When the leg hits the block, the mortise is the correct length.

SIDE VIEW   END VIEW

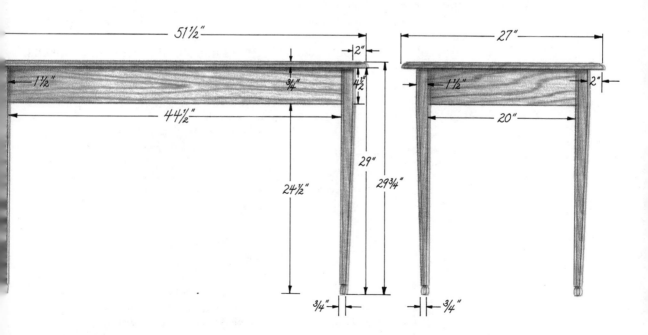

JOINERY DETAIL

¼" ¼" ¼"

¼"

1½" ¼"

1" ¼"

1½"

4½"

4½"

4½"

1"

APRON

LEG

3 Cut tenons on the aprons. Put a dado blade, set to cut ¾ inch wide, in the table saw. Position the fence ¼ inch away from the cutter and adjust the blade to make a cut ¼ inch deep.

Cut each side of the tenon in two passes. First, use the miter gauge to guide the cut along the fence. On the second pass, adjust the position of the board against the miter gauge so that the cut removes the rest of waste. Turn the board over and repeat.

After you've cut all the tenons, rout a ⅜ × ⅜-inch groove in the inside face, ⅜ inch below the top edge, as shown in the *Fastener Detail*. The wooden clips that attach the tabletop will fit into these grooves.

SHOP TIP: If the shoulders of your tenons don't align with each other, check the setup on the saw. Measure to make sure the fence is parallel to the blade. Check the miter gauge to make sure it really is set at 90 degrees. Cut a few test tenons on some scrap, until you're sure of your setup.

4 Taper the legs. After you have cut and fitted all of the mortises and ten-

ons, lay out the taper of the legs. You can cut out the tapers on the band saw or cut them on the table saw, as explained in "Table Saw Tapers" on opposite page.

After you've tapered the legs, lay out and chamfer the edges of the tapers. Put a chamfer bit in a router. Secure the router in a router table and cut the chamfers. Stop the chamfers 4½ inches from the top of the legs to allow for the aprons.

When the chamfers have been cut, use a band saw to cut the shape shown in the *Foot Detail* in the ends of the legs. Sand away the saw marks.

ONE SQUARE = ¼"

FOOT DETAIL

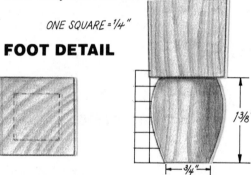

1⅜"

¾"

5 Assemble the legs and aprons. Sand the legs and aprons and test the fit of the joints. Make any necessary adjustments. Apply glue and clamp the legs and aprons.

After the glue has set and the clamps are removed, cut two dowel pins for each mortise. Drill ¾-inch-deep stopped holes in the legs and tenons. Drive a glue-coated dowel into each hole. Sand the dowels flush.

6 Glue up the tabletop. Joint, plane, rip, and cut boards to make up the tabletop stock. How many boards you need to cut depends, of course, on their widths; simply cut enough pieces to form the size given in the Cutting List.

TABLE SAW TAPERS

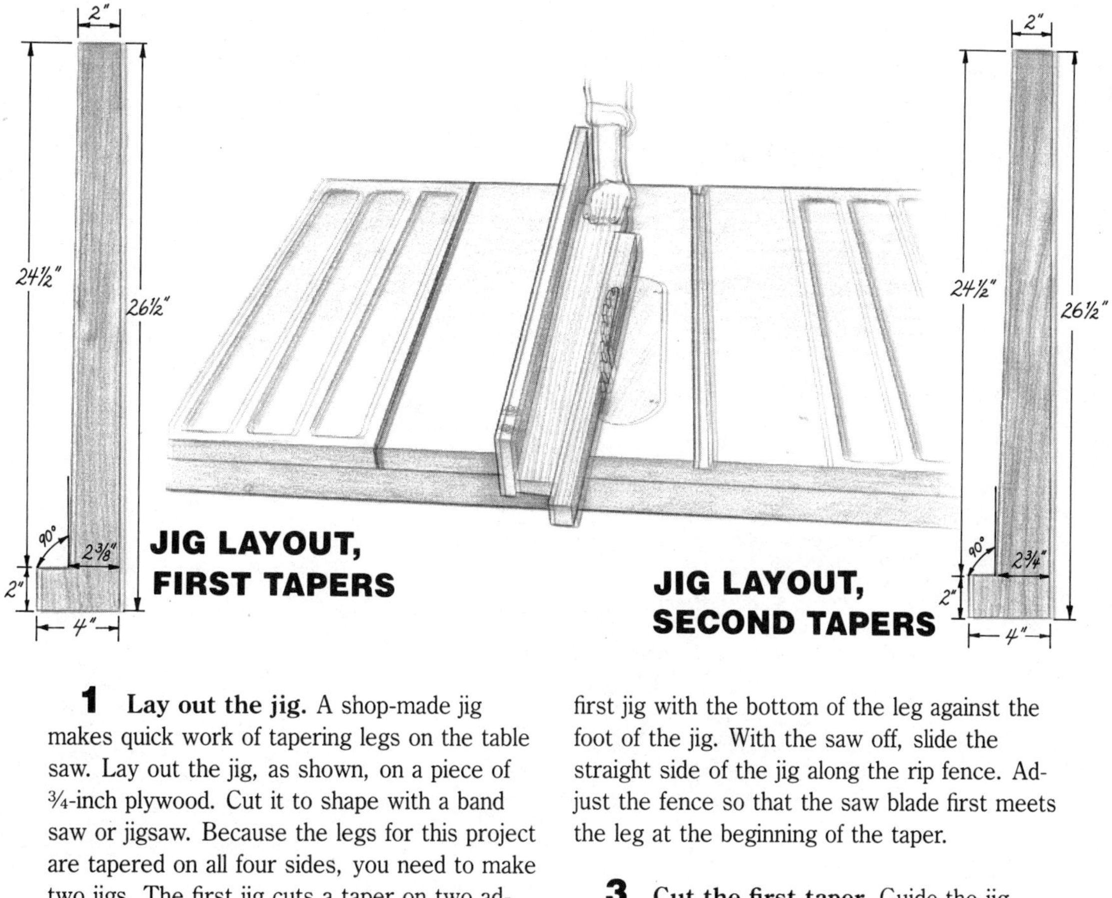

JIG LAYOUT, FIRST TAPERS

2"
24½"
26½"
90°
2⅜"
2"
4"

JIG LAYOUT, SECOND TAPERS

2"
24½"
26½"
90°
2¾"
2"
4"

1 **Lay out the jig.** A shop-made jig makes quick work of tapering legs on the table saw. Lay out the jig, as shown, on a piece of ¾-inch plywood. Cut it to shape with a band saw or jigsaw. Because the legs for this project are tapered on all four sides, you need to make two jigs. The first jig cuts a taper on two adjoining sides. The second jig cuts the taper on the remaining sides.

To lay out a taper other than the one shown here, draw the leg full size on a piece of plywood. Draw it so that a long edge of the leg is along the long edge of the plywood. Cut out the profile of the leg to make the jig.

2 **Set the rip fence.** Fit the leg into the first jig with the bottom of the leg against the foot of the jig. With the saw off, slide the straight side of the jig along the rip fence. Adjust the fence so that the saw blade first meets the leg at the beginning of the taper.

3 **Cut the first taper.** Guide the jig along the fence to cut the first taper. Then turn the leg a quarter turn and cut the adjacent face. Set the leg aside and make the same two cuts on the remaining legs.

4 **Cut the second taper.** Switch to the second jig and repeat the process, cutting the untapered faces.

Arrange the pieces with their most attractive faces up and in a sequence that yields the best appearance, then glue them together. After the glue sets, remove the clamps and sand the top.

Finally, put a ½-inch roundover bit in a router and rout the edges of top to the profile shown.

7 **Attach the tabletop to the frame.** The tabletop is attached to the aprons with wooden clips, as shown in the *Fastener Detail*. As the tabletop expands and contracts with changes in humidity, the fasteners slide in their grooves.

To make the clips, cut a ⅜ × ⅜-inch rabbet in a ¾-inch-thick board. Note the grain direction in the *Fastener Detail*. Rip a 1½-inch-wide strip from the board, then crosscut the board into 1½-inch squares.

Attach the top to the leg and apron assembly with the clips and flathead wood screws. Evenly space three clips along each end and four along each side.

8 **Apply finish.** Do any necessary touch up sanding, then apply a finish to the table. To help keep the tabletop from warping, be sure you finish the bottom as well as the top.

FASTENER DETAIL

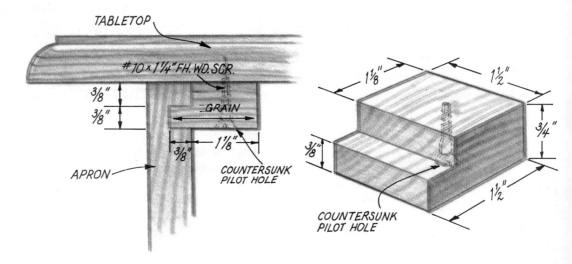

CHILD'S BENCH

This traditional bench could be mistaken for an old-fashioned school bench. It boasts the same straightforward lines and sturdy construction. With a 16½-inch seat height, average for most chairs, this bench fits adults and older children. If your bench is going into a young child's room, lower the seat height to about 12½ inches. Either maintain the same length and width, or scale down all the dimensions accordingly.

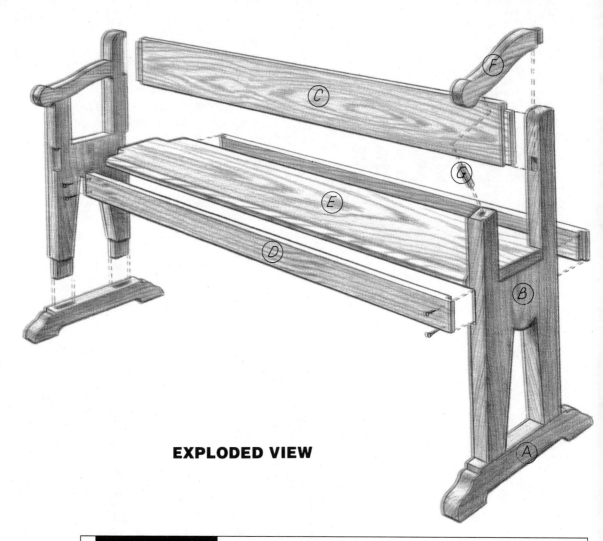

EXPLODED VIEW

CUTTING LIST

Part	Quantity	Dimension
A. Feet	2	$1\frac{9}{16}'' \times 2\frac{3}{4}'' \times 15''$
B. Bench ends	2	$1\frac{3}{8}'' \times 7\frac{3}{4}'' \times 26\frac{3}{4}''$
C. Back	1	$\frac{7}{8}'' \times 5\frac{3}{4}'' \times 40\frac{5}{8}''$
D. Seat supports	2	$\frac{7}{8}'' \times 2\frac{3}{4}'' \times 40\frac{5}{8}''$
E. Seat	1	$\frac{7}{8}'' \times 9'' \times 43''$
F. Arms	2	$1\frac{3}{8}'' \times 2'' \times 9\frac{5}{8}''$
G. Dowels	2	$\frac{1}{2}''$ dia. $\times 1\frac{3}{4}''$

Hardware

2 #10 $\times$ 1¾-in. flathead wood screws
12 #10 $\times$ 1½-in. flathead wood screws

1 **Select the stock and cut the parts.** Joint, plane, rip, and cut the parts to the sizes given in the Cutting List. If necessary, glue up boards to get the wider pieces.

2 **Mortise the feet.** Lay out the foot mortises with a sharp pencil. A plunge router with a ¾-inch straight bit and fence can cut theses mortises easily and cleanly. Clamp both foot blanks side by side in a vise with the tops flush. The two feet provide plenty of bearing surface for your router base. Adjust the fence so the bit is centered over the mortise. Rout the mor-

tise in several passes, lowering the bit about ¼ inch with each pass. If you do not have a plunge router, drill a series of adjacent ½-inch holes inside the layout lines. Cut along the layout lines with a sharp chisel to create the mortise.

3 **Shape the foot.** Draw a ¼-inch grid on a piece of paper and enlarge the *Foot Pattern* onto it. Transfer the pattern to the foot stock and cut out the shape on the band saw. Remove the band saw marks with a small-diameter sanding sleeve chucked in the drill press and by hand with files and sandpaper.

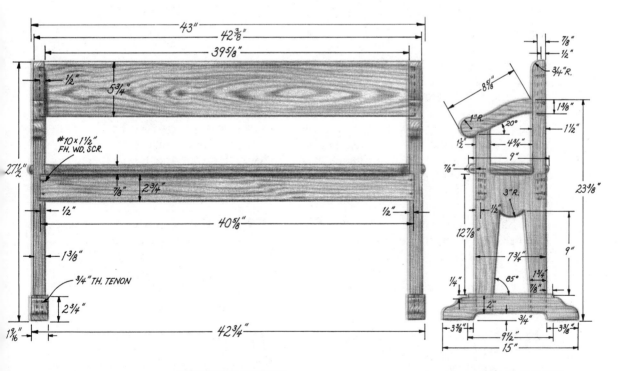

FRONT VIEW   **SIDE VIEW**

FOOT PATTERN

ONE SQUARE = 1"

4 **Tenon the bench end.** Cut all the joints in the bench end *before* you shape it. First, cut one long tenon across the bottom of the side. Put a dado blade in the table saw and raise the blade to make a 5/16-inch cut. Set the rip fence so that when you run the end of the board against it, it cuts a shoulder 2 inches from the end.

Check the setup by cutting a tenon on a sample piece 1⅜ inches thick. Put the scrap in the miter gauge, with the end of the scrap against the fence. Guide the sample across the saw blade with the miter gauge. Make several cuts, repositioning the sample in the miter gauge each time, until you've removed all the waste between the shoulder and the end of the sample.

Flip the board over and repeat. Test the fit of the tenon in the foot mortise and make any necessary adjustments to the setup.

Cut a tenon along the entire bottom of the bench ends.

5 **Rabbet for the back.** A tongue on the back fits into a rabbet in the bench end, as shown in the *Back Joinery Detail.* Mark what will be the two inside surfaces of the ends and lay out the rabbets on these surfaces. Put a ½-inch rabbeting bit

in the router and adjust the router to cut a ½ × ½-inch rabbet. Rout the rabbet in several passes. Square off the rounded ends of the rabbet with a chisel.

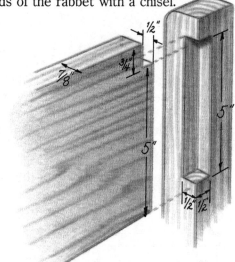

BACK JOINERY DETAIL

6 **Rabbet for the seat supports.** The seat supports also have tongues and fit in rabbets similar to the ones for the back. Lay out the rabbets, as shown in the *Front View* and *Side View,* and rout them as before.

7 **Cut the bench end to shape.** Lay out the legs, arm supports, and back supports on the bench ends, following the dimensions in the *Side View.* Cut the ends to shape with a jigsaw or band saw. Plane, scrape, and sand away the saw marks.

8 **Attach the feet.** Test fit the bench ends and feet. Make any necessary adjustments and glue them together.

9 **Cut tongues on the back and seat supports.** Set up the table saw,

148

dado blade, and rip fence to cut tenons. Raise the dado blade to remove ⅜ inch of stock; set the rip fence so that guiding the end of the board along it will cut away ½ inch of stock. Cut a tongue on the end of each piece, as shown in the *Back Joinery Detail*. With a backsaw, cut away part of the tongue on the back board, as seen in the *Front View*.

Clamp the seat supports and back in place with C-clamps. With a pilot hole bit, predrill two evenly spaced holes through the end of each part for #10 × 1½-inch screws. Screw the back and seat supports in place.

10 **Shape the seat.** Notch the front and back of the seat so that it will fit between the arm support and the back rest. With a compass, lay out a ⅞-inch radius on the front corners. Cut the radius on the band saw and sand any saw marks smooth. Rout a ⅜-inch roundover on the front and back of the seat.

11 **Make the arm.** Draw a ½-inch grid on a piece of paper and draw the *Arm Pattern* onto it. Transfer the pattern to the stock and cut the arm to shape on the band saw. Clean up the curved edges on a stationary belt sander or sanding sleeve in the drill press.

12 **Attach the arms.** The arms are attached to the arm supports with ½-inch-diameter dowels. First, drill the holes in the arm supports with the help of a doweling jig. For holes that are properly angled, position the jig so that there are no gaps between the jig and the end grain.

Put ½-inch dowel centers in the holes you've just drilled and position the arms on the bench. Push the arms firmly into the dowel centers; the points will make marks at the center of the dowel holes in the arms. Drill the holes with the help of a doweling jig as before.

The arms are screwed to the back of the chair. Put the arms and dowels in place. Hold the arms in place as you predrill through the back and into the arms with a ⅛-inch drill bit. Remove the arms and enlarge the holes in the back support with a ³⁄₁₆-inch drill bit. Countersink for a #10 screw.

Dowel and glue the arms to the arm supports; screw the arms to the back with #10 × 1¾-inch screws.

13 **Apply the finish.** The bench in the picture is finished with a spar varnish. A painted bench would have more of a country look.

ARM PATTERN

ONE SQUARE = 1"

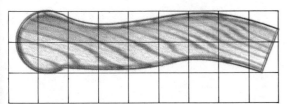

TILT TOP TABLE

This tilt top table is, in effect, a country card table. It is a good occasional table, but when you don't need it, it can be "folded" and stored out of the way. Set up as a table, it comfortably accommodates a pair of diners or game players. The top is nearly 3 feet square. With the top flipped up and the legs collapsed, the unit fits close to a wall.

EXPLODED VIEW

CUTTING LIST

Part	Quantity	Dimension	Comment
A. Top	1	$\frac{3}{4}'' \times 35'' \times 35''$	
B. Legs	2	$\frac{3}{4}'' \times 1\frac{1}{2}'' \times 29\frac{3}{4}''$	
C. Pivot posts	2	$\frac{3}{4}'' \times 1\frac{1}{2}'' \times 14''$	
D. Feet	2	$1\frac{1}{4}'' \times 2'' \times 11''$	
E. Posts	2	$1\frac{1}{4}'' \times 2'' \times 28\frac{11}{16}''$	
F. Bottom trestle	1	$1\frac{1}{4}'' \times 2'' \times 23''$	
G. Stretchers	4	$\frac{3}{4}'' \times 1\frac{1}{2}'' \times 13\frac{1}{2}''$	
H. Top trestle	1	$1\frac{1}{4}'' \times 2'' \times 23''$	
I. Pivot dowel stock	1	$\frac{1}{2}''$ dia. $\times 10''$	Makes 6
J. Pivot support	1	$1\frac{1}{16}'' \times 2\frac{1}{2}'' \times 23''$	
K. Battens	2	$1\frac{1}{4}'' \times 1\frac{1}{2}'' \times 32''$	

Hardware

As needed, #10 $\times$ 2-in. roundhead wood screws
As needed, $\frac{3}{8}$-in.-dia. flat washers

1 Select the stock and cut the parts. While you can make the tilt top table from an attractive hardwood, this is a country piece at heart. Keep the table utilitarian and economical by building it of pine and giving it a colorful paint job. Look for straight, flat stock, without knots. If you plan to apply a stain or clear finish, try to find boards with interesting grain patterns to make up the tabletop. Joint, plane, rip, and cut the parts to the sizes given in the Cutting List. Don't cut the feet to shape until after you have mortised them.

2 Glue up the tabletop. Lay out the boards that will make up the tabletop, choosing (and marking) the best face of each. Glue up the boards and set the piece aside while the glue dries.

3 Cut the mortises in the legs and pivot posts, feet, and posts. While the glue in the tabletop is drying, work on the rest of the table. Cut all the mortises at one time. All are through mortises.

Lay out each mortise carefully, as shown in the *Gate Assembly* and the *Post and Trestle Layout.* To cut the mortises, drill a series of adjacent holes between the layout lines with a bit as wide as the mortise. Before you drill, clamp a piece of scrap to the stock on the back side of the mortise. Drill completely through the stock and into the scrap. The scrap prevents the bit from splintering the wood as it exits. Square up the cavity with a chisel.

While you are cutting the mortises, also cut the dovetail slot at the top of each post. For more information on laying out

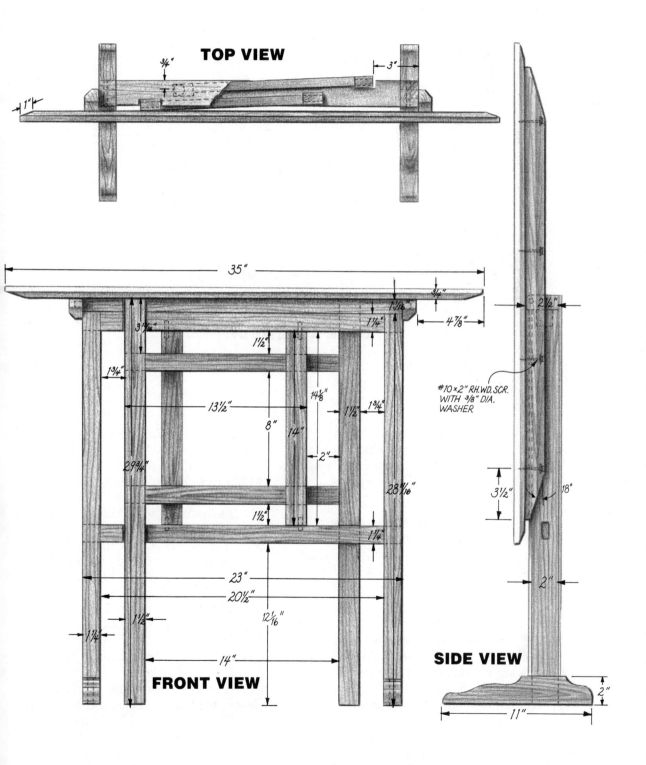

TOP VIEW

3/4"

3"

1"

35"

3/4"

1 1/16"

1 1/4"

4 7/8"

2 1/2"

3 13/16"

1 1/2"

1 3/4"

14 1/8"

1 1/2"

1 3/4"

13 1/2"

8"

14"

2"

#10 × 2" R.H.WD. SCR.
WITH 3/8" DIA.
WASHER

29 3/4"

28 11/16"

3 1/2"

18°

1 1/2"

1 1/4"

23"

20 1/2"

12 1/16"

2"

1 1/2"

1 1/4"

14"

FRONT VIEW

SIDE VIEW

2"

11"

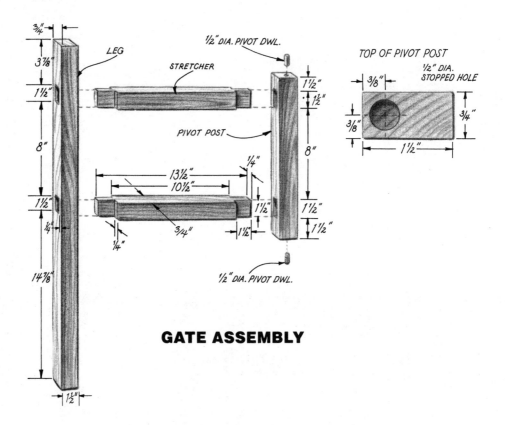

3/4"

3⅞"

1½"

8"

LEG

STRETCHER

½" DIA. PIVOT DWL.

TOP OF PIVOT POST

½" DIA. STOPPED HOLE

3/8"

3/8"

3/4"

1½"

1½"

1½"

PIVOT POST

13½"

10½"

¼"

¼"

¾"

1½"

8"

1½"

1½"

1½"

1½"

1½"

¼"

14⅞"

½" DIA. PIVOT DWL.

GATE ASSEMBLY

the joint see "Dovetailing" on page 42. Cut along the layout lines with a backsaw. Cut away most of the waste with a band saw. Remove the rest with a chisel.

4 Cut the foot to shape. Draw a ¼-inch grid on a piece of paper and draw the *Foot Pattern* onto it. Transfer the pattern to the stock and cut out the foot on the band saw. Sand the sawed edge smooth.

5 Cut the tenons on the posts, stretchers, and trestles. The tenons are not uniform: The posts have one size tenon; the stretchers, a second size; and the bottom trestle, a third. Lay out the tenons on the stock, as shown in the

Post and Trestle Layout and the *Gate Assembly.*

Cut all these tenons on the table saw with a dado blade. First, set up the dado blade to cut its maximum width. Then adjust the blade height so that a cut on both sides of the board leaves a tenon the proper thickness. Adjust the fence so that when you guide the end of a board along it with the miter gauge, it cuts the tenon shoulder in the right place.

Test your setup on a piece of scrap the exact thickness of the piece you will be tenoning. Butt one end against the fence and use the miter gauge to guide it over the dado blade. Slide the stock away from the fence and make another pass. Repeat until the first cheek is completed, then flip the work piece and repeat the full process to cut the tenon's second cheek.

Cut all the tenons.

With the dado blade still in the saw, cut two notches in each trestle, as shown in the *Post and Trestle Layout*. When the table is tilted up, the gatelegs fold up against the trestle and into these notches, as shown in the *Top View*.

After cutting all the tenons, cut the dovetail on each end of the top trestle. Use a backsaw to rough out the tail, then refine the fit by paring with a sharp chisel.

SHOP TIP: Set up your table saw using the mortised piece as a guide. Put the mortise next to the blade with its long edges parallel to the table. Raise the blade until it aligns with the bottom edge of the mortise. Next, position the rip fence to establish the length of the tenon. Line up the fence so that when you have one edge of the mortised piece butted against the fence, its opposite edge is aligned with the edge of the blade farthest from the fence.

POST AND TRESTLE LAYOUT

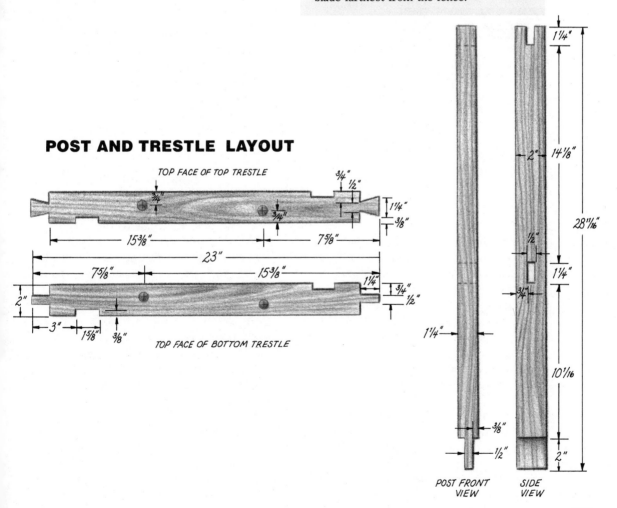

TOP FACE OF TOP TRESTLE

TOP FACE OF BOTTOM TRESTLE

POST FRONT VIEW

SIDE VIEW

155

6 **Assemble the gates.** The gates swing back and forth under the table to support it. Before gluing up the two gates, drill holes in the ends of the pivot posts for the pivot dowels that will link the gates to the trestle assembly. Position the holes as shown in the *Post and Trestle Layout.* Bore the ½-inch-diameter by ¾-inch-deep holes to accommodate the 1½-inch-long pivot dowels. Do *not* glue the pivot dowels to the gates.

SHOP TIP: A Forstner bit is the best bit to use for boring the pivot dowel holes. The bit cuts a precise and flat-bottomed hole. The absence of a protruding spur means you won't inadvertently penetrate the work piece before achieving the necessary depth for the pivot dowel.

Test fit each gate. If the joints fit properly, glue the gate together.

7 **Assemble the table base.** Test fit the table base. Insert the posts in the mortises in the feet, then connect them with the bottom trestle. Drop 1½-inch-long pivot dowels into their holes in the bottom trestle and fit the gate assemblies onto them. Put pivot dowels into the holes in the pivot posts, then top the unit with the top trestle.

Make any necessary adjustments and glue the trestle together.

8 **Complete the tabletop.** Remove the clamps from the tabletop, and sand or hand plane the glue joints smooth. On a table saw, cut a 10-degree chamfer around the bottom edge. Guide the tabletop against the rip fence as you cut.

To help steady the tabletop as you cut the chamfer, attach a plywood face to the rip fence. It should be as long as the fence and about 18 inches high. On most saws, you'll have to make the cut with the rip fence to the left of the blade. After cutting the chamfer, sand the tabletop smooth.

9 **Make the battens and pivot support.** Chamfer the battens on the table saw with the blade set at 45 degrees, as shown in the *Pivot Detail.* When the chamfer has been cut along the length of the battens, cut a 72-degree angle in the ends of the battens, as shown in the *Side View.* Lay out the angle with a protractor and straightedge and cut the angle with a jigsaw or band saw. Sand the sawed edge smooth.

The battens pivot when the top flips up. Drill a pivot dowel hole in each batten, as shown in the *Pivot Detail.*

The battens are screwed to the underside of the tabletop with #10 × 2-inch roundhead wood screws. Because the battens run perpendicular to the grain of the tabletop, allowance must be made for the top to expand and contract. To do this, drill ¼-inch-diameter screw pilot holes on 8-inch centers through the battens, as shown in the *Pivot Detail.* Then drill ⅜-inch-diameter by ³⁄₁₆-inch-deep washer recess holes as shown. Put washers between the screw and the wood to keep the screw from slipping through the hole. As the tabletop expands and contracts, the screws will move back and forth in the holes.

Turn to the pivot support next. Drill a pivot dowel hole in each end of this piece, as shown. Rout a ½-inch roundover in what will be the top of the pivot support, as shown in the *Pivot Detail.*

PIVOT DETAIL

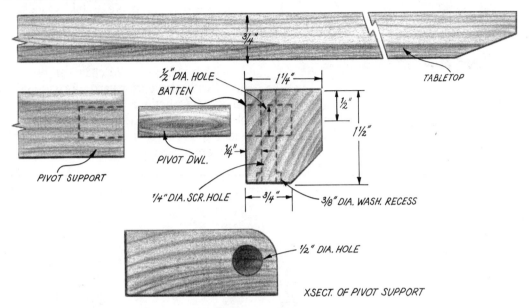

½" DIA. HOLE

BATTEN

TABLETOP

PIVOT SUPPORT

PIVOT DWL.

¼" DIA. SCR. HOLE

1¼"

½"

1½"

¾"

⅜" DIA. WASH. RECESS

¼"

½" DIA. HOLE

XSECT. OF PIVOT SUPPORT

10 **Assemble and install the table-top.** Turn the tabletop upside down on the bench and test fit the battens, pivot support, and pivot dowels on it. Poke an awl through the screw holes in the battens to lay out the screw holes in the top. Drill ⅛-inch-diameter pilot holes in the tabletop. Be careful not to drill all the way through the tabletop.

Check the pivoting action by rotating the pivot support. Make any necessary adjustments. Epoxy the pivot dowels in place and screw the battens to the tabletop.

Finally, set the table assembly—tilted—in place on the base assembly and clamp it. Drill screw holes through the pivot support into the trestle with a combination pilot hole bit. This bit drills a countersink hole, a clearance hole for the screw shank, and a slightly smaller pilot hole for the screw threads all in one operation. Combination pilot hole bits are available at most hardware stores and are sold according to the screw size.

11 **Apply the finish.** Sand the table and apply a finish. Be sure to apply the finish equally to all surfaces.

ONE SQUARE = ½"

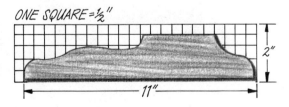

FOOT PATTERN

2"

11"

CHILD'S CHAIR

There's something about child-size furniture that can make a child's face light up. Having furniture that fits their small frames makes them feel important and grown up.

This pleasant little chair can be made with straightforward mortise-and-tenon construction. The unique mortise placement allows the chair front to be wider than the chair back without complicated angle setups.

EXPLODED VIEW

Part	Quantity	Dimension	Comment
A. Back legs	2	$1\frac{3}{16}'' \times 1\frac{3}{16}'' \times 22''$	
B. Front legs	2	$1'' \times 1'' \times 12\frac{1}{8}''$	
C. Front rails	2	$\frac{9}{16}'' \times 1\frac{1}{8}'' \times 9''$	
D. Back rails	2	$\frac{9}{16}'' \times 1\frac{1}{8}'' \times 7\frac{3}{4}''$	
E. Upper side rails	2	$\frac{9}{16}'' \times 1\frac{1}{8}'' \times 8\frac{1}{4}''$	
F. Lower side rails	2	$\frac{9}{16}'' \times 1\frac{1}{8}'' \times 8\frac{1}{4}''$	
G. Shaped rail	1	$\frac{9}{16}'' \times 1\frac{5}{8}'' \times 7\frac{3}{4}''$	
H. Top rail	1	$1\frac{3}{16}'' \times 1\frac{5}{8}'' \times 7\frac{3}{4}''$	
I. Peg stock	1	$\frac{1}{8}''$ dia. $\times 25''$	Dowel, makes 20
J. Seat boards	2	$\frac{1}{2}'' \times 4\frac{1}{8}'' \times 10\frac{1}{2}''$	

Hardware

8 #8 × 1¼-in. flathead wood screws

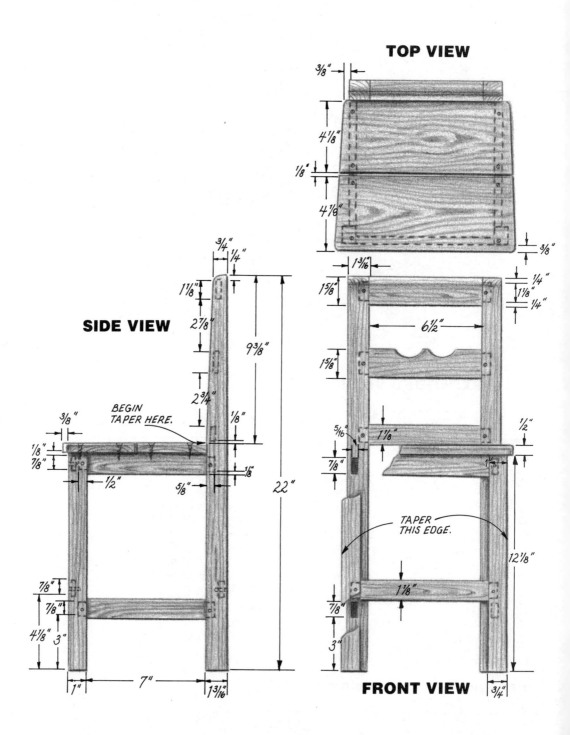

TOP VIEW

3/8"

4 1/8"

1/8"

4 1/8"

3/8"

1 3/16"

1 5/8"

1/4"
1 1/8"
1/4"

6 1/2"

1 5/8"

5/16"

7/8"

1 1/8"

1/2"

1 1/4"

TAPER
THIS EDGE.

7/8"

1 1/8"

12 1/8"

3"

FRONT VIEW

3/4"

SIDE VIEW

3/4"
1/4"

1 1/8"

2 7/8"

9 3/8"

2 3/4"

1/8"

3/8"

1/8"
7/8"

*BEGIN
TAPER HERE.*

1/2"

5/8"

1/8"

22"

7/8"

7/8"

4 1/8"

3"

1"

7"

1 3/16"

160

1 Select the stock and cut the parts. Make this chair from a user-friendly wood like pine. Hardwood isn't really necessary for a little chair like this one, and since pine is lightweight, a child will be able to move the chair easily. Joint, plane, rip, and cut the parts to the sizes given in the Cutting List.

2 Taper the back legs. The back legs are tapered above the seat. Lay out the taper, as shown in the *Side View*, directly on the stock and cut along the layout lines on the band saw. Stay about $\frac{1}{16}$ inch to the waste side of your layout lines as you cut and clean up the surfaces with a hand plane or on the jointer.

3 Lay out and drill the mortises. Lay out the mortises, as shown in the *Front View* and *Side View* and the *Joinery Detail*, with a sharp pencil and straight-edge.

Drill out the mortises with a series of adjacent $\frac{5}{16}$-inch holes. Because all of the mortises are $\frac{1}{8}$ inch from the edge of the legs, it's easiest to do this on a drill press. Clamp a fence to your drill press table and position it $\frac{1}{8}$ inch from the bit. Hold the

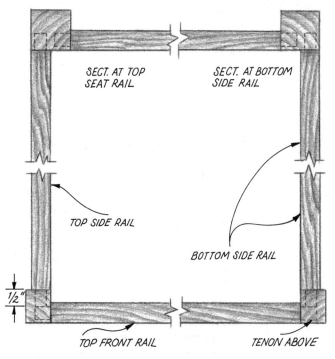

SECT. AT TOP SEAT RAIL

SECT. AT BOTTOM SIDE RAIL

TOP SIDE RAIL

BOTTOM SIDE RAIL

$\frac{1}{2}$"

TOP FRONT RAIL

TENON ABOVE

JOINERY DETAIL

legs against the fence as you drill the mortises. Adjust the drill press to drill $\frac{11}{16}$-inch-deep holes.

When you've drilled out all of the mortises, cut along the layout lines with a sharp chisel.

4 Cut the tenons. All the tenons, except for those on the top rail, are $\frac{5}{16}$ inch thick and have $\frac{1}{8}$-inch shoulders. They can be cut with one setup on the table saw.

Put a $\frac{5}{8}$-inch dado blade in your table saw and raise it to cut a groove $\frac{1}{8}$ inch deep. Clamp a wooden auxiliary fence to the table saw fence and adjust it so that the wooden fence just touches the edge of the dado blade.

Cut a test tenon in a piece of $\frac{9}{16}$-inch scrap. Guide the scrap as you cut with a

SHOP TIP: When laying out matching parts, such as the front legs and back legs on this chair, measure and mark one piece, then use that piece to lay out its partner. If you're making a number of chairs, you might want to mark the critical measurements on a piece of scrap wood and use that to lay out all the matching parts. Chairmakers often put every measurement for an entire chair on one of these layout aids, which they call a chair "stick" or "rod."

miter gauge set at 90 degrees. Test the width and length of the tenon in one of the mortises. Adjust the dado blade height and fence position, as necessary, and cut the actual chair tenons.

Trim the front tenon on each upper side rail so it is ½ inch long.

Reset the blade to tenon the top rail. Raise the dado blade to ¼ inch above the surface of the table to cut a ⁵⁄₁₆-inch-thick by 1⅛-inch-wide tenon on each end of the top rail. Test the setup on a piece of scrap and cut the tenons on the top rail.

5 **Test fit the chair.** Test fit the chair and check that all the joints fit properly. Make any necessary adjustments.

6 **Taper the front legs.** The front legs taper from 1 inch down to ¾ inch, as seen from the front. Lay out the taper, as shown in the *Front View,* on both front legs. Cut the taper down to the layout line with a sharp hand plane or cut away the waste on the band saw; clean up the saw marks with a hand plane or sander.

7 **Cut out the shaped rail.** Make a ¼-inch grid on a piece of paper and draw the *Shaped Rail Pattern* onto it.

SHAPED RAIL PATTERN

ONE SQUARE = ½ "

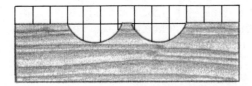

Transfer the pattern to the rail and cut it to shape on a band saw. Clean up the saw marks with files and sandpaper.

8 **Assemble the chair frame.** Assemble the chair in stages. First, glue the front rails between the front legs. Apply glue to the surfaces of the mortises and tenons. Pull the joints together with pipe or bar clamps with the assembly laying on a flat surface to ensure that the frames won't be twisted.

Then glue the rear rails between the rear legs. When the glue is dry, glue the front and back together.

With the front and back assemblies still in the clamps, drill ⅛-inch-diameter by ⁹⁄₁₆-inch-deep peg holes through the legs and into the tenons, as shown in the *Front View* and *Side View.* When the holes are drilled, cut the peg stock into 1-inch-long pieces, dip the pieces in some glue, and tap them into the holes. Because the holes don't go all of the way through the legs, you will have to trim the pegs flush with the surface of the legs.

When the glue is dry, remove the clamps and glue and clamp the side rails to the front and back of the frame. Set the chair upright on a flat surface, check to make sure the chair sits flat, and make any necessary adjustments.

With the chair still clamped, drill peg holes through the sides of the legs and into the side rail tenons, and then tap them in place.

Allow the glue to dry and remove the clamps.

9 **Attach and angle the seat boards.** First, center the seat boards across the top of the completed frame and leave a ⅛-inch gap between them, as shown in the *Top View*. Clamp the seat boards in place.

Next, drill holes for #8 × 1¼-inch flathead wood screws, as shown in the *Top View*. The best way to drill these holes is with an combustion pilot hole bit. Drill through the seat and into the rails. The combination pilot hole bit will drill a countersink hole, a clearance hole in the seat for the the screw shank, and a slightly smaller pilot hole in the rail for the screw threads all in one operation. Combination pilot hole bits are available in most hardware stores and are sold according to screw size.

Once you've drilled the pilot holes, put a ⅜-inch-thick piece of stock under the ledge created by the seat boards and guide a pencil against it to mark the ⅜-inch overhang on the bottom of the seat boards. Mark the ledge on both sides and remove the clamps.

Cut along the layout lines with a jigsaw or band saw and sand the sawed edges smooth. Reposition the seat boards on the frame and screw them in place.

10 **Sand and apply the finish.** Finish sand the chair. As you are sanding the chair, round-over any sharp corners. Round-over the top of the chair, as shown in the *Side View*, with files, a spokeshave, or a belt sander.

It might be a good idea to choose this chair's finish with the child for whom it's intended. But, of course, you might end up painting it hot pink or olive green.

FOOT-STOOL

If your kids can't reach the sink to wash their hands or an extra half foot would help you reach that book on the top shelf, consider building this footstool. It's sturdy, but portable enough to increase your reach anywhere in the house. It won't cost much to make, either. You can build it entirely from a single board 6⅜ inches wide and 25 inches long. It looks great, and it's a good way to show off some pretty slick dovetailing.

EXPLODED VIEW

CUTTING LIST

Part	Quantity	Dimension	Comment
A. Top	1	$1\frac{5}{16}'' \times 6\frac{3}{8}'' \times 12''$	Cut to size when beveling.
B. Legs	2	$1\frac{5}{16}'' \times 6\frac{3}{8}'' \times 7''$	Cut to size when beveling.

1 **Select the stock and cut the parts.** If you are not an experienced dovetailer, consider an easily workable wood like pine for your first attempt. If you've done some dovetailing, choose a more durable wood like walnut or cherry. Joint, plane, rip, and cut the stock to the sizes given in the Cutting List. For uniform grain pattern and color, cut the top and legs from a single board.

2 **Cut the bevels.** All the parts are beveled on both ends. Note that the bevels are parallel on the legs, but not on the top. Set the table saw blade to 12 degrees and, with the miter gauge as a guide, cut the miters shown in the *Front View*.

3 **Cut the dovetails.** Cutting an angled dovetail is made much like cutting a regular dovetail. If you haven't cut a lot of dovetails, practice on a piece of scrap. "Angled Dovetails" on page 168 shows you exactly how to cut the joint.

4 **Cut out the leg shape.** Draw a ½-inch grid on a piece of paper and draw the *Leg Pattern* onto it. With the legs removed from the top, transfer the pattern to the legs. Cut out the shape with a band saw or jigsaw.

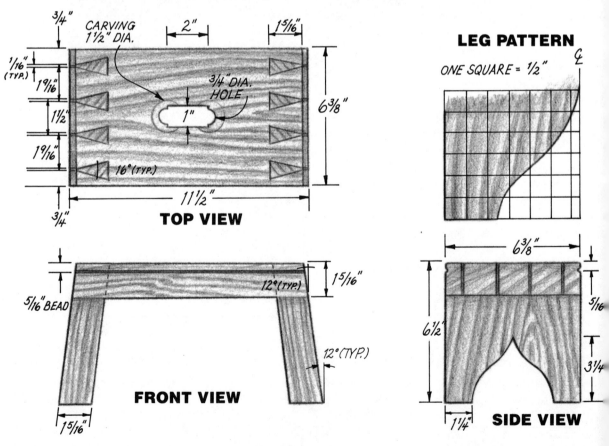

SHOP TIP: To get two identical legs, cut both at once. First stack the pieces together and secure by putting double-sided tape between them. Then cut both legs in one operation.

5 Cut the handhold in the top. Lay out and drill the holes in the top, as shown in the *Top View.* When the holes have been drilled, lay out and connect them by cutting away the wood between them with a jigsaw.

If you wish, carve around the handhold, as shown, with a V-shaped chisel called a parting tool.

6 Rout the bead in the top. Put a 5⁄16-inch beading bit in your router. Secure the router in a router table. Guide the top along the fence to cut a bead in the top, as shown in the *Front View.*

7 Assemble the stool. Spread glue on the tails and pins and clamp the legs to the top.

When the glue has dried, sand the dovetail joints even and scrape away any excess glue on the stool bottom.

8 Apply the finish. Finish sand the stool, removing all scribe marks. Stain and varnish, or paint the stool.

ANGLED DOVETAILS

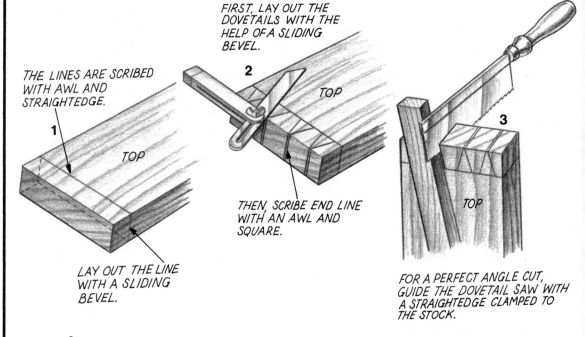

FIRST, LAY OUT THE DOVETAILS WITH THE HELP OF A SLIDING BEVEL.

THE LINES ARE SCRIBED WITH AWL AND STRAIGHTEDGE.

1

TOP

2

TOP

THEN, SCRIBE END LINE WITH AN AWL AND SQUARE.

LAY OUT THE LINE WITH A SLIDING BEVEL.

3

TOP

FOR A PERFECT ANGLE CUT, GUIDE THE DOVETAIL SAW WITH A STRAIGHTEDGE CLAMPED TO THE STOCK.

1 **Lay out the length of the pins and tails.** Angled dovetails are much like regular dovetails in that they are made of pins and tails. The tails are on the top of the stool; the pins are on the legs. You may notice that these dovetails are unique: The outside edge of the joint ends in half *tails* to make routing the bead easier. On most dovetail joints, the edges end in half *pins*.

The angled end of the stool makes it impossible to lay out the base of the tails with a marking gauge. Scribe the line with an awl and straightedge instead. Scribe the line $1\frac{5}{16}$ inches from the end of the board, as shown.

2 **Lay out the tails.** The *Top View* shows the exact location and shape of the tails. Lay out the tails with a sliding T-bevel on the tip face of the board. Then, lay out the angle of the tails on the back face of the board, so that they meet the lines you have just drawn.

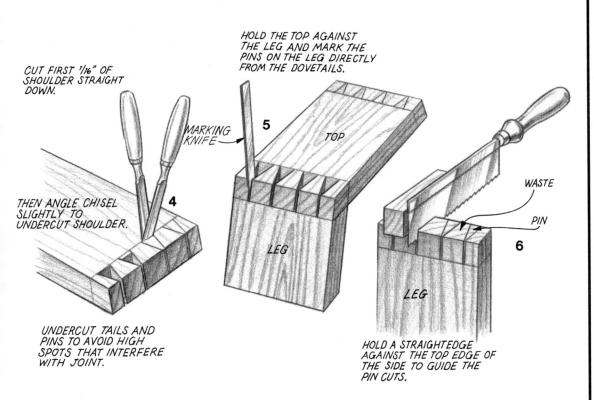

CUT FIRST ¹/₁₆" OF SHOULDER STRAIGHT DOWN.

THEN ANGLE CHISEL SLIGHTLY TO UNDERCUT SHOULDER.

MARKING KNIFE

UNDERCUT TAILS AND PINS TO AVOID HIGH SPOTS THAT INTERFERE WITH JOINT.

HOLD THE TOP AGAINST THE LEG AND MARK THE PINS ON THE LEG DIRECTLY FROM THE DOVETAILS.

TOP

LEG

WASTE

PIN

LEG

HOLD A STRAIGHTEDGE AGAINST THE TOP EDGE OF THE SIDE TO GUIDE THE PIN CUTS.

3 **Cut out the tails.** Saw down to the scribe line, cutting on the waste side of the layout lines. A Japanese Dozuki saw, like the one shown here, is easy to control and cuts crisp lines. Watch your layout lines carefully: Follow the angle of the pins and make sure you don't cut through either one of the scribe lines.

4 **Chisel out the waste between the tails.** Chisel halfway through the board from one side; turn the board over and chisel from the other side. Undercut slightly, as shown, to ease assembly of the joint.

5 **Lay out the pins.** For best results, lay out the pins by tracing around the tails. Hold the top and one leg together and lay out the pins with a marking knife directly from the tails. Carry your layout lines down to the scribe lines and clearly mark the waste with a pencil.

6 **Cut out the pins.** Saw along the layout lines to the scribe lines and chisel away the waste as before. Test fit the dovetails. Pare the pins to fit the tails if necessary. Do not glue them in place yet.

PART FOUR

TOYS

JUMPING JACK

He may not be Fred Astaire or Baryshnikov, but he'll dance and jump whenever you want him to. He will also help keep the kids entertained. Just pull his string and Jumping Jack will kick into action. He doesn't even need batteries.

The dancing man is a simple turning project. If you haven't done much turning, a good reference guide is *Creative Woodturning* by Dale L. Nish.

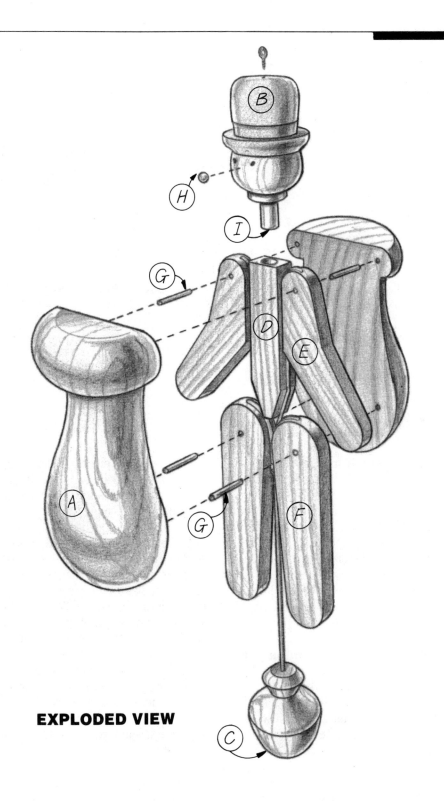

EXPLODED VIEW

CUTTING LIST

Part	Quantity	Dimension	Comment
A. Body	2	$1\frac{1}{2}'' \times 3'' \times 6\frac{1}{4}''$	Cut to length after turning.
B. Head	1	$3'' \times 3'' \times 4\frac{1}{4}''$	Cut to length after turning.
C. String pull	1	$2'' \times 2'' \times 2\frac{3}{4}''$	Cut to length after turning.
D. Divider	1	$\frac{3}{8}'' \times {}^{13}\!/_{16}'' \times 3\frac{3}{4}''$	
E. Arms	2	$\frac{5}{16}'' \times 2'' \times 4''$	
F. Legs	2	$\frac{5}{16}'' \times 1\frac{1}{4}'' \times 5''$	
G. Joint dowels	4	$\frac{1}{8}''$ dia. $\times \frac{7}{8}''$	
H. Nose*	1	$\frac{1}{2}''$ dia.	Wooden ball
I. Neck dowel	1	$\frac{3}{8}''$ dia. $\times 1\frac{1}{4}''$	

*The ½-in. wooden ball is available from Cherry Tree Toys, Inc., P.O. Box 369, Belmont, OH 43718. Part #42.

Hardware

1 15-in. string
2 standard toothpicks
1 ⁵⁄₁₆-in.-dia. × ⅞-in.-long eyescrew

1 Select the stock and cut the parts. Almost any hardwood can be used for this project. If you are going to paint the dancing man, don't bother choosing an expensive wood. Poplar or maple will prove adequate. Joint, plane, rip, and cut the parts to the sizes given in the Cutting List. Note that the body, head, and string pull stock are wider and longer than the finished dimensions of these parts to allow for turning.

2 Prepare the body for turning. The body is made from two halves that are glued together to form the $3 \times 3 \times 6\frac{1}{4}$-inch stock needed for turning. This is referred to as split turning. To allow the halves to be separated after the piece is turned, glue a piece of kraft paper between them. Kraft paper is the same paper from which heavy brown paper grocery bags are made.

3 Turn the body, head, and string pull. Set up the stock on a lathe and turn the parts to the shapes shown. When each part has been turned, sand it while it is still on the lathe. Turn off the lathe, saw off the waste with a backsaw, and sand the ends smooth and even.

When the body shape has been turned, separate the halves. Insert a chisel into the kraft paper sandwiched between the halves and carefully pry the halves apart. When the halves have been separated, sand away the kraft paper.

HEAD, FRONT VIEW

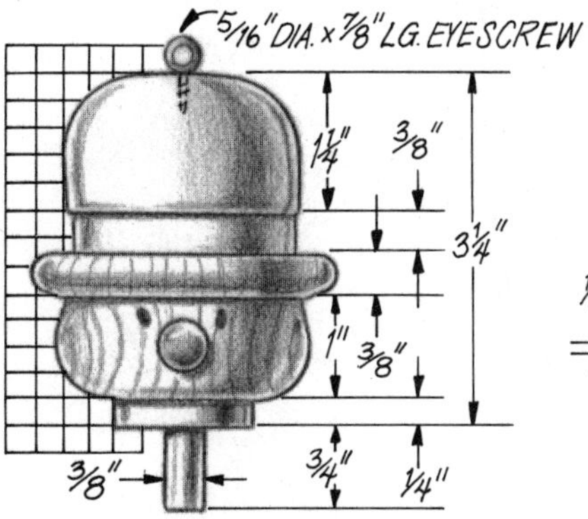
5/16"DIA. × 7/8"LG. EYESCREW
1¼"
3/8"
3¼"
1"
3/8"
3/8"
3/4"
1/4"

HEAD, SIDE VIEW

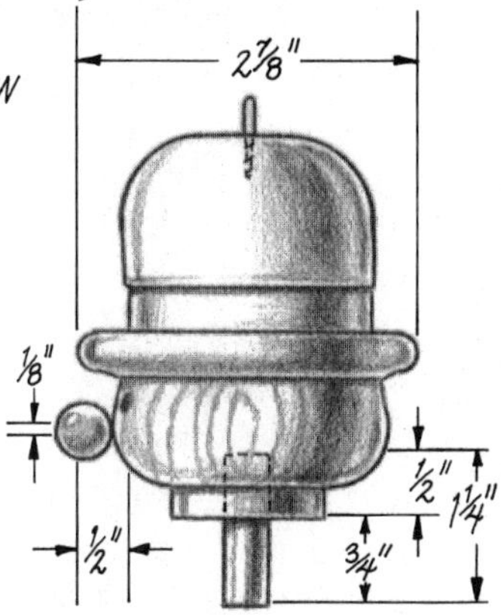
2⅞"
1/8"
1/2"
1¼"
1/2"
3/4"

BODY, TOP VIEW

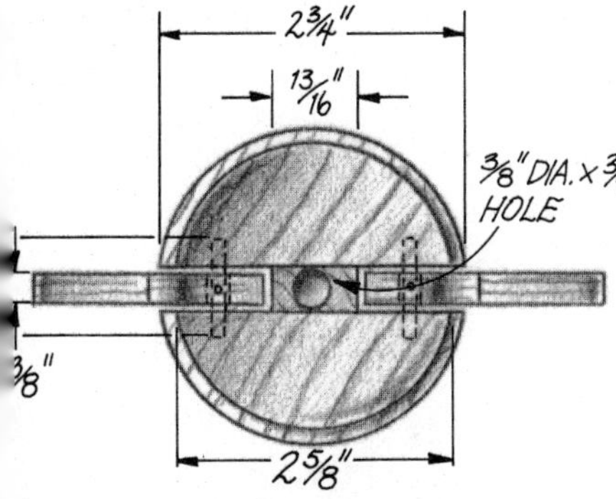
2¾"
13/16"
3/8"DIA. × 3/4" DP. HOLE
3/8"
2⅝"

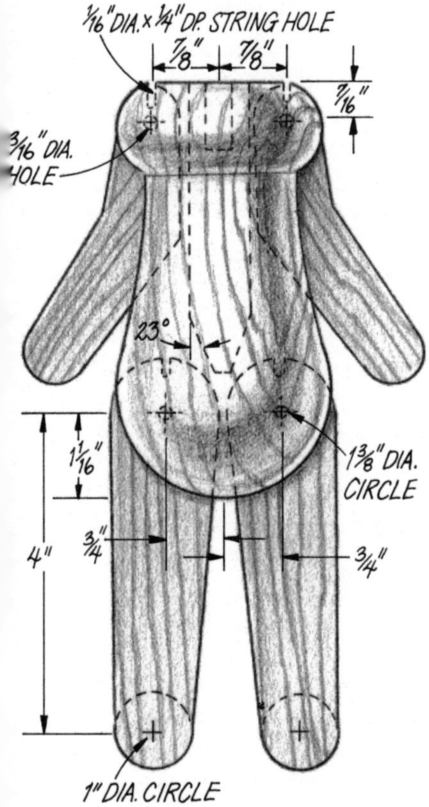
1/16"DIA. × 1/4"DP. STRING HOLE
7/8"
7/8"
7/16"
3/16"DIA. HOLE
23°
1 1/16"
1⅜"DIA. CIRCLE
4"
3/4"
3/4"
1"DIA. CIRCLE

BODY, FRONT VIEW

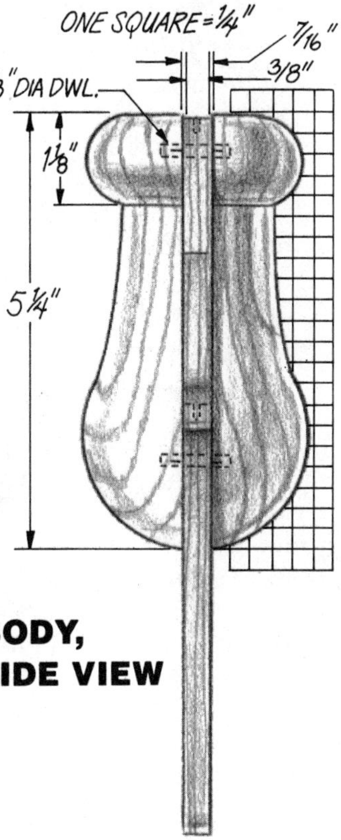
ONE SQUARE = 1/4"
7/16"
3/8"
1/8"DIA DWL.
1⅛"
5¼"

BODY, SIDE VIEW

ARM PATTERN

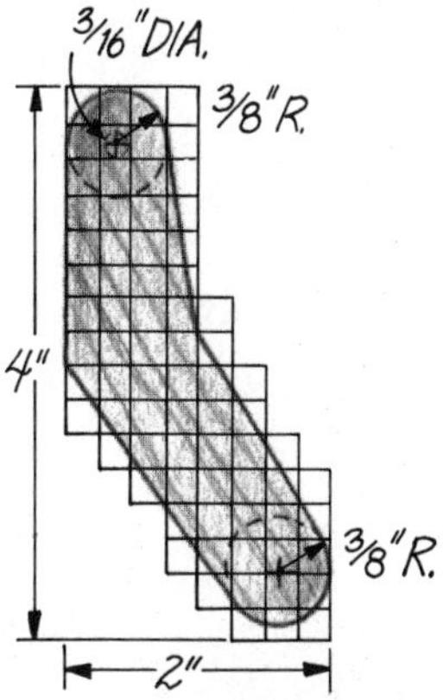
3/16"DIA.
3/8"R.
4"
3/8"R.
2"
ONE SQUARE = 1/4"

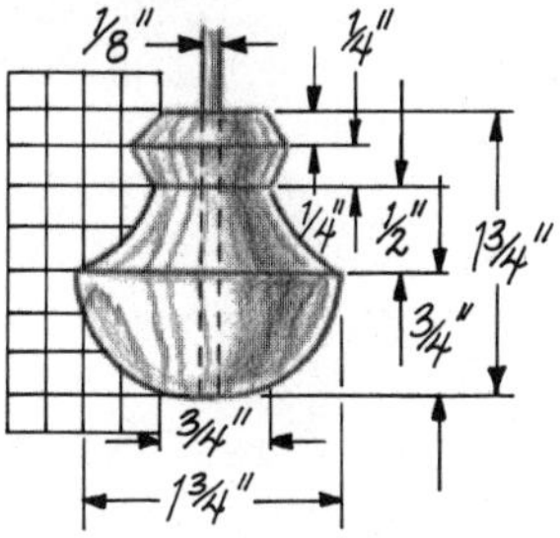
1/8"
1/4"
1/4"
1/2"
1¾"
3/4"
3/4"
1¾"

STRING PULL DETAIL

4 **Cut the angle in the end of the divider.** Mark and cut the angle, as shown in the *Body, Front View,* with the band saw or coping saw. When the angles have been cut, sand the divider edges. Round the corners well because the pull string will rub against them.

5 **Cut the arm and leg shapes.** Draw a ¼-inch grid on a piece of paper and draw the *Arm Pattern* onto it. Transfer the pattern to the wood. Be sure to follow the grain direction shown. Cut the arms with a band saw or coping saw.

Lay out the legs on the stock by drawing the circles shown in the *Body, Front View* and connecting them. Cut the legs with a band saw or jigsaw.

Sand the rough edges smooth.

6 **Drill the pivot holes in the arms and legs.** Drill ³⁄₁₆-inch pivot holes in the top joint of the arms and legs, as shown in the *Body, Front View* and the *Arm Pattern.*

7 **Drill the joint dowel holes and test fit the body.** Position the divider, arms, and legs on one half of the body, as shown in the *Body, Front View.* Make sure that the arms and legs can

swing freely. Mark through the pivot hole with an awl. Drill ⅛-inch-diameter by ¼-inch-deep holes at each mark.

To locate the holes on the other body half, slip #4 × ½-inch flathead screws into the existing dowel holes *head first.* Position the two body halves on top of each other and press gently. The points of the screws will mark the center of the second set of dowel holes. Drill the second set of holes, but don't glue the pieces together yet.

Glue the dowels into the holes in one side of the body and put the arms and legs in place over the dowels. Position the divider so that it will not interfere with the arm or leg movement. Mark the divider's position with a pencil and glue it to that half of the body. Wipe away any excess glue.

Test fit the body and make any necessary adjustments. Don't glue the rest of the body together yet.

8 **Drill the string holes and attach the string.** With the arms and legs hanging down, mark them for the string holes shown in the *Body, Front View.* Insert one end of a 15-inch-long piece of durable string into each hole. Apply a drop of glue to the top of each hole and wedge the string in the hole with a toothpick. Trim the toothpick flush.

Run the arm strings down along the divider and between the legs. Run the leg strings down between the legs. With the arms and legs still hanging down, tie the four strings together just above the bottom edge of the body.

Cut off three of the strings at the knot. Thread the remaining string through the hole in the pull and knot it to keep the string from slipping through the hole. If the string is strung correctly, the arms and legs should swing up when the string is pulled.

9 **Attach the nose to the head.** The nose is a wooden ball, which is attached to the head with epoxy. Position the nose, as shown in the *Head, Front View.*

10 **Apply the finish.** Because the body has moving parts, it will be easier to apply the finish before assembly. Prepare for the finish by covering any parts that will be glued with masking tape. Cover the exposed dowels, dowel holes, and divider surface. Also cover the area on the one body half that will be glued to the divider. The jumping jack shown was painted. It has a white body, bright red nose, blue eyes, and blue hat.

11 **Assemble the body.** When the finish has dried, place the arms and legs over their joint dowels. Make sure that the string is following its appropriate path and glue the two body halves together.

12 **Attach the head to the body.** Drill neck dowel holes in the head and body, as shown in the *Body, Front View* and the *Head, Side View.* Assemble the head to the body with the neck dowel and glue.

13 **Hang your jumping jack.** Put the eyescrew in place in the top of the hat and hang up the jumping jack with some strong string. Give the string pull a tug and your jumping jack will jump into action.

PICKIN' CHICKEN

This mechanical chicken is a wonderful learning toy for the curious child. It can help youngsters understand basic principles of weight, leverage, and motion. Simply swing the chicken's egg back and forth, and watch its head and tail bob up and down.

Best of all, it's fun to play with. The chicken will keep children busy for hours—if they can get it away from us big kids.

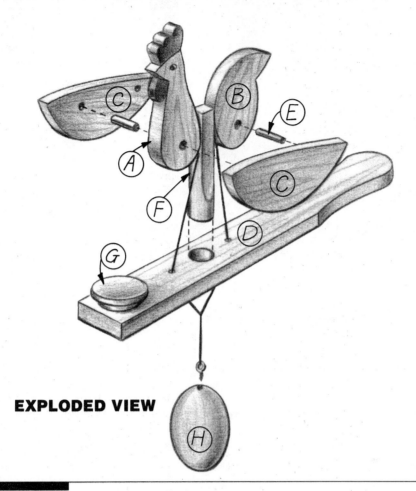

EXPLODED VIEW

CUTTING LIST

Part	Quantity	Dimension	Comment
A. Head	1	$3/8'' \times 2'' \times 4\frac{1}{2}''$	
B. Tail	1	$3/8'' \times 2\frac{1}{4}'' \times 3\frac{3}{4}''$	
C. Sides	2	$3/8'' \times 2\frac{1}{2}'' \times 4\frac{1}{2}''$	
D. Handle	1	$1/2'' \times 1\frac{3}{8}'' \times 12\frac{1}{2}''$	
E. Pivot dowels	2	$1/4''$ dia. $\times \, ^{15}/_{16}''$	
F. Center post	1	$7/16'' \times 7/16'' \times 3\frac{3}{8}''$	
G. Bowl	1	$1^{5}/_{16}''$ dia. $\times 1/2''$	
H. Egg*	1	$1\frac{3}{4}''$ dia. $\times 3\frac{3}{4}''$ long	Cut to size after turning.

*Wooden eggs are available from Trendlines, 375 Beacham Street, Chelsea, MA 02150. Specify Grade A, extra large.

Hardware

1 18-in. string
1 $1\frac{1}{4}$-in. dia. $\times \frac{1}{2}$-in. long eyescrew
2 standard toothpicks
As needed, 1-in. brads

1 Select the stock and cut the parts. Because this project has moving parts, make your chicken from a durable hardwood like poplar or maple. Joint, plane, rip, and cut the stock to the sizes given in the Cutting List.

2 Cut the head, tail, sides, and handle to shape. Draw a ¼-inch grid on a piece of paper and draw the head, tail, side, and handle patterns on it. Transfer the patterns to the wood and cut the parts to shape with a band saw or jigsaw.

To get two identical sides, cut both at once. First stack the pieces together and secure by putting double-sided tape between them. Then cut both sides in one operation.

3 Drill pivot and string holes in the head and tail. Lay out and drill the 5/16-inch-diameter pivot holes in the head and tail, as shown in the *Head Layout* and *Tail Layout.*

Mark the approximate position of the string holes shown in *Head Layout* and *Tail Layout.* The location isn't critical. An error of up to ⅛ inch won't affect the chicken's performance.

Put the head and tail in a vise and drill a hole 1/16 inch in diameter and ⅜ inch deep.

4 Round the edges of the sides. Put a ¼-inch roundover bit in your router. Secure the router in a router table and round-over the outer edges of the sides.

SHOP TIP: Always keep your hands well away from spinning cutters. Use two awls or ice picks as push sticks when routing small pieces like these.

5 Lay out and drill the dowel holes in the sides. Lay out the dowel holes on one side of the chicken, as shown in the *Side Layout.* Set up your drill press to drill ¼-inch-diameter by ¼-inch-deep holes on the inside surface of the sides. Be careful not to drill through the side.

Put a dowel center—available at most hardware stores—in each of the holes. Put the two halves of the chicken together. The dowel centers will mark the center of the holes in the second side. Drill the holes as before.

6 Mark the location of the center post. Once you've drilled the dowel holes, test fit the dowels in one of the sides and put the head and tail in position over them. With the head and tail in place, position the center post so that the head and tail pivot freely. Mark the location of the post.

7 Drill the holes in the handle. Lay out and drill the holes in the handle, as shown in the *Bottom View.* The two 3/16-inch holes are for the string that holds the egg. To prevent the string from wearing thin and breaking, chamfer the top and bottom edges of these holes with a countersink bit.

8 Turn or carve the bowl. Turn or carve the bowl to the approximate profile shown in the *Side View.* Don't worry if it doesn't look exactly like the one shown. The chicken won't notice.

9 Turn or purchase the egg. To get an accurate profile, make a template from ¼-inch plywood. Cut the plywood to the shape shown in the *Egg Layout.* When you turn the egg on the lathe, hold the

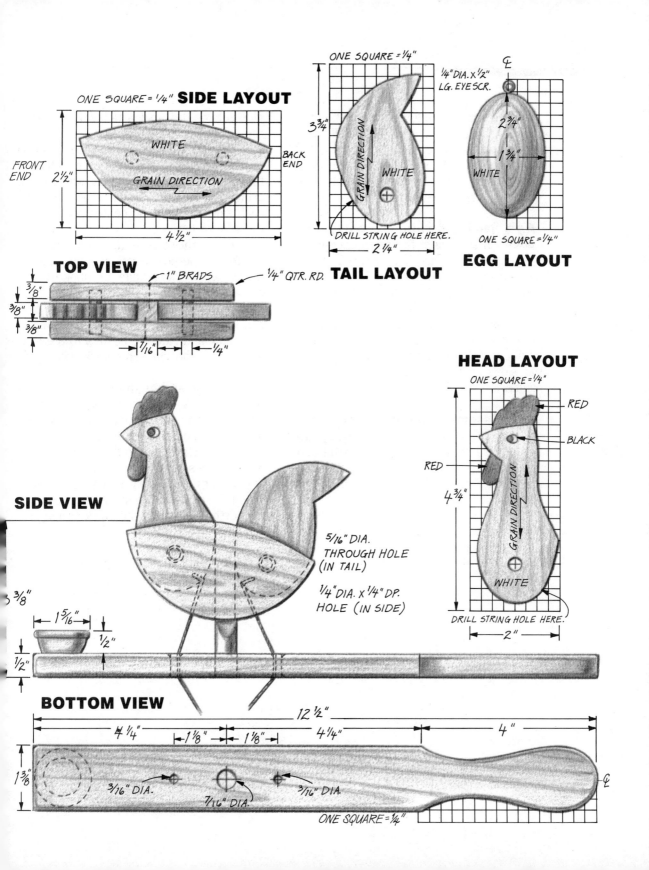

ONE SQUARE = ¼" **SIDE LAYOUT**

FRONT END

2½"

WHITE

GRAIN DIRECTION

BACK END

4½"

ONE SQUARE = ¼"

3¾"

GRAIN DIRECTION

WHITE

DRILL STRING HOLE HERE.

2¼"

TAIL LAYOUT

¼" DIA. x ½" LG. EYE SCR.

C̶L

2¾"

1¾"

WHITE

ONE SQUARE = ¼"

EGG LAYOUT

TOP VIEW

⅜"
⅜"
⅜"

1" BRADS

¼" QTR. RD.

7/16"   ¼"

HEAD LAYOUT

ONE SQUARE = ¼"

RED

BLACK

RED

4¾"

GRAIN DIRECTION

WHITE

DRILL STRING HOLE HERE.

2"

SIDE VIEW

3⅜"

5/16" DIA. THROUGH HOLE (IN TAIL)

¼" DIA. x ¼" DP. HOLE (IN SIDE)

1 5/16"

½"

½"

BOTTOM VIEW

12½"

4¼"   1⅛"   1⅛"   4¼"   4"

1⅜"

3/16" DIA.

7/16" DIA.

3/16" DIA.

C̶L

ONE SQUARE = ¼"

template against the egg to help gauge the proper shape. Sand the egg while it is turning on the lathe.

You can also purchase wooden eggs from many craft stores, or from the source given in the Cutting List.

10 **Sand and paint the parts.** Finish sand all of the parts except for the center post. Take special care in sanding the edges of the string holes in the handle. The smoother these holes, the longer the string will last.

Paint all of the parts except for the bottom ½ inch of the center post. Be careful not to get paint into the dowel holes in the sides or the center-post hole in the handle.

11 **Assemble the pickin' chicken.** Cut an 18-inch piece of string into two equal lengths, one for the head and one for the tail. Glue the strings into their appropriate holes and wedge with slivers of wood or toothpicks.

Put a small bit of glue in the pivot-dowel holes. Don't apply too much glue. Clean up any glue that squeezes out. If glue gets on the head or tail of the chicken, the chicken won't work.

Put the head and tail in place, position the center post, and clamp the chicken together. With the chicken still in the clamps, drive two 1-inch brads through each side and into the center post. Allow the glue to dry.

When the glue is dry, cut and sand the top of the post even with top edge of the sides. With a knife or spokeshave, round the bottom of the center post until it fits into the center-post hole in the handle. Glue the center post into the handle.

Brad and glue the bowl onto the handle so that the chicken's beak will hit its center.

Run the strings through the holes in the handle, as shown in the *Side View.* Knot the strings together 2 to 2½ inches below the handle, and then attach them to an eyescrew driven into the top of the egg 5 to 6 inches below the handle.

Do any necessary touch-up painting. When the paint is dry, swing the egg back and forth, and watch the chicken bob into action.

NOISE MACHINE

This delightful toy works on the same principle as a music box. However, unlike music boxes, which hide the mechanism, this noise machine lets you see the source of the sounds you make. Turn the handle and the pegs strike the thin wooden strips. When the strips vibrate, you hear four different tones.

Try building more than one noise machine. Build them with sticks of varying lengths or of different types of wood. Vary the striking order of the pegs. You may eventually wish to modify the design to elaborate the sound pattern, adding more pegs and sticks. This project invites experimentation.

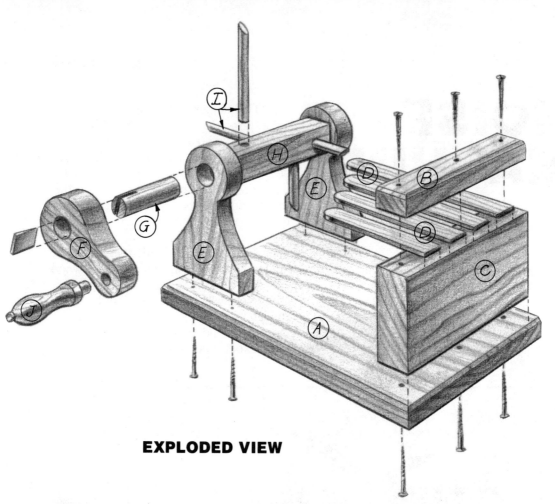

EXPLODED VIEW

CUTTING LIST

Part	Quantity	Dimension	Comment
A. Base	1	⅞″ × 6¾″ × 12⅜″	
B. Support cap	1	⅞″ × 1⅜″ × 5¾″	
C. Tongue support	1	1⅜″ × 3¾″ × 5¾″	
D. Tongues	4	⅛″ × ¾″ × 10″	Trim to fit.
E. Axle supports	2	⅝″ × 3¾″ × 6″	
F. Crank	1	⅞″ × 2½″ × 5¼″	
G. Axle dowel stock	1	⅞″ dia. × 5″	Cut to fit.
H. Peg block	1	1⅜″ × 1⅜″ × 4¾″	
I. Striking peg stock	1	⅜″ dia. × 12″	Adjust as needed. Makes 4.
J. Handle	1	1″ × 1″ × 4⅜″	Cut to length after turning.

Hardware

10 #8 × 1¾-in. flathead wood screws

TOP VIEW

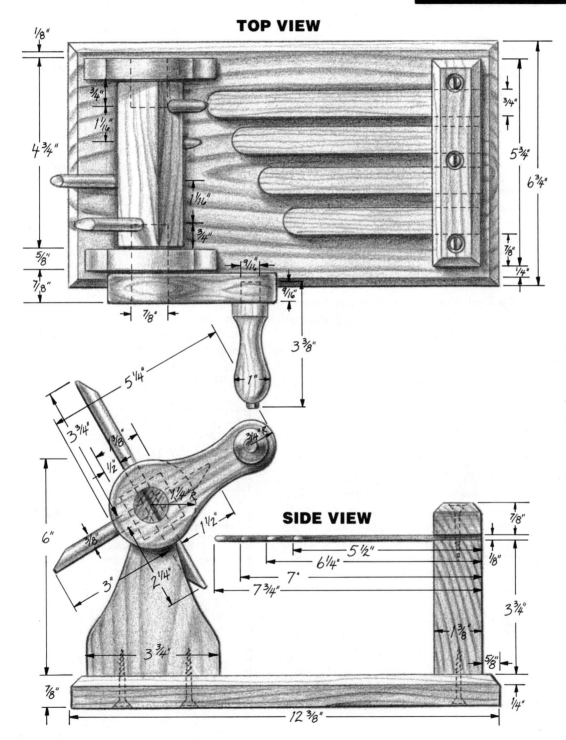

SIDE VIEW

1 **Select the stock and cut the parts.** Most hardwoods and softwoods are suitable for this project. Because the parts for this project are small, you can make them from scraps. Joint, plane, rip, and cut the parts to the sizes given in the Cutting List.

2 **Chamfer the edges of the base and tongue support cap.** Put a chamfer bit in your router. Secure the router in a router table and cut a chamfer all around the top edges of the base. Cut a matching chamfer on the support cap with a block plane.

3 **Drill screw holes in the tongue support cap and tongue support.** Clamp the tongue support cap on top of the tongue support and lay out the position of the three #8 × 1¾-inch flathead wood screws that hold the tongue support cap to the tongue support, as shown in the *Top View.* First, drill ⁷⁄₆₄-inch-diameter pilot holes down into the tongue support. Next, drill a ⁵⁄₃₂-inch-diameter clearance hole in the tongue support cap. Then countersink holes for the screw heads.

A combination pilot hole bit drills a countersink hole, a clearance hole for the screw shank, and a slightly smaller pilot hole for the screw threads all in one operation. These bits are available from most hardware stores and are sold according to the screw size.

4 **Shape the tongues.** Lay out a ⅜-inch-radius curve on the end of each tongue and cut them to shape on a band saw.

The noise machine's tongues become thinner near the edges. As you sand the

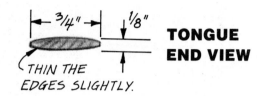

TONGUE END VIEW

THIN THE EDGES SLIGHTLY.

tongues to remove the saw marks, thin the edges slightly, as shown in the *Tongue End View.* Do not cut the tongues to their final lengths yet.

5 **Cut the axle supports and crank to shape.** Draw a ¼-inch grid on a piece of paper and draw the *Axle Support Pattern* and the *Crank Pattern* onto it. Transfer the patterns to the wood and cut the parts to shape on a band saw. If you wish, first tape the stock for the two axle supports together with double-sided tape and cut out both pieces simultaneously. Sand away any saw marks.

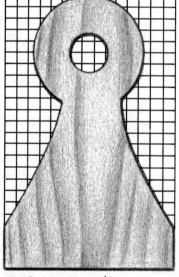

AXLE SUPPORT PATTERN

ONE SQUARE = ¼"

CRANK PATTERN

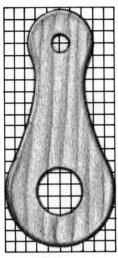

ONE SQUARE = 1/4"

6 **Drill the holes in the axle supports and crank.** On one axle support, mark the center of the top circular section. Align this support on top of the other and drill $^{15}/_{16}$-inch axle holes in both supports at the same time.

Lay out the holes on each circular section of the crank. Drill a $^7/_8$-inch-diameter hole in the large circle for the axle dowel. Drill a $^9/_{16}$-inch-diameter by $^9/_{16}$-inch-deep hole for the handle.

7 **Assemble the axle.** The axle is made up of a peg block and two axle dowels.

First, cut two axle dowels from the axle dowel stock. Cut one $2^3/_8$ inches long and one $1^3/_8$ inches long.

Next, drill a $^7/_8$-inch-diameter by $^3/_4$-inch-deep hole in each end of the peg block. Put a little glue in each hole, and insert an axle dowel.

When the glue is dry, cut a slot in the long axle dowel for a tightening wedge. To lay out the slot, slip the long axle dowel through the hole in one of the axle supports. Mark the axle dowel at the point where it protrudes. With a backsaw, cut a slot for a tightening wedge from the end of the axle dowel to the axle support mark.

Cut a thin $^7/_8$-inch square tightening wedge from some hardwood scrap and sand the edges smooth.

8 **Attach the striking pegs to the peg block.** Lay out the position of the striking pegs on the peg block, as shown in the *Top View*. Drill $^3/_8$-inch-diameter by $^1/_2$-inch-deep holes for the pegs.

Cut the four different length pegs shown in the *Side View* from the striking peg stock. Round and bevel the striking ends of the pegs, as shown, with sandpaper and glue them into their corresponding holes. The longest peg will strike the shortest tongue shown, and the shortest peg will strike the longest tongue. Allow the glue to dry.

9 **Turn the crank handle.** Turn the handle to the profile shown in the *Handle Pattern*. Sand the handle while it is still on the lathe, remove it from the lathe, and cut off the waste with a backsaw. If you are unfamiliar with turning, *Creative Woodturning* by Dale L. Nish is a good introduction. If you don't have access to a lathe, purchase a small drawer handle at a hardware store.

10 **Assemble the noise machine.** First, clamp the tongue support in

HANDLE PATTERN

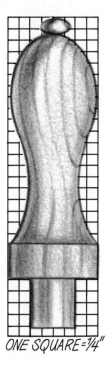

ONE SQUARE = ¼"

position on the base. From the bottom, drill three holes with a combination pilot hole bit for #8 × 1¾-inch screws, as shown in the *Side View*. Space the holes evenly. Drive the screws in place.

Next, slip the axle supports onto the axle and then clamp the axle supports in position on the base. Drill holes for #8 × 1¾-inch screws as before and drive the screws in place.

With the axle supports screwed in place, spread a little glue in the axle dowel hole in the crank. Push the crank over the slotted axle dowel until you have about a ¹⁄₃₂-inch gap between the crank and the axle support. Position the crank on the

axle so the slot is perpendicular to the crank's grain. Spread glue on the tightening wedge and carefully tap it into its slot.

When the glue dries, trim the wedge flush with the axle dowel. If the axles overhang the supports, trim them flush, too.

SHOP TIP: When fitting or gluing the axle and axle supports, place several folds of waxed paper between the parts. Once the glue has set, remove the paper for a free-spinning mechanism. You may also want to apply wax to the axle pins to prevent them from sticking. Be careful not to wax the slotted section of the dowel that is glued to the crank.

11 **Adjust the tongues.** Position the tongues on top of the tongue support and lightly screw on the tongue support cap. Notice that the screws do not go through the tongues.

Position the tongues, as shown in the *Top View*. Adjust the tongues so that as you turn the crank, the pegs just catch the ends of the tongues, causing them to sound. When the tongues are all adjusted, tighten the screws on the tongue support cap and trim the back ends of the tongues even with the tongue support.

12 **Apply the finish.** Give the noise machine a final sanding. A simple toy like this should have a simple finish, so rub on a one-step oil finish.

When the finish is dry, go make some noise.

RACE CARS

Imagine yourself speeding around the new racetrack at Indianapolis in your Mercer Race About. You zoom past a Blitzen Benz, and run head-to-head with a Lozier Gentleman's Roadster. The finish line approaches, your scarf whips in the wind, and you inch ahead to take the checkered flag.

The simple, durable design of these race cars makes them quick and easy projects that will last for years. Make these toy race cars as a gift for your children or grandchildren, or have them help you build them for a great learning experience.

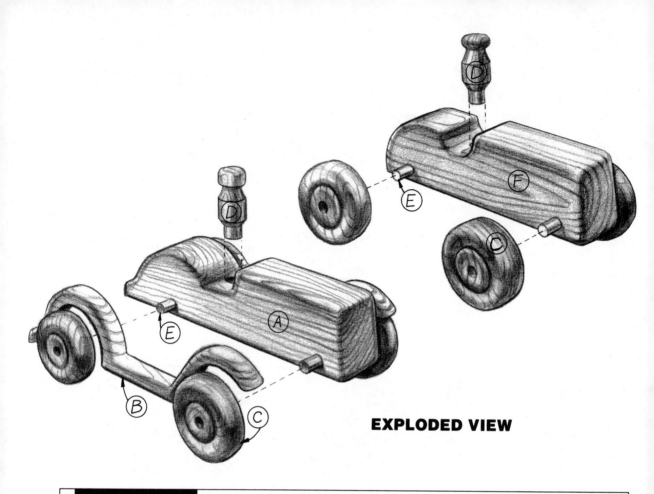

EXPLODED VIEW

CUTTING LIST

Part	Quantity	Dimension	Comment
#1 Gentleman's Roadster			
A. Chassis	1	1¾″ × 2¾″ × 11″	
B. Fenders	2	¾″ × 3½″ × 11½″	Cut to size when shaping.
C. Wheels*	4	¾″ × 2½″ dia.	
D. Driver†	1	1″ dia. × 3½″	Cut to length after turning.
E. Axles	2	⅜″ dia. × 3⅜″	
#2 Race About			
F. Chassis	1	1¾″ × 2¾″ × 9¾″	
C. Wheels*	4	¾″ × 2½″ dia.	
D. Driver†	1	1″ dia. × 3½″	Cut to length after turning.
E. Axles	2	⅜″ dia. × 3⅜″	

*Wheels are available from Cherry Tree Toys, Inc., P.O. Box 369, Belmont, OH 43718. Part #16 (oak, cherry, or walnut).
†Drivers are also available from Cherry Tree Toys, Inc. Part #22 for ⅞ × 2⅜-in. person.

1 **Select the stock and cut the parts.** The race cars shown are made of pine, but you can make yours out of almost any kind of wood. To add color and variety to the race cars, use various wood species for the different parts. Because these cars are basically the same, why not make both at once? Choose enough straight, flat stock to make both cars. Joint, plane, rip, and cut the stock to the sizes given in the Cutting List.

SHOP TIP: If you glue up stock for the chassis, consider gluing together different types of wood to get racing stripes. This project, like any other, takes on a whole new look with different types of wood.

2 **Shape the chassis.** Draw a ½-inch grid on a piece of paper and draw the chassis of the *Gentleman's Roadster Shape Pattern* and *Race About Shape Pattern* onto it. Transfer the patterns to the stock and cut the chassis to shape on a band saw. After you cut the chassis, sand away the saw marks.

3 **Drill the axle holes in the chassis.** Mark and drill ⁷⁄₁₆-inch axle holes in the chassis, as shown in the patterns. Drill the holes all the way through the stock.

SHOP TIP: When drilling a hole completely through a piece of wood, the wood often splinters where the bit exits the stock. To prevent this from happening, put a flat piece of scrap under the stock you are drilling. As the drill comes through the stock, the piece of scrap will support the edges of the hole and prevent it from splintering.

4 **Round the edges of the chassis.** Put a ¼-inch roundover bit in your router. Secure the router in a router table and round-over all of the edges of the chassis except where noted otherwise in the *Shape Pattern*. Use a push stick when routing and keep your fingers well away from the cutters.

5 **Cut out and glue the fenders to the Gentleman's Roadster.** Note that only the Roadster has fenders. While both of the Roadster's fenders are made from the same pattern, they are not identical. The right fender is rounded over on the right side; the left fender is rounded over on the left side.

Draw a ½-inch grid on a piece of paper and draw the fender shape onto it. Transfer the pattern to the two pieces of stock as called for in the Cutting List.

Start by cutting along the "first cut" line of the fender shapes, as noted in the *Shape Pattern*, and sand away the saw marks.

When the first cuts have been sanded smooth, round-over the appropriate edges with a ½-inch roundover bit set up in a table-mounted router. Remember: Round-over the left side of the left fender and the right side of the right fender. Round-over the square corner of the fenders with a chisel and file as noted in the drawing.

After you've routed the fender, make the cut along the bottom of the fender and sand away the saw marks.

Lay the chassis of the Gentleman's Roadster on its side and set the wheels in place. Place the appropriate completed fender above the wheels and mark its position. Spread some glue on the edge of the fender and clamp it in place with rubber bands. When the glue is dry, repeat the process with the second fender.

GENTLEMAN'S ROADSTER

TOP VIEW

SHAPE PATTERN

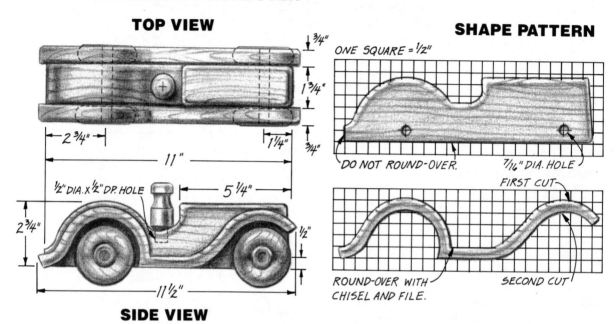

ONE SQUARE = 1/2"

3/4"

1 3/4"

3/4"

2 3/4"

1 1/4"

11"

1/2" DIA. X 1/2" DP. HOLE

5 1/4"

2 3/4"

1/2"

11 1/2"

DO NOT ROUND-OVER.

7/16" DIA. HOLE

FIRST CUT

SECOND CUT

ROUND-OVER WITH CHISEL AND FILE.

SIDE VIEW

RACE ABOUT

TOP VIEW

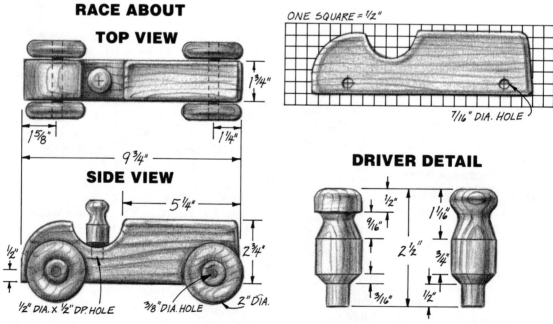

ONE SQUARE = 1/2"

1 3/4"

1 5/8"

1 1/4"

9 3/4"

7/16" DIA. HOLE

SIDE VIEW

5 1/4"

1/2"

2 3/4"

1/2" DIA. X 1/2" DP. HOLE

3/8" DIA. HOLE

2" DIA.

DRIVER DETAIL

1/2"

9/16"

1 1/16"

2 1/2"

3/4"

3/16"

1/2"

6 **Purchase the drivers or turn them on the lathe.** You can purchase drivers from the source listed in the Cutting List or turn them yourself on the lathe. If you decide to turn them yourself, turn the drivers to the dimensions shown in the *Driver Detail.* Sand the drivers while still on the lathe. When the drivers are turned and sanded, turn off the lathe, remove the drivers, cut off the tail stock with a backsaw, and sand the ends smooth.

If you are new to turning and want to give it a try, a good reference guide is *Creative Woodturning* by Dale L. Nish.

7 **Drill the holes for the drivers in the chassis.** If you turned the drivers to the specifications given, drill holes for your drivers in the chassis, as shown in the *Gentleman's Roadster, Side View* and *Race About, Side View.*

If you purchased the drivers from the source listed, drill a ⅞-inch-diameter hole, instead of the ½-inch-diameter hole indicated.

If you want to fasten the drivers to the chassis, simply glue them in place.

8 **Sand and finish the chassis and drivers.** Finish sand the chassis and drivers and remove any excess glue from the surface of the wood. As you sand, slightly round-over any sharp edges.

Give the chassis a coat of varnish and let the wood grain show through or paint them with stripes and racing numbers.

Allow the finish to dry.

9 **Add the axles and wheels to the race cars.** Glue one wheel to each axle. Lubricate the portion of the axle that will contact the chassis by rubbing some candle wax on it. Put the axles through the chassis and glue on the other wheels. Make sure that the wheels are not tight against the chassis, or they won't be able to turn. After all, a race car isn't much good if its wheels won't turn.

Allow the glue to dry, and you're off to the races.

FRONT-END LOADER

A simple weekend project, this toy might be fun to make with the child for whom it is intended. A young child could help sand, while an older child could do much of the work with hand tools.

Choose a nontoxic, child-safe finish for this piece and apply the finish to the separate subassemblies.

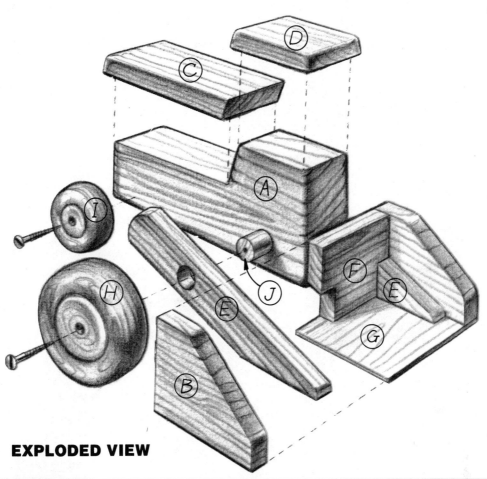

EXPLODED VIEW

CUTTING LIST

Part	Quantity	Dimension	Comment
A. Body	1	$1\frac{3}{4}'' \times 3\frac{3}{4}'' \times 7\frac{1}{2}''$	
B. Bucket sides	2	$\frac{5}{8}'' \times 2\frac{5}{8}'' \times 3\frac{1}{8}''$	
C. Engine cover	1	$\frac{5}{8}'' \times 2\frac{1}{4}'' \times 4\frac{3}{4}''$	
D. Cab roof	1	$\frac{5}{8}'' \times 2\frac{1}{4}'' \times 3\frac{1}{8}''$	
E. Bucket arms	2	$\frac{5}{8}'' \times 1\frac{3}{8}'' \times 7\frac{1}{8}''$	
F. Bucket back	1	$\frac{5}{8}'' \times 2\frac{5}{8}'' \times 3\frac{1}{16}''$	
G. Bucket bottom	1	$\frac{1}{16}'' \times 3\frac{1}{8}'' \times 4\frac{5}{16}''$	Plastic laminate
H. Front wheels	2	$1'' \times 3\frac{3}{8}''$ dia.	
I. Rear wheels	2	$\frac{7}{8}'' \times 2\frac{3}{8}''$ dia.	
J. Axle	1	$\frac{3}{4}''$ dia. $\times 3\frac{1}{16}''$	

Hardware

4 #12 × 1½-in. flathead wood screws
As needed, 4d finishing nails

1 Select the stock and cut the parts. The loader can be made of softwood, as shown in the photo, or hardwood—perhaps making different parts with hardwood scraps of different colors. For durability, the bottom of the bucket is made of a plastic laminate. If you don't have a scrap laying around, substitute ⅛-inch tempered hardboard. Joint, plane, rip, and cut all the parts except the wheels to the sizes given in the Cutting List.

SHOP TIP: When you're making a project with lots of small parts, do as much work as possible on larger pieces of stock, then cut the smaller ones from it. On this project, cut all the ⅝-inch-thick parts for the loader from a single board 3 × 36 inches. Planing one long board to correct thickness is easier—and safer—than planing lots of short pieces.

2 Shape the body and bucket sides. Draw a ¼-inch grid on a piece of paper and draw the *Body Detail* and *Bucket Side Detail* onto it. Transfer the patterns to the stock and cut the parts to shape on a band saw.

3 Bore the hole for the axle. Lay out and drill a $^{13}/_{16}$-inch-diameter axle hole in the body, as shown in the *Body Detail*. Put a flat piece of scrap under the stock you are drilling. As the drill comes through the stock, the piece of scrap will support the edges of the hole and prevent it from splintering.

4 Bevel the engine cover. Bevel the end of the engine cover to fit against the back of the cab. Set your table saw blade to 13 degrees and guide the cut with

the miter gauge set at 90 degrees. Test fit the engine cover to the body and adjust the bevel if necessary.

5 Round-over the edges of the body, cab roof, and engine cover. Put a ¼-inch roundover bit in your router. Secure the router in a router table and rout the appropriate edges of the body, cab roof, and engine cover. Edges to be routed are shown in the *Side View* and *Bottom View*.

6 Assemble the chassis. Glue the cab roof and engine cover to the body. Clamp them securely and allow the glue to dry.

Sand and finish the chassis.

SHOP TIP: Pieces assembled with glue only often slip around when you use clamps. To prevent this, position the pieces exactly, drive thin brads into the body, and clip them off ⅛ inch or so above the surface. Press the mating surface onto the brads with clamps: The brads keep the parts from slipping.

7 Make the bucket arms. Lay out and drill $^{13}/_{16}$-inch axle holes in the bucket arms. Then lay out and cut the angle on the end of the arms with the band saw, as shown in the *Side View*. Cut the radius shown in the opposite end on the band saw and sand any saw marks or roughness smooth.

8 Cut the bucket arm notches. The bucket arms run through the bucket back. Lay out and notch the bucket back for the arms, as shown in the *Side View*

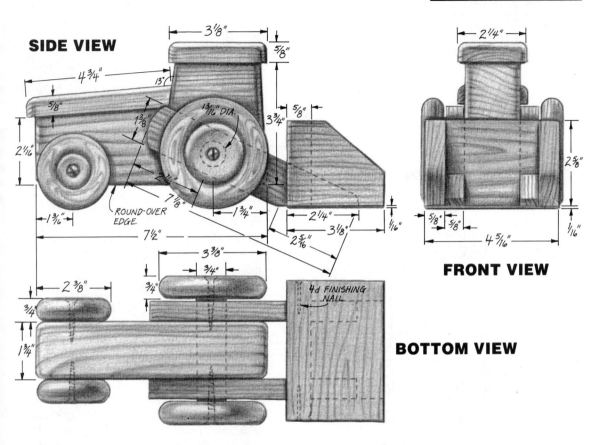

SIDE VIEW

FRONT VIEW

BOTTOM VIEW

and *Front View*. Note that the top of the notch is angled. It's quicker to cut the notch with a backsaw or dovetail saw than to set up a machine to cut them. Make sure both notches are the same size and angle.

9 **Assemble the bucket.** Glue and clamp the bucket sides, back, and bottom together. For wood-to-wood joints, white or yellow glue is fine, but epoxy the bottom of the bucket in place if you are using plastic laminate.

When the glue has dried, slip the bucket arms into the notches in the bucket back. If there's any difference between the notches, you'll notice it now. Remove the bucket and trim the notches with a chisel until they fit correctly. Then apply glue to the mating surfaces of the arm and bucket and clamp them together. Secure the sides and back to the bucket arms by driving 4d finishing nails through the sides and bucket arms and into the back. Sand and finish the bucket.

10 **Make the wheels.** If you have a lathe, you can turn the wheels. Mount band-sawn blanks onto a small faceplate and shape them as indicated in the *Cross Section through Wheels*.

The wheels are attached to the body by #12 × 1½-inch flathead wood screws. Drill ¼-inch axle screw holes in the center of each of the wheels and countersink the holes.

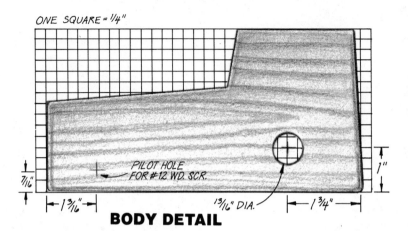

ONE SQUARE = ¼"

PILOT HOLE
FOR #12 WD. SCR.

7/16"

1 3/16"

13/16" DIA.

1 3/4"

1"

BODY DETAIL

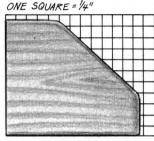

ONE SQUARE = ¼"

**BUCKET
SIDE DETAIL**

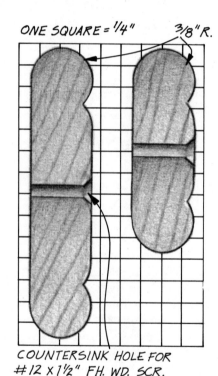

ONE SQUARE = ¼"

3/8" R.

COUNTERSINK HOLE FOR
#12 X 1½" F.H. WD. SCR.

**CROSS SECTION
THROUGH WHEELS**

If you don't have a lathe, consider buying a wheel and circle cutter for your drill press. This special cutter can cut wheels from 1 to 6 inches in diameter.

Wheel and circle cutters are available from Woodcraft, 210 Wood County Industrial Park, P.O. Box 1686, Parkersburg, WV 26102. You can also find these cutters in many hardware stores.

Still another option is to purchase wooden wheels from a craft store, but the dimensions may differ slightly. If you do purchase the wheels, adjust the dimensions of your front-end loader accordingly.

Sand and finish the wheels.

11 Assemble the front-end loader. First, drill ⁹⁄₆₄-inch-diameter pilot holes for the axle screws. Drill a pilot hole for the front wheels centered on each end of the axle. Drill a hole for the rear wheels in each side of the body, as shown in the *Body Detail*.

Next, wax the axle with paste wax and screw one of the front wheels securely to it. Then, put the bucket arms in place on either side of the body and slide the axle through the bucket arms and body. Screw the remaining front wheel to the axle.

When the front wheels, axle, and bucket are in place, screw the back wheels to the sides of the body. Don't drive these screws in all the way. The back wheels must rotate freely on the screws.

Do any necessary touch up sanding and finishing.

DUMP TRUCK

Here's a fine addition to the hallway and sandbox highway department. This rugged dump truck is designed to survive years of hard play, and its simple structure makes it easy to build. This dump truck is the perfect toy for young children because there are no dangerous small parts that can be broken off and swallowed. The dump truck is also a great project to get your children or grandchildren involved in building.

EXPLODED VIEW

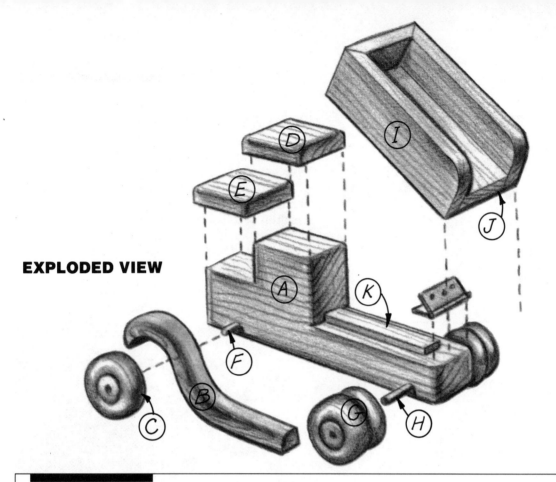

CUTTING LIST

Part	Quantity	Dimension	Comment
A. Body	1	$1\frac{3}{4}'' \times 3\frac{3}{4}'' \times 9\frac{3}{4}''$	
B. Fenders	2	$\frac{5}{8}'' \times 5'' \times 6\frac{3}{4}''$	
C. Front wheels*	2	$\frac{3}{4}'' \times 2''$ dia.	
D. Cap	1	$\frac{5}{8}'' \times 2\frac{1}{4}'' \times 2\frac{5}{8}''$	
E. Hood	1	$\frac{5}{8}'' \times 2\frac{1}{4}'' \times 2\frac{1}{2}''$	
F. Front axle	1	$\frac{3}{8}''$ dia. $\times 3\frac{3}{8}''$	
G. Rear wheels*	4	$\frac{1}{2}'' \times 2''$ dia.	
H. Rear axle	1	$\frac{3}{8}''$ dia. $\times 3\frac{7}{8}''$	
I. Dump sides/back	1	$\frac{3}{8}'' \times 1\frac{3}{4}'' \times 16''$	Makes 3 pieces; miter to fit.
J. Dump bed	1	$\frac{5}{8}'' \times 2\frac{3}{4}'' \times 5\frac{3}{4}''$	
K. Spacer	1	$\frac{1}{2}'' \times \frac{3}{4}'' \times 4''$	Rip to thickness of closed hinge.

*Wheels are available from Cherry Tree Toys, Inc., P.O. Box 369, Belmont, OH 43718. Part #14 for front wheels and part #28 for rear wheels.

Hardware

1 $1\frac{1}{2}$-in. butt hinge

1 Select the stock and cut the parts. The dump truck shown here is made of pine, but you can make yours from any wood you have on hand. Choose straight, flat stock. Joint, plane, rip, and cut all of the parts, except the spacer, to the sizes given in the Cutting List. You may need to glue a couple of pieces together for the body. Purchase the wheels from the source given in the Cutting List.

2 Cut the body and fenders to shape. Draw a ¼-inch grid on a piece of paper and draw the body and fender shapes from the *Cutting Pattern* onto it. Transfer the body pattern to the wood and cut out the body on the band saw. Sand the saw marks smooth.

Cut the fenders next. The fenders are not identical: The left fender is rounded over on the left side and the right fender is rounded over on the right side. Transfer the fender pattern to the stock.

Cut the fenders along the line marked "cut first" in the *Cutting Pattern*. Sand away the saw marks.

Once you've sanded the first cuts, round-over the appropriate edge. Put a ½-inch roundover bit in your router. Secure the router in a router table. Remember: Round-over the left edge of the left fender and the right edge of the right fender. Use push sticks and keep your fingers well away from the cutter.

When you've rounded-over the fenders, cut along the bottom of the fenders and sand away any saw marks.

3 Drill the axle holes in the body. Drill ⁷⁄₁₆-inch axle holes in the body, as shown in the *Cutting Pattern*. These holes go all the way through the body.

When drilling a hole completely through a piece of wood, the wood often splinters where the bit exits the stock. To prevent this from happening, put a flat piece of scrap under the stock you are drilling. As the drill comes through the stock, the piece of scrap will support the edges of the hole and prevent it from splintering.

4 Glue the fenders in place. Lay the body of the dump truck on its side and set the front wheels in place. Set the appropriate completed fender in place and make sure that it doesn't interfere with the wheel. Mark the fender's position. Spread some glue on the fender's inside edge, put it on the body, and clamp it in place with rubber bands. When the glue is dry, repeat the process with the second fender.

5 Glue the cap and hood to the body. To round-over the edges of the cap and hood, put a ½-inch roundover bit in your router. Secure the router in a router table. Round-over all the top edges of the cap, but only the front and sides of the hood. Use push sticks and keep your fingers away from the cutter.

Spread glue on the bottom of the cap and hood and position them as shown in the *Top View* and *Side View.* Clamp them in place with some strong rubber bands and allow the glue to dry.

6 Attach the axles and wheels to the body. Glue one ¾-inch-wide wheel to the front axle. Lubricate the portion of the axle that will contact the body by rubbing some candle wax against it. Put the axles through the body and glue on the other ¾-inch-wide wheel. Make sure that the wheels are not tight against

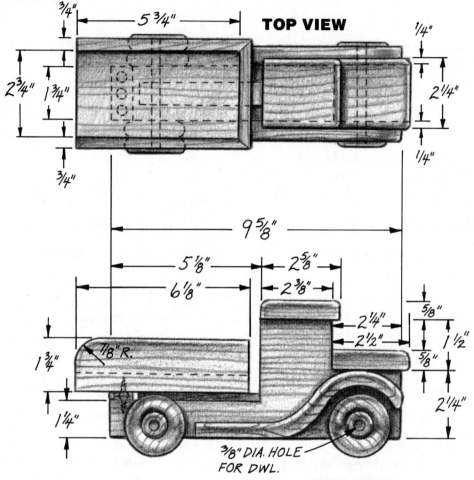

TOP VIEW

3/4"
5 3/4"
1/4"
2 3/4"
1 3/4"
2 1/4"
3/4"
1/4"

9 5/8"
5 1/8"
2 5/8"
6 1/8"
2 3/8"
2 1/4"
5/8"
2 1/2"
1 1/2"
1 3/4"
1/8" R.
5/8"
2 1/4"
1 1/4"
3/8" DIA. HOLE
FOR DWL.

SIDE VIEW

the body, or they won't turn.

Glue two of the ½-inch-wide wheels side by side on one end of the back axle, as shown in the *Top View*. Rub some candle wax on the axle and put the axle through the body. Glue the two remaining wheels to the axle and make sure that they can turn freely.

Allow the glue to dry.

7 Miter and shape the dump sides and back. Miter the dump sides and back to fit around the dump bed. Set the

table saw blade to 45 degrees and guide the cuts with a miter gauge set at 90 degrees. Test fit the dump sides and back as you go.

To get accurate miters, check your mitering setup on some pieces of scrap. Put the miters together and make sure that the resulting angle equals 90 degrees. Adjust the blade as necessary.

Round the corners of back ends of the sides to approximate the shape shown in the *Side View*. Round the corners with a band saw or jigsaw and sand the saw marks smooth.

8 **Measure, rip, and attach the spacer to the body.** A spacer, between the dump and the body, supports the dump. Immediately behind the spacer, the dump and body are hinged together. The thickness of the spacer depends on the thickness of the hinge. Measure the closed thickness of the hinge and rip the spacer to this measurement on a table saw. Glue the spacer in place on the body, as shown in the *Top View.*

9 **Hinge the dump to the body.** Position the hinge, as shown in the *Top View,* and screw it in place.

10 **Apply the finish.** Finish sand all of the exposed surfaces of the dump truck.

When the dump truck has been sanded, you can give the truck a coat of varnish like the dump truck shown. You could also paint your truck and add details like headlights, windows, and a company logo.

CUTTING PATTERN

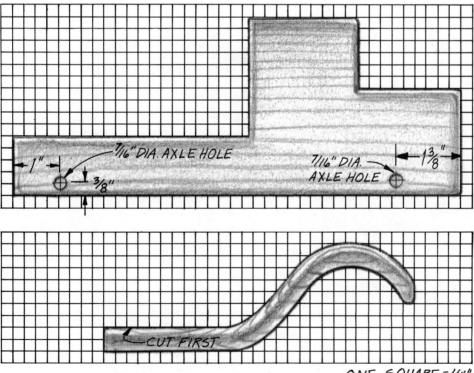

ONE SQUARE = 1/4"

PLEASURE BOAT

Wooden boats are a great excuse for child and adult alike to get good and soaking wet. And because simple projects like this don't take much time or wood, you can build a whole fleet. If the admiral is a young woodworker, pick a wood like pine that's easily worked by young hands. For a showier fleet, mix and match a variety of hardwoods.

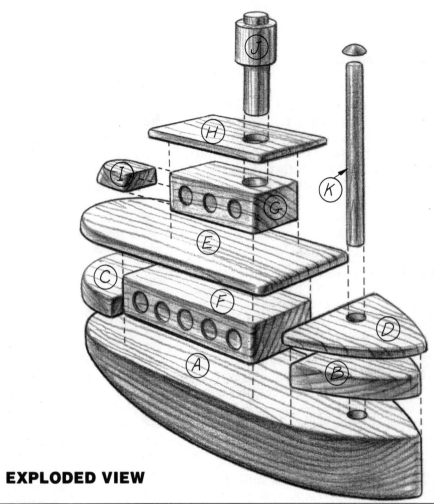

EXPLODED VIEW

CUTTING LIST

Part	Quantity	Dimension	Comment
A. Hull	1	$1\frac{9}{16}'' \times 3\frac{1}{2}'' \times 11\frac{1}{2}''$	
B. Foredeck	1	$\frac{5}{8}'' \times 3'' \times 2\frac{1}{2}''$	
C. Aft deck	1	$\frac{5}{8}'' \times 2\frac{3}{4}'' \times 2''$	
D. Foredeck cap	1	$\frac{3}{16}'' \times 3\frac{1}{4}'' \times 2\frac{3}{4}''$	Cut to shape and length.
E. Top deck	1	$\frac{3}{16}'' \times 3\frac{1}{2}'' \times 7\frac{3}{8}''$	
F. Cabin	1	$1\frac{1}{8}'' \times 2\frac{1}{8}'' \times 5''$	
G. Wheelhouse	1	$1\frac{1}{8}'' \times 1\frac{3}{4}'' \times 3\frac{1}{4}''$	
H. Wheelhouse roof	1	$\frac{3}{16}'' \times 2\frac{1}{8}'' \times 3\frac{3}{4}''$	
I. Ventilator cap	1	$\frac{1}{2}'' \times 1'' \times 5''$	Cut to length after shaping.
J. Smokestack*	1	$\frac{7}{8}''$ dia. $\times 3''$	Cut to length after turning.
K. Mast*	1	$\frac{1}{2}''$ dia. $\times 5''$	Cut to length after turning.

*Similar parts are available from Cherry Tree Toys, P.O. Box 369, Belmont, OH 43718. Specify smokestack #6 and headlamp #54 for top of mast.

1 **Select the stock and cut the parts.** Joint, plane, rip, and cut the parts to the sizes given in the Cutting List. It's safest to work with boards that are at least 15 inches long, particularly as you joint and plane the stock.

Cut small pieces like these on the band saw: You can rip them to width without danger of the saw kicking the piece back at you.

2 **Make a pattern for the hull.** Draw a ½-inch grid on a piece of paper and draw the hull shape onto it, as shown in the *Top View.* Transfer the pattern to what will be the *bottom* of the boat.

3 **Attach the foredeck and aft deck.** It's easier to glue these parts together before you've sawn them to shape. If you don't have clamps, use large rubber bands to hold the pieces while the glue dries. If you're planning to sail the boat, use a waterproof glue, like resorcinol.

4 **Shape the assembled hull.** Draw a ½-inch grid on a piece of paper and draw the stern profile onto it, as shown on the *Side View.* Transfer the stern profile to the hull and cut out the shape. Flip the boat upside down on the band saw and cut along the layout lines you drew there earlier. Remove the saw marks and finish shaping with files and sandpaper.

5 **Make the foredeck cap.** Position the straight back edge of the cap so it overhangs the foredeck by ⅛ inch. Then trace the shape of the foredeck onto the cap. Hold the side of the pencil flat against the hull and foredeck as you trace. The thickness of the pencil automatically creates the overhang of the cap. Cut to the line on the band saw. Sand to remove any saw marks and glue the cap in place.

6 **Make the top deck.** Trace around the hull to establish the shape of the top deck. The top deck does not overhang the hull: Draw the deck so that it is the same size as the section of hull below it. Cut to shape as before.

7 **Make the portholes.** Mark the centerlines for the portholes on the cabin and wheelhouse, as shown in the *Side View.* Bore holes ⅛ inch deep with a ⅝-inch bit.

8 **Assemble the superstructure.** Glue the cabin, top deck, wheelhouse, and wheelhouse roof in place on the hull. Note that they're all centered across the hull's width.

9 **Make the ventilator cap.** To rout the roundover on both long edges of the ventilator cap stock, put a ½-inch roundover bit in your router. Secure the router in a router table and guide the stock against a fence. Round the end grain on one end to a ½-inch radius with a file and sandpaper. Cut to length. Glue the cap in place on the top deck.

10 **Add the smokestack and mast.** Turn the mast and smokestack to the profile shown. If you don't have a lathe, substitute a similar chimney, available from the source listed in the Cutting List. To make the mast, epoxy a wooden headlamp, available from the same source, on top of a dowel.

11 **Add the finishing touches.** Clean off any excess glue with a sharp chisel. Round-over any sharp edges of the boat with sandpaper. You can paint the boat or seal it with a clear finish.

TOP VIEW

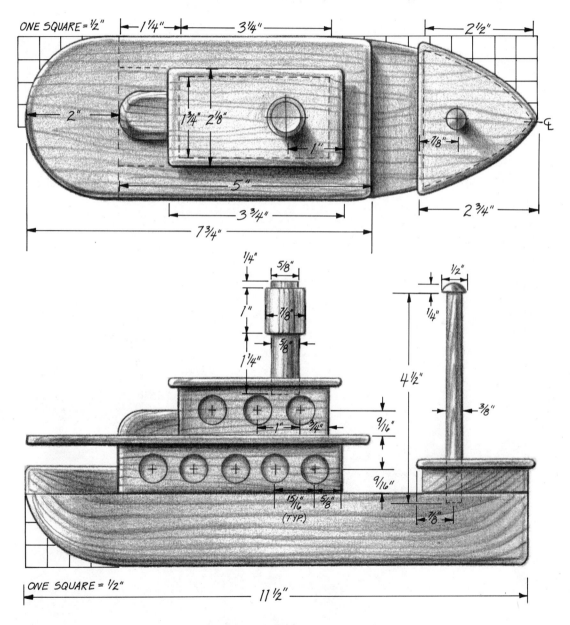

ONE SQUARE = ½"

SIDE VIEW

ONE SQUARE = ½"

BIPLANE

Have you ever wished that you were a flying ace rolling and twisting through the blue yonder, locked in a dogfight with the Red Baron? Or have you ever dreamed of dropping down to dust a rolling green field of soybeans and then swooping up again at the last possible moment? You can pass these and other dreams of flight on to your children or grandchildren with this sturdy biplane.

The biplane shown here is made from pine. Pine is a good choice because it will keep the biplane lightweight for that tough maneuvering under the lamp stand and up over the mountainous couch terrain.

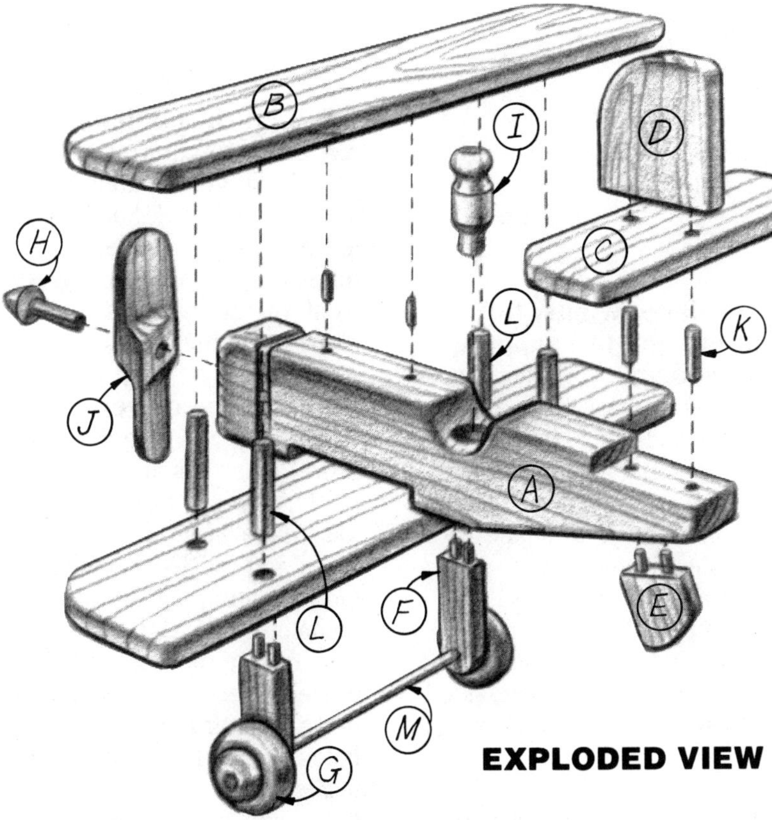
B
I
D
H
C
L
K
J
A
F
E
L
M
G
EXPLODED VIEW

CUTTING LIST

Part	Quantity	Dimension	Comment
A. Fuselage	1	1⅜″ × 2¾″ × 13½″	
B. Wings	2	9/16″ × 3¾″ × 15″	
C. Tail wing	1	9/16″ × 2¾″ × 6″	
D. Tail fin	1	9/16″ × 2¾″ × 3¼″	
E. Tail support	1	9/16″ × 1½″ × 2″	
F. Axle supports	2	9/16″ × 1 5/16″ × 2⅞″	
G. Wheels*	2	¾″ × 2″ dia.	
H. Prop shaft*	1	1″ × 1″ × 3″	Cut to length after turning.
I. Pilot*	1	1″ × 1″ × 3″	Cut to length after turning.
J. Propeller	1	¾″ × 1 3/16″ × 6½″	
K. Dowel stock	1	¼″ × 12″	For dowel joints
L. Wing struts	4	½″ dia. × 2¾″	Dowel
M. Axle	1	½″ dia. × 7¾″	Dowel

*Available from Cherry Tree Toys, P.O. Box 369, Belmont, OH 43718. Specify person #22 for pilot, multiuse peg #53 for prop shaft, and part #16 for ¾-in.-thick × 2½-in.-dia. wheel (oak, cherry, or walnut).

1 Select the stock and cut the parts. Choose straight, flat wood without knots. Joint, plane, rip, and cut the parts to the sizes given in the Cutting List.

2 Cut the fuselage, wings, tail wing, tail fin, and tail support to the shapes shown. Draw a ½-inch grid on a large piece of paper and draw the fuselage, wing, tail wing, tail fin, and tail support shapes on it, as shown in the *Cutting Pattern*. Transfer the shapes to the wood and cut the parts to shape with a band saw or jigsaw. Remember to make two wings that are the same shape.

To get two identical wings, cut both at once. First stack the wing stock together and secure by putting double-sided tape between them. Then cut both wings in one operation.

3 Cut the radius in the axle supports and drill the axle holes. Lay out and cut the radius shown in the *Side View* on the band saw or jigsaw. Mark and drill the axle holes.

4 Round the appropriate edges of the fuselage, wings, tail wing, tail fin, tail support, and axle supports. Put a ¼-inch roundover bit in your router. Secure the router in a router table and round all the edges that will be exposed when the plane is assembled. Do not round the sections of the parts that meet other parts. For example, don't round the bottom wing where it meets the fuselage.

Use a push stick when routing and keep your hands well away from the cutter. A pair of scratch awls makes excellent push sticks for small parts.

5 Rout the engine groove in the fuselage. Put a ⅜-inch-diameter round nose bit in your router. Secure the router in a router table and rout the engine groove shown. Guide the fuselage with a miter gauge set at 90 degrees and run the front of the fuselage against a fence to ensure a straight cut.

6 Drill the dowel holes in the parts. Set up a drill press to drill the dowel holes for attaching the wings, tail, tail fin, tail support, axle support, and pilot. Make sure that you drill the dowel holes and mortises to the depths shown. Only the tail wing's dowel holes are drilled completely through the piece.

Locate the exact position of matching dowel holes with commercially available dowel centers. For example, drill dowel holes in one of the axle supports, as shown in *Side View*. Put the dowel centers in the holes and position the axle supports on the bottom of the lower wing. Press the points of the dowel centers into the wing to mark the exact position of the matching dowel holes.

SHOP TIP: Substitute drywall screws for dowels for a simpler construction. Drill the holes with a combination pilot hole bit, available at most hardware stores. The bit will also drill a counterbore, which you can fill with a wooden plug. Glue the plug in place and sand it flush—it will be nearly invisible.

7 Drill the axle holes in the wheels. Most wooden wheels that you can buy will have no larger than a ⅜-inch-diameter axle hole. Drill out the holes in the wheels to a ½-inch diameter.

TOP VIEW

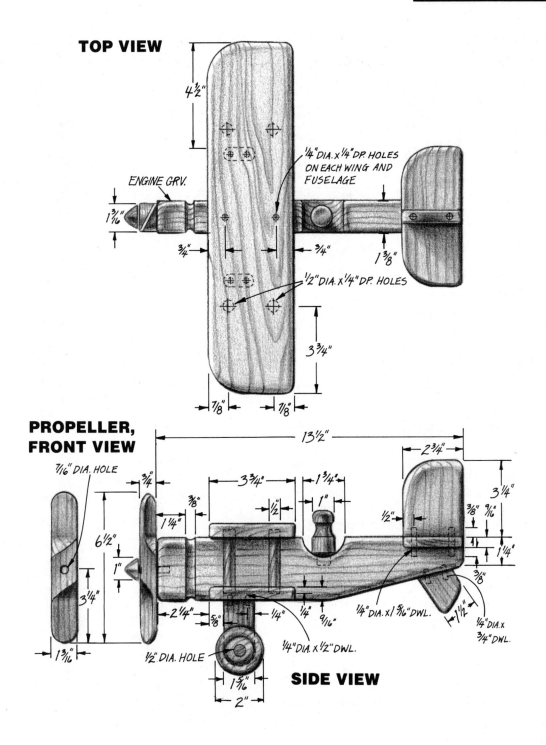

ENGINE GRV.

1/4"DIA. x 1/4"DP. HOLES
ON EACH WING AND
FUSELAGE

1 3/16"

3/4"

3/4"

1 3/8"

4 1/2"

1/2"DIA. x 1/4"DP. HOLES

3 3/4"

7/8"   7/8"

**PROPELLER,
FRONT VIEW**

7/16" DIA. HOLE

13 1/2"

2 3/4"

3/4"

3 3/4"

1 3/4"

1"

3/8"

1/2"

3 1/4"

6 1/2"

1 1/4"

1/2"

3/8"   9/16"

1"

1 1/4"

3/8"

3 1/4"

1/4" DIA. x 1 5/16" DWL.

1 1/2"

1/4"DIA. x
3/4"DWL.

1 3/16"

2 1/4"

5/8"

1/4"

1/4"   9/16"

1/4"DIA. x 1/2"DWL.

1/2" DIA. HOLE

SIDE VIEW

1 5/16"

2"

CUTTING PATTERN

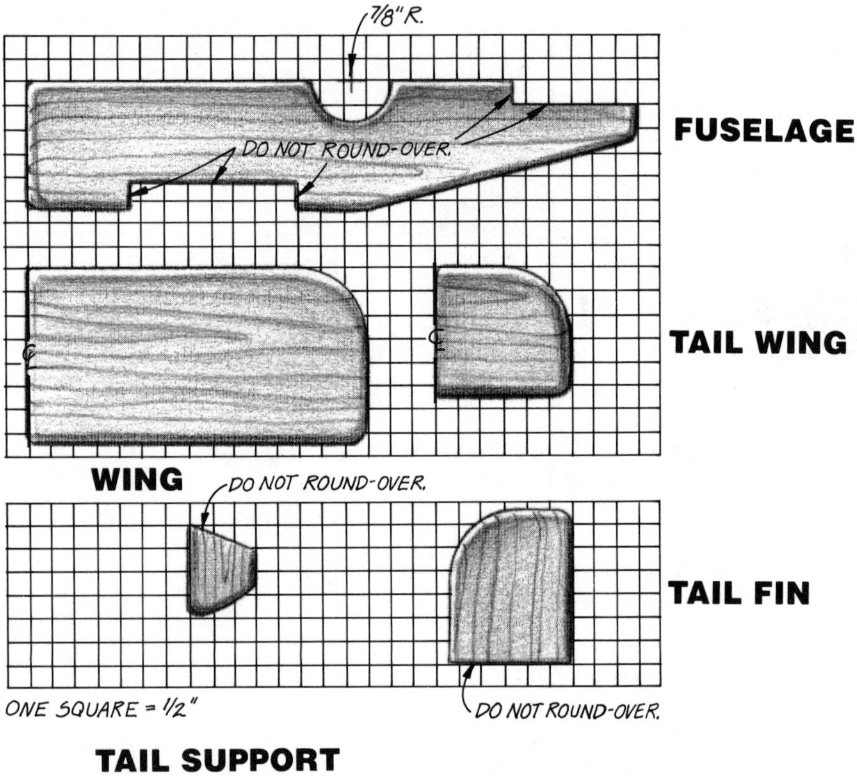

7/8" R.

DO NOT ROUND-OVER.

FUSELAGE

TAIL WING

WING DO NOT ROUND-OVER.

TAIL FIN

ONE SQUARE = 1/2"

DO NOT ROUND-OVER.

PILOT LAYOUT

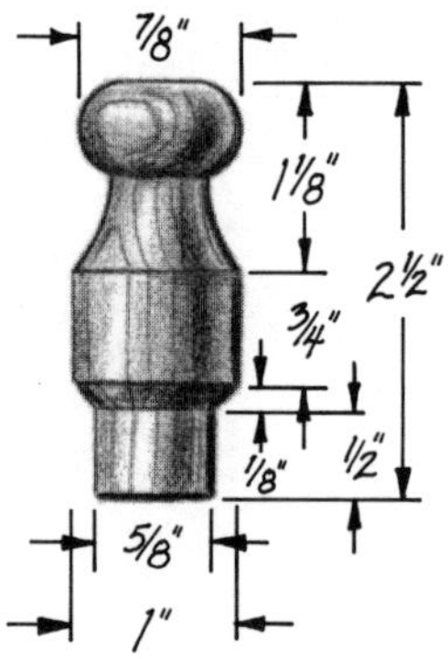

7/8"
1 1/8"
2 1/2"
3/4"
1/8"   1/2"
5/8"
1"

PROP SHAFT LAYOUT

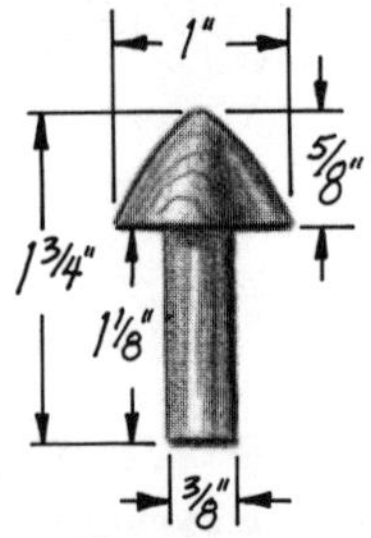

1"
5/8"
1 3/4"
1 1/8"
3/8"

TAIL SUPPORT

8 Turn the prop shaft and pilot. Set up the stock on a lathe, put on your safety glasses, and turn the parts to the shapes shown in the *Prop Shaft Layout* and *Pilot Layout*. When each part has been turned, sand it while it is still on the lathe. Turn off the lathe, saw off the waste with a backsaw, and sand the ends smooth and even.

If you're not an experienced turner, *Creative Woodturning* by Dale L. Nish is a good beginner's guide.

If you don't have access to a lathe, you can order similar parts from the source given in the Cutting List and adjust the size of the necessary holes accordingly.

9 Drill and shape the propeller. Mark and drill the prop shaft hole in the propeller shown in the *Propeller, Front View.*

Lay out and cut the radius on each end of the propeller with a band saw or jigsaw. Shape the blade angle on a stationary belt sander, as shown in the *Propeller Shaping Technique*. Put on some leather gloves to protect your hands. Then hold the propeller at a slight angle, as shown, and slowly sand away stock to form the blades.

Always wear safety glasses when working on the belt sander. The moving belt can grab a piece and throw it at you with surprising force.

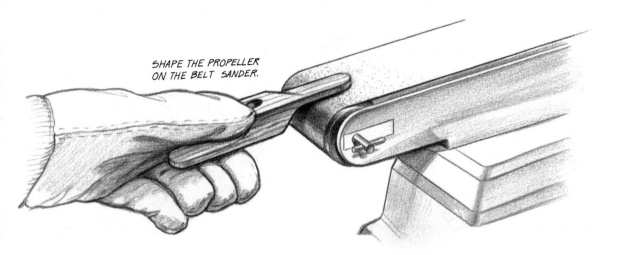

SHAPE THE PROPELLER ON THE BELT SANDER.

PROPELLER SHAPING TECHNIQUE

10 **Assemble the biplane.** Cut the different lengths of dowel required for the dowel joints. Test fit the biplane to make sure that it goes together well and make any necessary adjustments.

Assemble the wing to the fuselage first. Glue the dowels between the lower wing and the fuselage. Glue the wing struts in place, and then glue and dowel the upper wing above the wing struts and fuselage.

Next, glue the 1⁵⁄₁₆-inch-long dowels through the tail wing leaving equal amounts of the dowels exposed on each surface. Glue the tail fin above the tail wing and glue the entire assembly to the fuselage.

Glue and dowel the tail support below the tail and the axle supports below the wing.

Hold the parts together with small clamps and rubber bands. Wipe away any excess glue with a damp cloth.

When the glue is dry, glue the wheels and axle in place. Then put the prop shaft through the propeller and glue it in place. Don't apply too much glue or it will squeeze out and the propeller will seize up, causing the biplane to crash in flames.

The last thing you need to add is the pilot—somebody has to drive. The pilot can either be glued in place or left removable.

11 **Finish the biplane.** Finish sand the biplane. Wipe off the sanding dust and paint, stain, or apply a clear varnish. Allow the finish to dry, and then take off on an adventure.

STEAM TRAIN

What child hasn't dreamed of having a toy train of his or her own? From old wooden toy trains to the fancy modern electric train sets, we have passed the railroad mystique on to our children.

The simple design of this steam train allows you to be creative. The basic chassis design for the cars stays the same, only the body changes. You could make a few extra car chassis and add your own body designs to the ones shown.

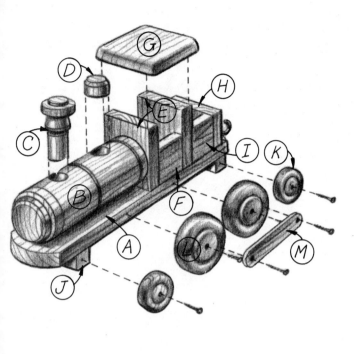

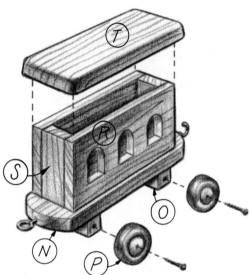

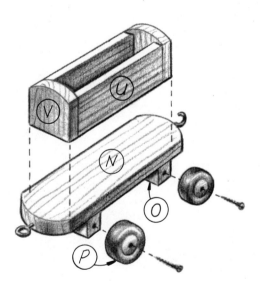

EXPLODED VIEW

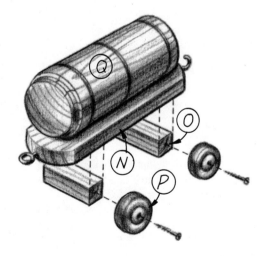

CUTTING LIST

Part	Quantity	Dimension	Comment
Engine			
A. Chassis	1	⅝″ × 2¾″ × 12¾″	
B. Boiler	1	2⅝″ dia. × 8″	Cut to length after turning.
C. Smoke stack	1	1½″ dia. × 3¾″	Cut to length after turning.
D. Steam dome	1	1¼″ dia. × 2″	Cut to length after turning.
E. Cabin front/back	2	⅝″ × 2¾″ × 3⅜″	
F. Cabin sides	2	⅝″ × 1¾″ × 2″	
G. Cabin roof	1	¾″ × 3¼″ × 3½″	
H. Coal bin back	1	⅝″ × 2¾″ × 2″	
I. Coal bin sides	2	⅝″ × 1¾″ × 2″	
J. Axle beams	2	¾″ × ¾″ × 2⅞″	
K. Small wheels*	4	½″ × 1½″ dia.	
L. Large wheels*	4	½″ × 2⅞″ dia.	
M. Drive rod	2	⅛″ × ½″ × 3⅞″	
Car Chassis			
N. Chassis	3	⅝″ × 2¾″ × 8½″	
O. Axle beams	6	¾″ × ¾″ × 2⅞″	
P. Wheels*	12	½″ × 1½″ dia.	
Tank Car Body			
Q. Tank	1	3⅜″ × 8″	Cut to length after turning.
Passenger Car Body			
R. Sides	2	⅝″ × 3⅜″ × 7″	
S. Ends	2	⅝″ × 3⅜″ × 1½″	
T. Roof	1	¾″ × 3¼″ × 7½″	
Gondola Car Body			
U. Sides	2	⅝″ × 2″ × 5¾″	
V. Ends	2	⅝″ × 2¾″ × 2¼″	

*Wheels are available from Woodcraft, 210 Wood County Industrial Park, P.O. Box 1686, Parkersburg, WV 26102. Part #50N21, 1½-in.-dia. wheels and part #50N51, 2⅞-in.-dia. wheels.

Hardware

16 #12 × 1¼-in. flathead wood screws
6 #8 × 1¼-in. flathead wood screws
4 #5 × ½-in. roundhead wood screws
As needed, 1¼-in. brads
4 sets ¾-in.-dia. hook screws and eyescrews

1 Select the stock and cut the parts. The steam train shown is made from pine, but almost any kind of wood will work fine. Choose straight, flat stock. You may find it necessary to glue together two or more pieces for the engine boiler and tank car's tank. Joint, plane, rip, and cut all the parts, except for the wheels, to the sizes given in the Cutting List.

2 Turn the boiler, smokestack, and steam dome for the engine and the tank for the tank car. Set up and turn the parts one by one on the lathe to the shapes shown in the *Smokestack Detail, Steam Dome Detail,* and *Tank Car with Chassis, Side View.* Sand the parts while they are still on the lathe. When the parts are thoroughly sanded, remove them from the lathe. Cut them to length and sand the ends smooth.

If you haven't done much turning, a good reference guide is *Creative Woodturning* by Dale L. Nish.

Next, make slight flat spots along the length of the boiler and tank by rubbing them back and forth over a piece of sandpaper. These flat areas allow you to attach the boiler and tank to their chassis. Sand away about 1/8 inch of wood on each.

3 Drill smokestack and steam dome holes in the boiler. Lay out the hole centers on the boiler, as shown in the *Engine, Top View.* Drill the 1/2-inch-deep holes, as shown in the *Engine, Side View.*

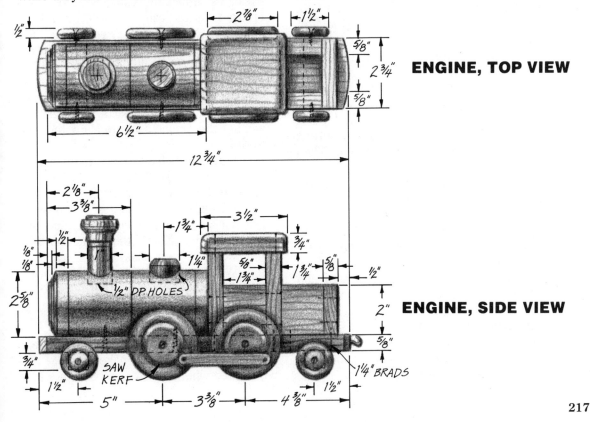

ENGINE, TOP VIEW

ENGINE, SIDE VIEW

SMOKESTACK DETAIL

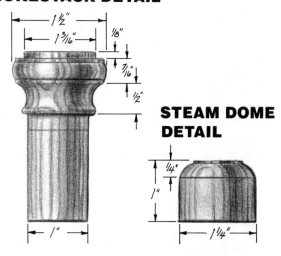

STEAM DOME DETAIL

4 **Cut the curves in the engine chassis, car chassis, and gondola car ends.** Draw a ¼-inch grid on a piece of paper and draw the *Gondola Car, End View* on it. This pattern represents the curves in the gondola car and the chassis. Transfer the pattern to the stock and cut the curves on a band saw.

To get two or more pieces with identical curves, cut all at once. First stack the pieces together and secure by putting double-sided tape between them. Then cut the pieces in one operation.

When all the curves have been cut, sand the saw marks smooth.

5 **Round-over the edges of the engine cabin roof and the passenger car roof.** Rout the roundover in the top edges of the engine cabin roof and passenger car roof, as shown. Put a ¼-inch roundover bit in your router. Secure the router in a router table. Use push sticks and keep your hands well away from the cutter. A pair of awls make good push sticks for handling small parts.

6 **Cut the windows in the passenger car sides.** Lay out the windows on the stock, as shown in *Passenger Car, Side View.* Drill a ¼-inch hole through each of the windows and slip your coping saw or jigsaw blade through the hole. Cut out the window shapes and sand the saw marks smooth.

7 **Attach the body parts to the chassis.** Begin this step by assembling the engine. First, lay out and drill clearance and countersink holes for #8 × 1¼-inch flathead wood screws in the chassis and corresponding pilot holes in the boiler. Glue and screw the boiler to the engine chassis.

Once you've screwed the boiler in place, assemble the cabin with glue and brads. Glue the cabin in place behind the boiler, as shown in the *Engine, Side View* and the *Exploded View.* Next, assemble the coal bin with glue and brads. Then glue and brad it to the engine cabin, as shown.

Clamp any of the parts, if necessary, and set the engine aside to allow the glue to dry.

Screw and glue the tank to its chassis in the same way that you attached the boiler to the engine chassis.

Assemble the bodies of the passenger car and gondola car with glue and brads, as shown, and then glue and brad the bodies to their chassis.

Wipe away any excess glue with a damp rag and allow the glue to dry.

8 **Make or purchase the small wheels and attach them to the axle beams.** You can make the 1½-inch-diameter wheels in two steps with a hole

GONDOLA CAR, SIDE VIEW
(CHASSIS REMOVED)

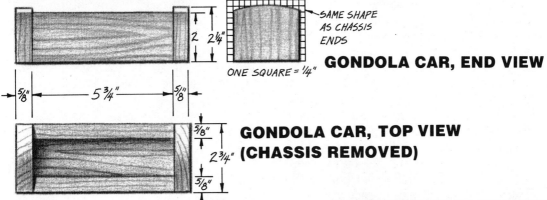

2 2¼"

SAME SHAPE
AS CHASSIS
ENDS

ONE SQUARE = ¼"

GONDOLA CAR, END VIEW

5/8"   5 ¾"   5/8"

GONDOLA CAR, TOP VIEW
(CHASSIS REMOVED)

5/8"
2¾"
5/8"

PASSENGER CAR, SIDE VIEW
(CHASSIS REMOVED)

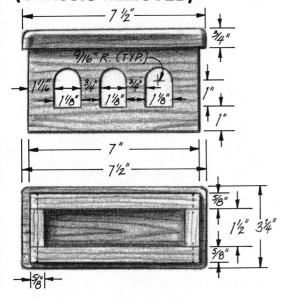

7 ½"

¾"

9/16" R. (TYP.)

1 1/16"   ¾"   ¾"
1⅛"   1⅛"   1⅛"

1"

1"

7 "

7½"

5/8"
1½" 3¾"
5/8"

5/8"

PASSENGER CAR, BOTTOM VIEW
(CHASSIS REMOVED)

TANK CAR WITH CHASSIS,
SIDE VIEW

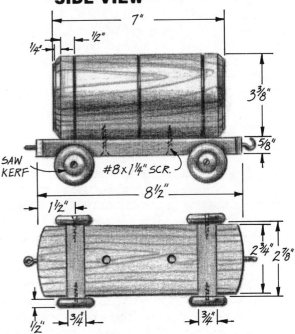

7"

½"

¼"

3⅜"

5/8"

SAW
KERF

#8 × 1¼" SCR.

8½"

1½"

2¾" 2⅞"

½"   ¾"   ¾"

CHASSIS, BOTTOM VIEW

219

saw. First, put a ⅞-inch-diameter hole saw in a drill press and cut a 1/16-inch-deep kerf into the wheel stock, as shown. Then, put a 1⅝-inch-diameter hole saw in the drill press and cut completely through the stock to make the wheel. Repeat the process for each of the small wheels.

Most hole saws have ¼-inch pilot hole bits, and this pilot hole will serve as the axle hole in the wheels. Attach the wheels to the axle beams through this hole with #12 × 1¼-inch flathead wood screws. Chamfer the outside edges of the axle holes with a countersink bit to accept the screw heads. Drill a pilot hole in the exact center of the ends of each axle beam and screw the wheels in place. Remember, these are wheels, and wheels must be able to turn freely; so don't screw the wheels too tightly in place.

Wheels can also be purchased from the source given in the Cutting List. The purchased wheels will work fine, but they are ⅜ inch thick as opposed to ½ inch thick. Also, the purchased wheels have ⅛-inch axle holes, so adjust the hole size or axle screw size accordingly.

9 **Attach the axle beams to the chassis.** Position the axle beams under the engine and car chassis, as shown in the *Engine, Side View* and the *Chassis, Bottom View.* Attach them with glue and 1¼-inch brads.

10 **Make or purchase the large wheels and attach them to** the engine chassis. The large wheels can also be cut with hole saws. First, make the 1/16-inch-deep saw kerfs shown with a 1¾-inch-diameter hole saw. Then cut all the way through the stock with a 3-inch-diameter hole saw. As with the small

wheels, chamfer the edges of the axle holes to accept the heads of the axle screws.

Lay out the position of the large wheels on the engine, as shown in the *Engine, Side View.* Make sure that the layout allows all the wheels to touch the ground. Make any necessary adjustments and drill the pilot holes. Screw the large wheels in place.

11 **Attach the drive rods to the large wheels.** The drive rod is held to the wheels with #5 × ½-inch roundhead wood screws. Drill pilot holes for these screws exactly ⅜ inch from the outside edge of the wheels, as shown in the *Engine, Side View.* Drill the screw clearance holes in the drive rod, as shown in the *Drive Rod Detail,* and screw the drive rod in place. Don't tighten the screws too much; the drive rod must be able to move freely.

DRIVE ROD DETAIL

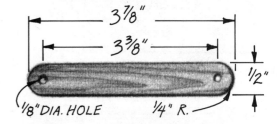

12 **Sand, finish, and add the hook screws and eyescrews to the steam train.** Sand the train engine and cars and, as you sand, round-over any sharp corners. You can finish the train in any way you choose. The train shown simply has a clear varnish to protect the wood. You could finish your train in the same way or paint it to look like a real train.

SLED

This child's sled will make you feel like hot chocolate and marshmallows even on a summer's day, and it will provide hours of snowy fun on winter days when the kids need to get out of the house. Make this sled as a gift or get your kids to help you make it. There are plenty of screws for young children to drive and holes for older children to drill.

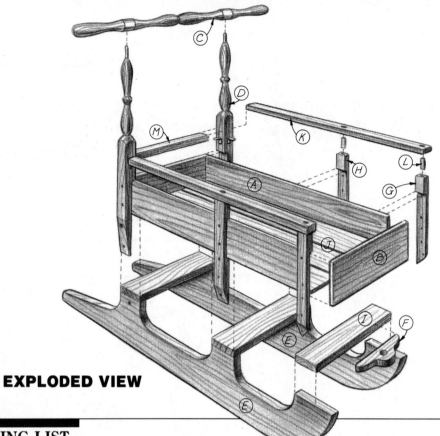

EXPLODED VIEW

CUTTING LIST

Part	Quantity	Dimension	Comment
A. Sides	2	¾″ × 4¾″ × 31″	
B. Front/back	2	¾″ × 4¾″ × 15½″	
C. Handle	1	1¾″ × 1¾″ × 28¾″	Trim after turning.
D. Handle supports	2	1¾″ × 1¾″ × 31″	Trim after turning.
E. Runners	2	1″ × 6⅝″ × 48″	
F. Nose piece	1	1″ × 2½″ × 8¾″	
G. Front posts	2	¾″ × 1¾″ × 12¼″	
H. Middle posts	2	¾″ × 1¾″ × 13⁷⁄₁₆″	
I. Cross supports	3	1″ × 2¾″ × 16″	Trim to fit.
J. Floor slats	3	¾″ × 4⅜″ × 30¼″	
K. Side rails	2	1″ × 1⅜″ × 31½″	
L. Dowels	4	⅜″ dia. × 2″	
M. Back rail	1	1″ × 1⅜″ × 14½″	Cut to fit.

Hardware

As needed, #8 × 1½-in. flathead wood screws
As needed, #8 × 1¼-in. flathead wood screws
As needed, #8 × 1-in. flathead wood screws
As needed, #8 × 1¾-in. flathead wood screws
2 ¼-in.-dia. × 2½-in. carriage bolt
4 ⅝ × 2-in. metal corner braces

1 **Select the stock and cut the parts.** Oak is a good choice of wood for this project, but other hardwoods could also be used. Choose straight, flat stock without knots. Joint, plane, rip, and cut the parts to the sizes given in the Cutting List. Notice that the handle and handle supports are 1 inch longer than their finished dimensions to allow for turning.

2 **Assemble the box frame.** The box frame is made up of the sides, front, and back. Simply butt the sides between the front and back, and screw through the front and back into the sides, as shown in the *Front View.* Predrill for #8 × 1½-inch flathead wood screws with a commercially available combination pilot hole bit. A combination pilot hole bit drills a countersink hole, a clearance hole for the screw shank, and a slightly smaller pilot hole for the threads all in one operation. Make sure that the top edge of the sides aligns with the top edge of the front and back.

3 **Drill holes in the handle and turn the handle and handle supports.** Before turning, lay out and drill ¾-inch-diameter handle support holes in the handle.

Turn the handle and handle supports on the lathe to the profile shown in the *Handle Detail* and *Handle Support Detail.* Turn the ¾-inch-diameter tenons at the

FRONT VIEW

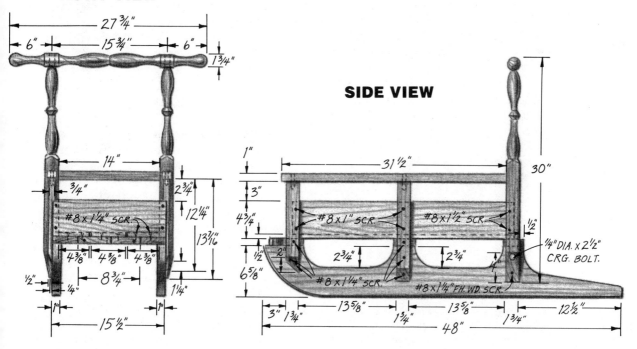

SIDE VIEW

tops of the handle supports slightly longer than the thickness of the handle so they can be trimmed flush after assembly.

HANDLE SUPPORT DETAIL

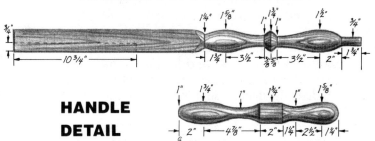

HANDLE DETAIL

4 **Cut the runners and nose piece to shape.** Draw a ½-inch grid on a piece of paper and draw the runner and nose piece patterns onto it, as shown in the *Runner Detail* and *Nose Detail*. Transfer the patterns to the wood and cut the parts to shape with a band saw or jigsaw. Sand the sawed edges smooth.

After you cut the nose piece to shape, lay out and drill the ¾-inch-diameter rope hole, as shown in the *Nose Detail*.

SHOP TIP: After you have cut one runner to shape, use it as a template to lay out the second runner.

5 **Fit the front posts, middle posts, and handle supports to the box frame.** The front posts, middle posts, and handle supports are all notched to fit around the box frame. Lay out the ¼-inch-deep notches on the front and mid-

dle posts starting 2¾ inches from the top, as shown in the *Front View*. Lay out the ¾-inch-deep notch on the handle supports, as shown in the *Handle Support Detail*.

Notch the parts on a band saw. To ensure a straight cut, set up a fence on the band saw table to guide the long cuts.

While you are still at the band saw, cut the 45-degree angles on the bottom ends of the front posts, as shown in the *Side View*.

Taper the bottom ends of the posts and handle supports on a stationary belt sander to the profiles shown in the *Front View*.

6 **Fit the cross supports and screw them to the runners.** Cut the cross supports to the exact width of the box frame. Predrill with a pilot hole bit and attach the nose piece to the front cross support with glue and #8 × 1¾-inch screws, as shown in the *Front View*. Predrill and attach the cross supports to the tops of the runners.

7 **Assemble the posts and handle support to the box frame and runners.** First, set the box frame in position on top of the cross supports and runners and then clamp the front and middle posts and handle supports to it. Position the parts as shown in the *Side View*.

Next, lay out and drill pilot holes for #8 × 1-inch, #8 × 1¼-inch, and #8 × 1½-inch flathead wood screws, as shown in the *Side View*. Also drill a ¼-inch-diameter hole through each handle support and runner for a carriage bolt, as shown.

Drive the appropriate screws into their pilot holes and attach the carriage bolts to the handle supports and runners. Remove the clamps.

8 **Attach the floor slats.** Drop the floor slats in place, as shown in the *Front View,* spacing them evenly to allow snow to melt through. Drill pilot holes for #8 × 1¼-inch screws through the floor slats and into the cross supports and screw them in place.

9 **Attach the side and back rails.** The side rails are doweled to the front and middle posts and then fastened to the handle support with metal corner braces. The back rail is attached between the handle supports with metal corner braces. First, position the side rails on top of the front and middle posts and against the handle support, as shown in the *Side View* and *Front View.* Clamp the rails in place and drill ⅜-inch-diameter by 2-inch-deep dowel holes through the side rails and into the front and side posts.

Next, spread glue on the dowels and tap them down into the dowel holes.

When the dowels are in place, position the metal corner brace, as shown in the *Side View.* Drill screw pilot holes through the existing holes in the brace and into the handle support and side rails. The screw hole diameter in metal corner braces may vary, so choose screws to fit your brace. Drive the screws in place.

Next, cut the back rail to fit between the handle supports and position it as shown in the *Front View.* Attach the back rail to the handle supports with screws and metal corner braces.

10 **Attach the handle.** The holes in the handle fit over the tenons on the handle supports. Test fit the handle to the handle supports, and if the tenons are too tight, remove some stock from them with sandpaper. When the tenons fit properly, spread glue on them and attach the handle. Allow the glue to dry.

11 **Apply the finish.** Finish sand the sled and apply a varnish or paint capable of handling lots of moisture.

Mush, you huskies!

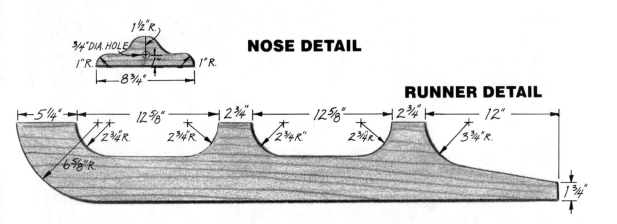

NOSE DETAIL

1½"R.

¾"DIA. HOLE

1"R.   1"R.

8¾"

RUNNER DETAIL

5¼"   12⅝"   2¾"   12⅝"   2¾"   12"

2¾"R.   2¾"R.   2¾"R."   2¾"R.   3¾"R.

6⅝"R.

1¾"

CHILD'S WAGON

What better toy for adult and child alike than a wagon? This particular wagon recalls a simpler time, when toys were handmade of wood.

Construction, too, is surprisingly simple. The wood is dimensioned lumber available at lumberyards. The hardware for this project is available at larger hardware and building supply stores.

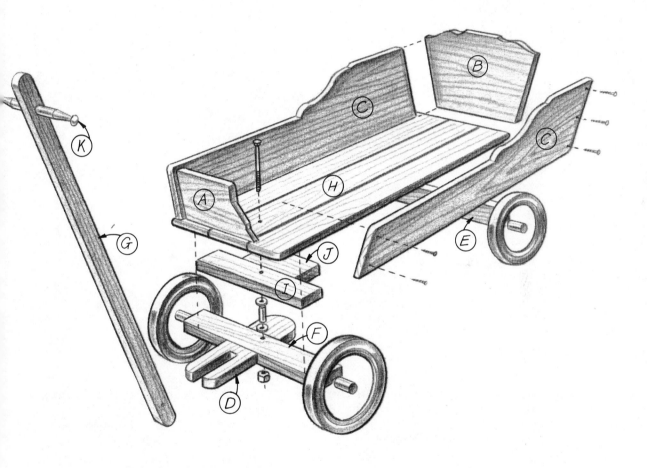

EXPLODED VIEW

CUTTING LIST

Part	Quantity	Dimension	Comment
A. Front	1	¾″ × 6¼″ × 15¾″	
B. Back	1	¾″ × 10¾″ × 18½″	
C. Sides	2	¾″ × 10½″ × 40″	
D. Yoke	1	1½″ × 3¾″ × 13″	
E. Rear axle support	1	1½″ × 2¾″ × 18½″	
F. Front axle support	1	1½″ × 2¾″ × 19½″	
G. Handle	1	1½″ × 1¾″ × 42″	
H. Bottom boards	3	¾″ × 5″ × 41″	
I. Cleat	1	1½″ × 2¾″ × 14½″	
J. Brace	1	1½″ × 3¾″ × 7½″	
K. Handholds*	2	⅞″ dia. × 3⅜″	Shaker pegs

*Available from The Woodworker's Store, 21801 Industrial Boulevard, Rogers, MN 55374. Specify part #B1501 for birch, #B1502 for oak, or #B1503 for walnut.

Hardware

As needed, #8 × 1½-in. flathead wood screws
As needed, #8 × 1¼-in. flathead wood screws
As needed, #8 × 1-in. flathead wood screws
1 ⅜ × 5-in. carriage bolt with two washers and a stop nut
1 ¼ × 4-in. carriage bolt with a washer and stop nut
4 ½-in.dia. push nut caps
4 ½-in.-dia. washers
1 ½-in.-O.D. × 1-in. bushing (⅜-in. I.D.)
4 ⅝ × 2-in. angle brackets
8 ½ × 2-in. metal mending plates
4 10-in.-dia. ball-bearing wheels with ½-in.-dia. axle holes. Available from Youngs, P.O. Box 1, Route 309, Line Lexington, PA 18932. Part #A-WH-9082-SP.
2 ½-in.-dia. × 36-in. steel rods

1 Select the stock and cut the parts. You can get the wood you need for this wagon preplaned from the lumberyard. Cut the thicker pieces from 2 × 4s and 2 × 6s. Cut the thinner stock from 1 × 6s and 1 × 8s. Glue up stock to make the sides and back.

Cut the angles in the front and back as you cut them to the sizes given in the Cutting List. Lay out the angles directly on the stock and cut the angles on the table saw with a miter gauge set at 75 degrees. Rip 15-degree bevels on the bottom edge of the sides, as you cut the parts to width.

Get your hardware before you begin construction, in case you need to make alterations. Sturdy ball-bearing solid wheels replace the wire-spoked wheels of the original wagon; if you prefer to use spoked wheels, you may be able to salvage them from a baby carriage. The axles are made of ½-inch-diameter steel rod. The bronze bushings in the yoke can be found in hardware stores or at electrical supply stores.

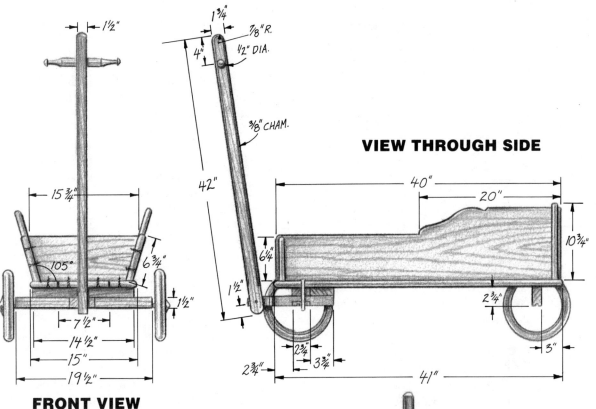

VIEW THROUGH SIDE

FRONT VIEW

BACK VIEW

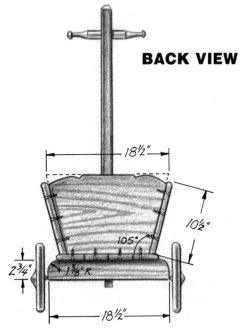

2 Cut the parts to shape. With a compass, lay out the radii on the yoke and rear axle support and the handle. Then draw a ½-inch grid on a piece of paper and draw the side and back shapes onto it, as shown in the *Side Detail* and *Back Detail*. Transfer the patterns to the stock and cut the parts to shape on the band saw. Sand any saw marks smooth.

3 Rout for the axles. In the next few steps, you'll make the wagon's chassis. After that, you'll make the box that sits on top of the chassis.

First, lay out and rout ½ × ½-inch axle grooves in the front and rear axle supports. Put a ½-inch straight bit in your

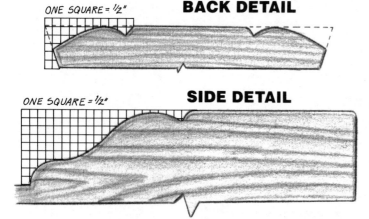

BACK DETAIL

ONE SQUARE = 1/2"

SIDE DETAIL

ONE SQUARE = 1/2"

router. Secure the router in a router table and guide the axle supports against a fence as you rout. Center the groove in each axle support, as shown in the *View through Side* and the *Support Bottom View.*

4 Assemble the bottom. First, place the cleat and the rear axle support on a flat work surface, parallel to one another and 31½ inches apart. Put a shim under the yoke, so that the top of the yoke and the rear axle support are at the same level. Mark the location of the cleat and support in pencil on the bench, so that you'll know if you've nudged them out of place.

Put the bottom boards on top of the cleat and rear axle support, positioning them as shown in the *Front View* and *View through Side.* Make sure that the bottom boards are perpendicular to the cleat and support and then check that the cleat and support haven't strayed from the pencil marks.

Drill screw holes for two #8 × 1½-inch flathead wood screws through both ends of each board and into the cleat and support. A #8 pilot hole bit will drill the appropriate-size holes in each piece and

countersink for the screw head in one pass.

Next, put the brace in position behind the front cleat, as shown. Drill holes with the pilot bit through the bottom boards and into the brace. Attach the cleat with #8 × 1½-inch flathead wood screws.

5 Cut the handle notch in the yoke. The yoke houses both the handle and the front axle. Lay out the notch for the handle on the yoke stock to the dimensions shown in the *Support Bottom View.* Cut out the notch on the band saw, then file and sand away any saw marks or irregularities. Lay out and drill a ¼-inch-diameter hole through the tongues of the yoke for the bolt that secures the handle.

6 Cut the lap joint. The front axle support and the yoke are joined by a lap joint. Lay out the ¾-inch-deep lap joints on the axle support and yoke, as shown in the *Support Bottom View.* Cut the joints on the table saw with a dado cutter. To cut the lap, screw a piece of straight scrap to your miter gauge as an extension, set the gauge to 90 degrees, and guide your stock over the dado cutter.

When the laps have been cut, put the yoke and axle support together and make sure that the corners form 90-degree angles. Attach the two parts with glue and four metal angle brackets, as shown.

7 Attach the yoke. Lay out and drill the ½-inch-diameter hole for the steering bushing in the yoke, as shown in the *Support Bottom View.* Tap the bushing in place.

With the wagon body still upside down, position the yoke assembly on the cleat. Put a pencil through the bushing to

SUPPORT BOTTOM VIEW

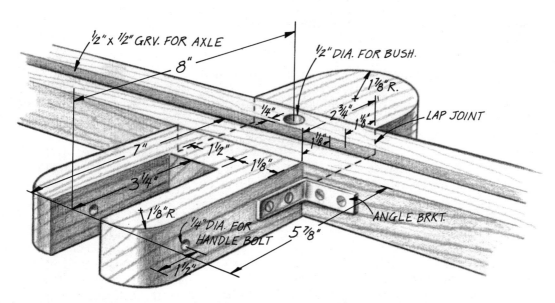

mark the position of the steering bolt hole on the cleat and drill a ⅜-inch bolt hole all the way through the cleat and bottom board.

Bolt the yoke in place. As you do, put a nut washer between the yoke and axle and between the stop nut and yoke. Be sure to use a stop nut. Stop nuts have a nylon collar just above the threads that keeps the nut from slipping off. Don't put the nut on too tightly because the yoke should move freely.

8 Assemble the front, sides, and back. Assemble the front, sides, and back independently of the rest of the wagon, then attach them as a unit.

To assemble the front, sides, and back, lay out and drill screw holes in the parts, as shown in the *Front View* and *Back View*. The distance between the

screws isn't critical, but each row of screws should be ⅜ inch from the edge of the stock.

To drill the holes, have a helper hold the two parts together. Drill through the side and into the adjoining piece using a pilot hole bit. The bit will drill the appropriate size hole in each piece and countersink for the screw head. Drill all the necessary holes, then screw the parts together.

Center the assembled front, sides, and back on the chassis. With a pencil, mark the position of the sides along the bottom. Remove the box assembly and, on 3-inch centers, drill a series of ¹⁄₁₆-inch-diameter holes between the pencil lines. Clamp the box to the chassis and flip the assembly over. Enlarge each hole with a #8 pilot hole bit. Drill through the chassis and into the box. Screw the chassis to the box with #8 × 1½-inch flathead wood screws.

9 **Attach the axles and wheels.** The ½-inch-diameter steel rod stock used for the axles is typically sold in 3-foot pieces. Cut the axles to length with a hacksaw and allow enough margin on either side of the axle supports for a flat washer, the hub of the particular wheel you've chosen, and a push nut cap. Secure the wheels by hammering the push nut in place.

With the wagon upside down, place the front axle in the groove. Screw four metal mending repair plates across the axle and into the wood with #8 × 1-inch flathead screws.

Place the rear axle in the groove in its support and secure it with four metal mending plates. Put the wheels on the axles and secure them with caps or cotter pins.

10 **Chamfer the edges of the handle.** Put a chamfering bit in your router. Secure the router in a router table and rout a ⅜-inch stopped chamfer in all four edges of the handle. Stop the chamfer 4 inches from the bottom of the handle on all four edges.

Lay out and drill the bolt hole in the handle, 1½ inches from the handle's bottom end.

Drill a ½-inch-diameter hole centered 4 inches from the top end of the handle for the two handholds.

11 **Attach the handle.** Glue the handholds in place. Fasten the handle to the yoke with a ¼-inch-diameter bolt, secured by a washer and stop nut.

12 **Finish the wagon.** Sand the wagon, taking care to round-over any sharp edges for the safety of young passengers. Finish with two coats of either exterior polyurethane or exterior paint.

Finally, make a note on your calendar to check all of the wagon's bolts and screws for tightness after a couple of weeks of use.

Rodale Press, Inc., publishes AMERICAN WOODWORKER™, the magazine for the serious woodworking hobbyist. For information on how to order your subscription, write to AMERICAN WOODWORKER™, Emmaus, PA 18098.